A Toolkit for the Effective Teaching Assistant

Second Edition

A Toolkit for the Effective Teaching Assistant

Second Edition

Maureen Parker, Chris Lee, Stuart Gunn,
Kitty Heardman, Rachael Hincks,
Mary Pittman and Mark Townsend

Los Angeles | London | New Delhi
Singapore | Washington DC

Second edition first published 2009

Reprinted 2012

First edition published 2004. Reprinted 2006 (twice), 2008

SAGE Publications Ltd
1 Oliver's Yard
55 City Road
London EC1Y 1SP

SAGE Publications Inc.
2455 Teller Road
Thousand Oaks, California 91320

SAGE Publications India Pvt Ltd
B 1/I 1 Mohan Cooperative Industrial Area
Mathura Road
New Delhi 110 044

SAGE Publications Asia-Pacific Pte Ltd
3 Church Street
#10-04 Samsung Hub
Singapore 049483

Library of Congress Control Number: 2008935451

British Library Cataloguing in Publication data

A catalogue record for this book is available from the British Library

ISBN 978-1-84787-942-4
ISBN 978-1-84787-943-1 (pbk)

Typeset by C&M Digitals (P) Ltd, Chennai, India
Printed in Great Britain by CPI Group (UK) Ltd, Croydon, CR0 4YY
Printed on paper from sustainable resources

CONTENTS

ABOUT THE AUTHORS

Maureen Parker is the Senior Tutor for Educational Development, Partnership and Enterprise and formerly the Programme Director for the Foundation Degree (Education) Teaching Assistants at the University of Plymouth. Her research interests include all aspects of emotional health and well being as it relates to educational settings and the developing roles of support staff across all aspects of the Children's Workforce in relation to 'professional identity', specifically HLTAs.

Chris Lee was Head of the School of Continuing Professional Development at the University of Plymouth until 2008. His main researching and lecturing foci are bullying and behaviour management. Prior to his career in higher education he taught in both secondary and special schools.

Stuart Gunn has a degree in Psychology and in his early career worked in a unit for pupils with severe behavioural difficulties. Prior to his appointment at Plymouth University, he lectured in Psychology in Further Education.

Kitty Heardman has held two primary headships in Derbyshire and Aberdeenshire, where she also worked in school improvement and quality assurance in both primary and secondary schools. She has also worked with Teaching Assistants to design and implement a new pay and grading framework arising from the National Agreement and subsequent School Workforce Reforms. She has a BA (Hons) in music and considerable experience as a performer as a violinist in both symphony orchestras and string quartets. She also has an MA in Applied Linguistics. Her research interests focus on music, language acquisition and leadership.

Rachael Hincks graduated from the University of Sheffield with a BSc in Medical Biochemistry before gaining her PGCE from the University of Warwick and working as a science teacher in secondary schools. She has enjoyed posts as both a SENCO and Assistant Principal, during which time she studied for her MA in Inclusive Education from the Open University. Rachael has research interests in inclusive science education as well as enjoying life with her partner Simon, playing with their son and daydreaming by the sea.

Mary Pittman has worked with children who have autism and other complex learning needs for more than 28 years. In 1999 she received a UK National Teaching Award for her work in this field. From 2001 to 2005 Mary worked on the Foundation Degree for Teaching Assistants at the University of Plymouth developing SEN aspects of the programme, and participated in the developement of HLTA routes for Teaching

Assistants. Mary currently works as an independent trainer and classroom advisor and is based at the Oasis Centre (Outreach, Advice, Support, Information Service) at Longcause School, Plympton, Plymouth.

Mark Townsend has been a member of the Faculty of Education at the University of Plymouth for seven years, teaching on the Foundation Degree (Teaching Assistants) and Initial Teacher Education programmes. His specialist areas are ICT in education, and supporting children with Special Educational Needs. His research interests currently cover two key areas: e-learning, and the impact of workforce reform on schools, with a series of papers being presented at national and international conferences. He is also co-chair of the University's e-learning conference, which has gained an international reputation for its engagement with 'cutting edge' themes. Publications include peer-reviewed journals and chapters on ICT in education for four prominent books. Prior to joining the University, Mark's educational career developed over many years in the special education schools sector, where his last post was assistant head teacher.

ACKNOWLEDGEMENTS

- To all current and former students on the Foundation Degree (Education) Teaching Assistants at the University of Plymouth who continue to inspire us in our work with the difference they make *every day* to children and young people in their education and achievements. Their stories and experiences are part of this book too.
- To all CPD admin staff from the Faculty who have worked so diligently to support the Programme.
- To our Local Authority colleagues in Devon, Torbay, Dorset, Poole, Plymouth, Bournemouth and Cornwall for their belief and commitment to accredited CPD for TAs and HLTAs.
- To Richard, the former Programme Director who guided the first edition.
- To John an inspirational teacher who truly demonstrated belief in those for whom education was a challenge and Susannah who introduced me to Transactional Analysis.
- Finally to Claire, Rachel, Abi, Andy and Katie for their patience and help in the final stages!

ABBREVIATIONS

AfL	Assessment for Learning
AST	Advanced Skills Teacher
CAF	Common Assessment Framework
CD	Compact Disc
CPD	Continuing Professional Development
CRB	Criminal Records Bureau
DCSF	Department for Children, Schools and Families
DDA	Disability Discrimination Act
DVD	Digital Versatile Disc or Digital Video Disc
EAL	English as an Additional Language
ECM	Every Child Matters
EIP	Education Improvement Partner
EYPS	Early Years Professional Status
GT	Gifted and Talented
HMI	Her Majesty's Inspector
HLTA	Higher Level Teaching Assistant
ICT	Information and Communication Technology
INSET	In-Service Education and Training
LA	Local Authority (formerly Local Education Authority)
LAC	Looked After Children
LDD	Learning Difficulties and Disabilities
NC	National Curriculum
NRwS	New Relationship with Schools
NSF	National Service Framework
OFSTED	Office for Standards in Education
PDF	Portable Document Format
PE	Physical Education
PPA	Planning, Preparation and Assessment
PRU	Pupil Referral Unit
PSHE	Personal, Social and Health Education
PSHCE	Personal, Social, Health and Citizenship Education
QA	Quality Assurance
QCA	Qualifications and Curriculum Authority
QTS	Qualified Teacher Status
SEAL	Social and Emotional Aspects of Learning
SEF	Self Evaluation Form

SEN	Special Educational Needs
SENCO	SEN Coordinator
SENDA	Special Educational Needs and Disability Act (2001)
SIP	School Improvement Partner
TA	Teaching Assistant
TDA	Training and Development Agency for Schools (formerly Teacher Training Agency)

INTRODUCTION

When the first edition of the 'toolkit' was published in 2004 we had no idea that it would prove to be as successful or realize that we would soon be thinking about this second edition.

Now, almost five years later, we have tried to encapsulate the current world of the Teaching Assistant (TA) and the Higher Learning Teaching Assistant (HLTA) and the variety of support staff in schools. This has been achieved through updating the former chapters, bringing new ideas to the fore in new chapters and embracing the new 'HLTA Standards'. Despite these changes the book remains constant to its initial principles in that it draws upon the work of a team who set up a single short course for TAs in 1995 which evolved into a highly successful Foundation Degree in Education for Teaching Assistants. It also continues with its aspiration to enhance the skills and practice of the Teaching Assistant, based upon what they themselves say about their experiences. Throughout the book, the shortened form 'TA' will be used.

A 'TOOLKIT'?

Including the idea of a 'toolkit' in the title is one of the few items that remains unchanged as the book retains its resemblance to a toolkit in that the contents are not all used at the same time. Some 'tools' are more useful for specific tasks and some provide exactly the right solution for those awkward jobs that have been left too long, while others have a variety of creative uses for numerous tasks – some of which they were never intended for! But like any form of toolkit there is a need to replace, adjust and refine the tools from time to time in order that a professional outcome is achieved. Although the subjects tackled herein could well be of interest to teachers, student teachers and other education professionals, it is the following groups that are our focus.

Teaching Assistants (TAs)

These are teaching assistants who work with teachers in the classroom, helping pupils with their learning on an individual or group basis and include specialist TAs and those referred to as Learning Support Assistants and Education Assistants.

Higher Level Teaching Assistants (HLTAs)

These are experienced teaching assistants who plan and deliver learning activities under the direction of a teacher and report on pupils' progress. They may also manage other support staff or may supervise a class in a teacher's absence.

Nursery Nurses

Nursery Nurses work alongside teachers, looking after the social and educational development of children. Their work includes planning, supervising activities and keeping parents informed of their child's progress.

Learning Mentors

These staff have specific skills in guiding and supporting young people to enable them to continue to engage with their learning and achieve their potential.

Cover Supervisors

Cover Supervisors are usually trained school staff who supervise pupils when teachers are absent.

Source: http://www.tda.gov.uk/support/support_staff_roles/learningsupportstaff.aspx (accessed 14 August 2008).

It is these groups who combine a unique blend of skills, knowledge and understanding with a role that allows sometimes different forms of engagement with pupils and classroom processes. This book gives the course team the opportunity to begin to reflect more clearly on the integrated nature of Children's Services and is an opportunity to, 'work across professional boundaries … to ensure that joining up services is not just about providing a safety net for the vulnerable – it is about unlocking the potential of every child' (Children's Plan, 2008: 18).

There is an emphasis on reflection and active engagement with your practice as the 'toolkit' provides TAs from all types of educational setting and Key Stages with the opportunity to stand back and to consider their values, ideas and practices. It is hoped that this is undertaken alongside colleagues, preferably in the context of study in higher or further education or in working towards HLTA status, but it may be that it simply helps to fulfill the individual TA's professional aspirations to be a better practitioner.

STRUCTURE AND CONTENT

This new toolkit explores themes which Teaching Assistants engage with almost every day of their working life and is also appropriate for those studying for their HLTA status or on Foundation Degrees. The book is divided into three broad sections:

1. The TA's role with colleagues and the management of the school system.
2. The TA's role with pupils, especially those experiencing difficulty.
3. The TA's role with learning and teaching colleagues.

In the first section there are chapters on roles and responsibilities, distributed leadership, the process of change and how TAs engage with other adults and the school systems in which they work. This brings opportunities to look at the broader concepts and systems of education. The second section looks at how TAs work alongside pupils and teachers in a supportive role, with the focus on self esteem, well being and managing difficult pupil behaviour. The third and final section considers learning and teaching and the potential of ICT to support it.

How to use this book

It is impossible to prescribe exactly how any book might best be used but the following have been considered by the writing team in preparation of the text.

Each chapter contains:

(a) Activities, designed for individuals, groups or both, related to the issue being discussed or the topic being reported.
(b) Diagrams and other representations which illustrate key topics.
(c) An introductory summary of each chapter to help focus the reader.
(d) Explicit references to the HLTA Standards in the text. In the margins, you will also find boxes which show you which HLTA standards are addressed in the text or chapter. The full HLTA standards are available as an appendix on p. 211.
(e) Questions that aid reflection.
(f) Further reading which will help those wishing to look at a breadth of materials;
(g) Useful websites, where applicable.

If used as part of a formal study there are preparatory stages that will help you. These include:

- Find a colleague who will help as a critical friend, advisor or mentor.
- Collect other materials including relevant books, research papers and website addresses.
- Always remember the crucial ethical issues that come with issues related to children and schools, e.g. informed consent and confidentiality.

How can I become an even more effective TA or HLTA?

This is a key question to reflect on as you read and connect this with your practice. The subsequent chapters in this text will guide you in identifying areas that you can develop irrespective of the age range of the pupils you work with or the setting and context in which you work and whether you are a TA or HLTA or in another support staff role. However, in any setting good communication is critical and will aid you in establishing a professional dialogue with colleagues that will enable you to be both effective in your role and to develop as a reflective practitioner. Broadly you should seek to:

- Have a clear and (shared!) understanding of your role and responsibilities (clarify vague points on your job description). Revisit this often as your role may subtly change during an academic year.
- Know the relevant school policies and seek clarification if you are unsure of the part you play in supporting and implementing them.
- Seek opportunities for professional development that encourages you to deconstruct and examine your practice both within your setting and through your LA or an accredited qualification such as a foundation degree with a university.
- Try to establish what are the key characteristics of your professional self that would describe you in your role.
- Develop this to consider what opportunities exist in your setting to further promote this and acknowledge what are the barriers that are holding you back in your role development.

Throughout your reading, be prepared to challenge ideas and be challenged by them. Now almost a decade after the government systematically developed the role of the TA the HLTA and the workforce remodeling initiatives are now firmly embedded into the contemporary educational landscape. Teaching Assistants and HLTAs are significant players in nearly all schools and with their developing roles come new found responsibilities and a consequent need for increased professional knowledge. The speed of change is unlikely to slow down, and, as supporting references, important web addresses have been included as part of the further reading of this Introduction. However, it is essential to step beyond these and engage with a literature base that might ask difficult questions or even dare to counter the prevailing views emanating from a centralized system. Critical and informed analysis of the current beliefs and practices is central to the growing professionalism of the TA and the HLTA.

Keeping a reflective diary or log

Many of you are required to record events, interactions and the effectiveness of strategies and interventions as part of your current role, however you can develop this further and begin a reflective diary that enables you to systematically examine areas of your practice that are successful and areas for further development. You may wish then to refer to relevant chapters in this book to further guide your thinking and reflections. It is important that this is a document that is personal to you and that it is one that records celebrations as well as challenges. Writing regularly will enhance the skills of those of you on higher education courses and provide a record both of achievements linked to meeting standards (perhaps?) and the success and the uniqueness of the role you have in enhancing learning and teaching.

The contents

Each chapter is written by a member of a University team who has worked extensively with TAs in their studies and also alongside teaching assistants in practical settings. They contain helpful professional development exercises, supporting tables, key web addresses and further reading for those wishing to probe issues more extensively or perhaps in greater depth.

In terms of layout all **Activities** are clearly indicated in boxes and where the subject is explicitly relevant to the **HLTA Standards** they are clearly indicated in shaded boxes. There are quotations from TAs and HLTAs, and, in keeping with good ethical principles all the names have been changed to preserve the participants' anonymity. Additional suggestions for further reading and resources or areas of study are added at the end of each chapter.

Section 1

In Chapter 1, Maureen Parker and Mark Townsend consider why the number of TAs has grown and the changes in philosophy that have supported this expansion. The bulk of the chapter, however, draws on a series of perceptions, both by and about TAs, on their role, responsibilities and place in school provision. This gives you an opportunity to begin to examine your own strengths and weaknesses and consider your professional identity.

In Chapter 2 Kitty Heardman examines the way in which leadership has been distributed across and within different educational settings as a result of the initiatives such as Every Child Matters, Extended Schools and the National Agreement 2003; this will be considered in the specific context of the developing roles and responsibilities of Teaching Assistants.

Chapter 3 sees Chris Lee considering the influence of TAS and HLTAs as agents of change. You are invited to consider and reflect upon you own attitude to change and how change in school practice and policy can be planned and supported.

In Chapter 4, Mary Pittman looks at the importance of being part of a team not just in terms your TA colleagues but also she acknowledges the importance of teacher and TA partnerships in providing for pupil learning and suggests ways in which good collaborative practice can be developed and enhanced within schools.

Section 2

In Chapter 5 Maureen Parker considers the complex, sometimes controversial subject of self esteem and how TAs have a central role in identifying, supporting and raising levels of self esteem. She considers how developing an understanding of self esteem and identifying specific strategies to support individual pupils can have an impact on learning. She has also identified aspects of self esteem that relate to the developing professional role of a TA and the emerging 'professional self'.

In Chapter 6 Maureen Parker continues to explore the role of the TA in supporting the development of emotional health and well being. The theory of Transactional Analysis is introduced and suggestions are made as to how to embed this into practice. Developments in the roles of TAs in relation to Children's services and Children's Trusts are considered.

Chris Lee returns in Chapter 7 to consider ways in which TAs can approach difficult classroom behaviour through three broad approaches and the skills that are associated with them.

In Chapter 8 Rachael Hincks explores inclusion in relation to the school as a community. Every Child Matters and EAL is considered in some detail with relevant examples related to a range of support staff roles.

Section 3

In Chapter 9 Stuart Gunn provides a stimulus for reflecting on the complexity of pedagogy. He provides a brief theoretical background, before looking at some practical facets of learning and teaching. The important contribution to raising academic standards by TAs should be underpinned by the development of equal levels of skill, knowledge and understanding about teaching, learning and inter-personal relationships.

In Chapter 10 Mark Townsend considers the contribution of ICT to raising achievement and helping pupils, teachers, schools and TAs to improve their standards. In this he provides an overview of some of the contemporary key developments which are affecting TAs, both in their roles as educators and as learners in this large and rapidly evolving subject area.

Finally Rachael Hincks in Chapter 11 examines aspects of the curriculum in relation to the role of the TA. She also explores in some detail personalized learning and creativity with a range of case study examples.

Appendix 2 contains all the latest HLTA Standards and relevant website addresses. If you are considering applying for HLTA status, you will need to identify and record evidence of your practice and begin to maintain a Professional Development Record (PDR) in which you can collect and record data and evidence alongside the HTLA Standard as guided by the TTA (www.hlta.gov.uk).

Further Reading 📖

Department for Education and Skills (2002) *Consultation on Developing the Role of School Support Staff*. London: DfES.

www.canteach.gov.uk – Teacher Training Agency's definitive website.

www.dcsf.gov.uk – website for the Department for Children, Schools and Families. Information available on The Children's Plan and regular reviews and updates.

www.hlta.gov.uk – website providing easy access to up-to-date developments on higher level Teaching Assistant developments.

www.lg-employers.gov.uk – website providing information on the National Occupational Standards (NOS) which form the basis for National Vocational Qualifications (NVQs) at levels 2 and 3. Follow A–Z on web page, click 'T' and select relevant pages.

www.teachernet.gov.uk

SECTION 1

ROLES, RESPONSIBILITIES AND RELATIONSHIPS

CHANGING SCHOOLS, CHANGING ROLES FOR TEACHING ASSISTANTS

Mark Townsend and Maureen Parker

This chapter will:

- Document and explain the phenomenal increase in the number of Teaching Assistants (TAs) and Higher Level Teaching Assistants (HLTAS) in schools.
- Explore the increasingly diverse roles of support staff.
- Define and explore the notion of the TA as the 'new professional' in the classroom.

The traditional classroom, staffed by a single teacher, is rapidly disappearing in schools across the UK. (Wilson *et al.*, 2003)

RE-DEFINING THE ROLE OF THE TEACHING ASSISTANT IN A CLIMATE OF CHANGE

It is an exciting time to be a TA or HLTA. The role is evolving rapidly with its own dynamic structures and emerging professional identity. Indeed, if you have been working in schools over the past 10 years you will have seen the impact of a raft of initiatives, driven mostly by central government policy-making departments, and overseen by the Department for Children, Schools and Families. How schools have responded to this wave of change, varies widely, and will largely depend on those factors which underpin change and leadership described in Chapters 2 and 3. Nowhere are these changes more clearly exemplified than in the increase in numbers of school support staff, and in the responsibilities for teaching and learning that many of these staff have now acquired. Indeed, as Ofsted (2007) reports, there has been a 'revolutionary shift in the culture of the school workforce' resulting from school workforce reform. The number of support staff working in schools in England has more than doubled within 10 years (Blatchford *et al.*, 2006), and the Training and Development Agency for Schools (TDA, 2008) recorded, by early 2008, over 21,000 Teaching Assistants gaining Higher Level Teaching Assistant Status (HLTA), a new educational role only introduced in 2002.

Let's return to the TDA's definition of the roles of the TA and HLTA, highlighted in the introduction:

> Teaching assistants work alongside teachers in the classroom, helping pupils with their learning on an individual or group basis. Some specialise in areas such as literacy, numeracy, special education needs, music, English as an additional language, and the creative arts.
>
> Higher level teaching assistants (HLTAs) are experienced teaching assistants who plan and deliver learning activities under the direction of a teacher and assess, record and report on pupils' progress. They may also manage other classroom-based staff or may supervise a class in a teacher's absence. (http://www.tda.gov.uk/support/support_staff_roles/learningsupport staff.aspx (accessed 14 August 2008))

Whilst statistics and definitions clearly exist that describe the range of roles that TAs/HLTAs have, an actual understanding of effective support in the classroom is more difficult to achieve than one might anticipate. Research findings question the fundamental belief that providing additional educators in the classroom will always guarantee greater levels of achievement for pupils (Blatchford, 2003; Muijis and Reynolds, 2003; Peddar, 2006). However, Blatchford *et al.* (2006) certainly report on the positive factors, cited by many teachers, that TAs bring to the classroom: reduced workloads, lowered levels of stress, shared engagement in planning, and the benefits that additional one staffing brings to the delivery of intervention strategies. Our work with TAs/HLTAs suggests that an extra dimension is certainly added to schools where roles are clearly defined and understood for TAs/HLTAs and teachers.

ALL CHANGE: NEW POLICIES, NEW PRACTICES

The current government were, in part, elected because of their commitment to education. As the then Prime Minister Tony Blair is famously quoted as saying one of his top priorities for the country was 'education, education, education'. Indeed, since 1945 central government has become increasingly involved in directing what goes on in schools and how schools themselves should be organised. It can also be argued that since 1978 all successive governments have had two key objectives in mind: to raise educational standards in terms of measuring quantifiable learning outcomes, and to allow marketplace economics to be the main vehicle for driving up those standards. In other words, governments would instigate frameworks which allowed all to see the results and performance of schools, and, importantly, enable parents to make highly informed decisions about which school they wanted their children to attend. With the role of overseeing in great detail and reporting on the performance of all schools, would be the regulatory body, Ofsted giving detailed curriculum guidance, including that offered by the Qualifications and Curriculum Authority for those pupils with severe and complex learning difficulties (as exemplified by the 'P-scales'). The year 1997 was also a key date for a government focus upon 'inclusion' rather than integration, with an accompanying increase in support staff to begin to facilitate this process.

Changes made to the education system during the last 10 years include the consolidation of summative assessment processes, the revision of core curriculum frameworks, the extended schools initiative, workforce reforms, and perhaps most significantly of all, the introduction of the Every Child Matters agenda in 2004 and the Children's Plan in 2008. Perhaps almost of equal importance, in terms of impacting especially on the role of the HLTA, has been the introduction of statutory Planning, Preparation and Assessment (PPA) time for teachers. This has encouraged many schools to formally employ HLTAs (and sometimes TAs) in the role of leading the teaching of whole classes, without the direct supervision of a teacher – although the content and delivery of the lesson will have been planned under the guidance of the appropriate teacher. For many support staff, this is a very significant development of their role.

HLTA
Standards
14, 16,
19, 20 &
31

WHY ARE TAs CONSIDERED FUNDAMENTAL TO THE IMPLEMENTATION OF THE GOVERNMENT'S VISION FOR SCHOOLS?

If the government is going to succeed in its vision for achieving a world class education system (Balls, 2008), there may yet need to be more changes to the way schools are currently organised and the roles and responsibilities of the adults in them. You, as a TA, may certainly have noted that the days of the 'traditional' classroom staffed by one adult (the teacher) who is responsible for delivering all aspects of teaching and learning are almost over. Townsend and Parker (2006, 2007) reported that schools have developed the role of the TA, and especially the HLTA in very different ways to begin to address the need for change in both the opportunity for management roles for TAs and how they are managed.

Wilson *et al.'s* extensive 2007 report found that just over half of all schools had developed a specific role for HLTAs. To that effect HLTAs are integral to helping to achieve the current Every Child Matters (DfEs, 2004) agenda which focuses on developing an 'integrated approach' for all those in agencies working for the welfare of children. The latest initiative, the Children's Plan, announced in 2008, will drive forward ideas on improving partnerships with parents, and build on both the Extended Schools and the Inclusion agendas.

The government certainly believes that increasing the number of support staff in the classroom will help to impact on children's academic achievement (Blair, 2005), and overall performance of pupils in Standard Assessment Tests (SATs) has, by the indicators set by the DfES, certainly been raised as the role of TAs has become one of increasing direct teaching and learning suppport. However, the direct correlation between educator numbers and effective raising of pupil achievement is a complex and under-researched area (Vincett *et al.*, 2005).

In terms of contributing generally towards helping schools meet the demands of these government strategies, the TA role and can be defined, according to the TDA (date unknown, accessed 12 July 2008) in terms of providing effective practice as one which:

- seeks to enable pupils to become more independent learners
- fosters the participation of pupils in the academic and social processes of the school
- helps to raise standards of learning for pupils.

DRIVING FORCES FOR CHANGE

In Chapter 3, Chris Lee discusses the importance of identifying 'drivers of change', and how an understanding of these 'drivers' can help us to manage changes. Indeed, it is evident from well-documented research that the educational landscape is shifting with increasing rapidity (Blatchford, 2003; Townsend and Parker, 2006; Wilson *et al.*, 2003). Whilst it is always impossible to categorically isolate reasons for change – whether it happens as a result of deliberate interventions, or is a reflection of wider issues in society at large – there are clearly several pieces of government legislation which are affecting the roles of TAs. Workforce reform has been the prime factor, which the government saw as being fundamental to implementing its future education policies.

The Workforce Reform Agenda

HLTA Standard 6

Driven initially by the Green Paper of 1998, Teachers: Meeting the Challenge of Change (DfEE, 1998) and the subsequent Workforce Reform Agenda (of 2003), teachers have seen several key aspects of their roles transferred to support staff. Apart from moving the responsibilities of some 25 routine tasks from teacher to TA as part of the School Workforce Reform Agenda (Teachernet, 2003), the provision of planning, preparation and assessment (PPA) time for all teachers in English primary schools has involved most TAs in a greater level of responsibility for teaching and learning than could have been predicted even 10 years ago. Indeed, there are many TAs (primarily HLTAs) now who are teaching whole classes under the direction or supervision of a teacher, leading small groups of pupils in 'catch-up' sessions, assisting teachers with their planning and preparation, and even taking on subject coordination roles including that of the role of Assistant SENCO in many primary schools. As a result of workforce reform, Ofsted (2007) believes that there has been a 'revolutionary shift in the culture of the school workforce'. They also report that:

HLTA Standards 17, 18 30 & 31

- Teacher's time and work are now focused more directly on teaching and learning.
- The substantial expansion of the wider workforce at all levels is allowing schools to extend the curriculum, provide more care, guidance and support for pupils, and monitor children's progress more effectively.

Pupils benefited from increased support from members of the wider workforce. In addition, deploying adults with different skills allowed the schools to improve care and guidance for vulnerable pupils and those at risk from exclusion from mainstream education, thus meeting the government's drive for inclusion of all pupils through the development

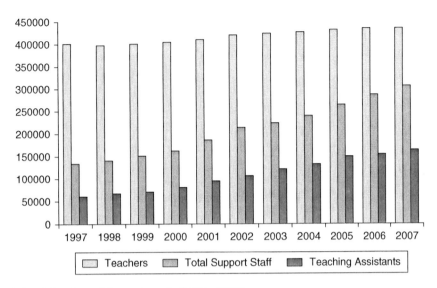

Figure 1.1   School workforce trends (DfES, 2007)

of the Common Assessment Framework (2006) and latterly, the Children's Plan which 'aims to make [England] the best place in the world for our children and young people to grow up' (Balls, 2008).

The increase in the number of teaching assistants (full-time equivalent positions) in England has been phenomenal, rising from approximately 60,000 in 1997 to nearly 163,000 in 2007. Figure 1.1 illustrates the consistent growth which has taken place in the school workforce (now referred to as the Children's Workforce) over the past 10 years.

As stated earlier in this chapter, the TDA has also recorded over 21,000 TAs gaining Higher Level Teaching Assistant Status (HLTA). Those with HLTA status will have demonstrated that can meet 33 newly revised Standards (January 2008) (Appendix 2), including providing evidence that they can teach whole classes as well as small groups of pupils, under the direction of a qualified teacher. These standards are the beginnings of moving towards a structure that may in the future also relate to pay and conditions of service. Attainment of the status does not for the vast majority mean a post, however research conducted by the authors does indicate that it may bring a change in role and status within the school setting.

Wilson *et al.* (2007), translates these numbers into a detailed analysis of statistics relating to the deployment and experiences of HLTAs. Some 68% of schools in the sample surveyed now had one or two members of staff with HLTA status, although not all of these worked in an HLTA post since only around 53% of schools employed either one or two members of staff to carry out what they considered to be HLTA-level duties.

Activity

Having read about the growth in the numbers of school support staff, consider how your own school has evolved in the time you have been working there in terms of:

- The increase in numbers of support staff now employed?
- What key areas of developments, and new initiatives, have support staff been able to facilitate in school (for example, lunchtime clubs, specific learning support strategies)?
- Has the rapid growth of support staff been successful in your setting? What have been the challenges and opportunities that they presented?

Many of you as TAs who have been working in schools for any length of time will have seen considerable changes to both your roles and job titles. Five years ago the role may have been described as primarily logistical, offering practical support to the teacher, notably preparing resources and tidying the classroom, today you are much more likely to have enhanced responsibilities for supporting learning and teaching, including involvement in planning and assessment, and even subject coordination.

HLTA Standards 1, 2, 3, 4, 13, 14, 17, 30 & 31

Case study

Jane, a TA who we also meet later on in Chapter 10, decided to become a TA 12 years ago when her two children were both in primary school. She had a background in the banking sector, but had spent seven years looking after her children, an experience which prompted a real interest in learning development, and a decision to change career to one which involved working in the classroom. After 6 months of working as a school volunteer, she successfully applied for the job of Classroom Assistant. For the first few years she worked in a Reception class, and was mainly occupied with offering very practical support to the class teacher, including setting up activities and tidying resources, and managing the various 'corners' (role-play, book) of the classroom. Within two years, the school had changed her job title to that of Learning Support Assistant and Jane also noticed a shift in the emphasis of her role: she was now charged with helping individual pupils to meet very specific learning objectives drawn from the Foundation Stage Profile. She acquired an in-depth knowledge of relevant curriculum documentation, and met regularly with her class teacher to plan and review her work. By 2000, her job title changed again: the term Teaching Assistant became the DfES' preferred title for classroom support staff, and Jane once again felt an impact on her role. Moving up to a Year 5 class a year later, she demonstrated particular strengths in her work with children who demonstrated learning difficulties. She took several groups of pupils on a regular basis for 'catch up' literacy and numeracy activities, and developed a real insight into the needs of pupils with complex learning difficulties, notably Autistic Spectrum Disorders. She worked closely with the school's SENCO, developing activities to meet individual pupil's IEP targets, and played an increasingly important role in monitoring and reviewing a number of children's progress. The SENCO, along with her head teacher encouraged Jane to undertake a short route to achieving HLTA Status, which she subsequently successfully gained. In the past two years, Jane has seen her role transformed; promoted to the post of Assistant SENCO, she now carries additional responsibilities for developing IEPs and resources for teachers throughout the school, attends annual review meetings, and has led a number of training programmes on Special Educational Needs.

HLTA
Standards
4, 6 & 15

As with Jane, you may have started out as a TA, but your role may have evolved into those such as a Specialist TA for Behaviour, Autism, Speech and Language, Literacy, Learning Mentors, Cover Supervisors, or ICT Technicians, where your focus of responsibility is much narrower and the accompanying job descriptions require very specific skills and attributes to perform the role effectively.

 Activity

Consider how your own role has changed throughout the time you have been working as a TA, and reflect upon these questions:

- How has the degree of responsibility you now have for teaching and learning in the classroom changed over the time you've been a TA?
- Which of these responsibilities may have been driven forward by a central government agenda?

HOW ARE TAs TAKING ON THE ADDITIONAL ROLE OF SUPPORTING TEACHING AND LEARNING?

Many Teaching Assistants are increasingly taking on aspects of what would have been considered to have been in the teacher's remit. Vincett *et al.* (2005: 32) note that 'Today, TAs are thought of assistants who teach, and not merely as assistants to the teacher'. It is clear that what would have been a controversial statement 10 years ago, is now gaining a considerable degree of acceptance amongst teachers. Townsend and Parker (2007) undertook research into how teachers themselves felt about the changing notion of 'what is a teacher?' A series of interviews, with extracts contained in the following pages, indicate the high level of enthusiasm evident amongst teachers when questioned as to whether they felt their own professional identities were being eroded as a result of TAs taking over some aspects of their roles. Ginny, a primary school teacher, was highly supportive of her HLTA's enhanced role, and the impact on her own thinking:

I even think that the new roles have changed us. Not just in doing menial tasks, but the HLTAs actually engaging with teaching and learning ... Like having two teachers in the classroom ... they've [HLTAs] have had a lot of training - Literacy and Numeracy - just as good as us [teachers] ... Planning is shared, and they're involved with the SEN interviews with parents.

Wilson *et al.* (2007) found that almost three-quarters of senior managers (73%) indicated that the HLTA role had reduced teacher workload, at least to some extent. This response by a geography teacher in a large, inner city school was typical from participants.

> My HLTA has made a real difference to my workload … I meet with her each Friday and plan the activities she needs to do with John who's got ASD for the next week. To be honest, she understands the boy's needs much more than I do, been on quite a few courses, whereas I'm just a geography teacher. She has lots of really good ideas for motivating him, and he's made great progress since she started working in my lessons.

In the primary sector, the significance of change and the evolving TA/HLTA role was perhaps even clearer to see:

> I'm totally dependent on my TA now. She intuitively knows how to work with the pupils, even the challenging ones. The pupils really respect her, see her on the same level as me. They produce really good work, and she's a real whizz in the computer – a real boon given some of the great ICT resources we've got. Our SATs results have been really good this year, I think she can take a lot of the credit for this. (Year 6 class teacher, large suburban primary school)

Whilst there does now appear to be an emerging overlap between aspects of TAs' and teachers' roles, Farrell *et al.* (1999, cited in Blatchford, 2003: 91) concluded that there was still a clearly understood demarcation between teacher and TA roles by all the stakeholders involved, and evidence from practitioners and observers would tend to support this observation made on Governornet (2006):

> The National Agreement states that teachers and support staff are not interchangeable and that each class or group for timetabled core and other foundation subjects and for religious education must be assigned a qualified teacher to teach them. The fact that HLTAs may be working with whole classes for some of the time does not make them substitutes for a qualified teacher.

However, Vincett *et al.* (2005: 32) strongly state that 'TAs can and should be involved in the broadest range of activity in the classroom … and … fulfil a wide range of tasks that parallel or shadow those of the teacher'.

Is there now a need for educators to re-assess their definition of what constitutes the role of 'teacher', given the context of changes taking place not only within education but in society itself? Margaret, a head teacher of a large primary school certainly thinks so, acknowledging that perhaps the notion of 'what a teacher is' itself needs to be re-thought:

> Interesting – the role of the teacher has changed a lot. Teachers may now not be so much the practitioner, more the planner and manager of the curriculum … it's now about supporting other adults, a wider sphere of working. (Head teacher, primary school)

The Training and Development Agency for schools, in the development of the Higher Level Teaching Assistant Status, acknowledged the evolving role of the TA, and the potential it has for impacting on school structures. Responsibilities for many tasks which were once the sole remit of the teacher have shifted, including leading whole classes – although the teacher is still charged with directing and overseeing these activities. Importantly, there has been a cultural shift in attitudes towards HLTAs by many school management teams. For them, this new role is seen as one which can bring about changes which are potentially dynamic and refreshing.

HLTA
Standard
33

> The HLTAs are flexible – responding to their new roles ... they're adapting to change, different ways of engaging with teaching and learning, because it's new. [They are] taking things forward in different ways. [They have] space in their head for things, ... Teachers are unable to take on any more - TAs will embrace new ideas. (Head teacher of a large market town primary school)

Teaching Assistants and HLTAs, it would appear, are impacting not only on school structures and systems, but becoming embedded into the pedagogical processes to such an extent that they are able to demonstrate real skills in teaching and learning practices. This senior manager in a large inner city secondary school holds this vision about seeing HLTAs: 'moving towards being like a teacher ... good HLTAs can be the teacher'. And she was not alone in this view, although Charlie, working in an infant class, took a contrasting view about the *practitioner* component: 'These changes have been coming for a long time ... we're [teachers and support staff] all practitioners, I'm the lead practitioner, but we're all equal here in terms of status'.

Understanding how the role of the TA is currently developing and the expectations all have of each others' roles is paramount if support staff and teachers are to co-exist in ways which are conducive to the production of a harmonious learning environment. Research by the authors indicated a lack of common understanding of the various roles performed by TA/HLTAs in schools. Whilst tensions between teachers and TAs over their roles were not identified as an issue, nevertheless, many participants in this research cited a lack of training to support the development of collaborative working skills. The role of manager of other adults in the classroom is clearly a new responsibility for most teachers in mainstream education, and one for which many may not feel adequately prepared. A TDA funded project 2005–2006, seeking to explore this concern, offered the opportunity to begin to understand the range of roles support staff had through a project that initiated a dialogue between trainee teachers, TAs, teacher educators and Foundation Degree staff. Third-year students on initial teacher training identified what had helped or hindered them in developing effective practice in working with TAs on school experience placements. Trainees who were placed in schools with HLTAs indicated that it was difficult at times to understand this role in the context of how it was presented to them. They were just beginning to construct their identity as teachers and as James-Wilson (2001: 29) cited in Day *et al.* (2007: 105) notes:

> The ways in which teachers form their professional identities are influenced both by how they feel about themselves and how they feel about their students. This professional identity helps them to position or situate themselves in relation to their students and to make appropriate and effective adjustments in their practice and their beliefs about and engagement with students.

The trainees were clearly indicating how they were aware of how to position themselves and construct their identities in relation to pupils but were less sure of this in relation to the roles of support staff, specifically HLTAs. It is worth considering that trainees, therefore, may not be aware of the range of skills and expertise you and your colleagues may have, so opening a conversation may both help them and offer you further opportunities for collaboration and professional development. Chapter 4 offers strategies to begin to initiate such a dialogue if you are unsure.

HLTA Standard 17

Rueda and Monzo (2002) suggested that power differences between teacher and para-educators (TAs), affect collaboration and interaction. The addition of a new role such as HLTA to a school staff could be both a challenge and an opportunity to forge more meaningful and effective professional dialogues both within a school staff and as part of a multi-agency team within an extended provision. Mary Pittman, in her chapter on teamwork, discusses how an ethos of collaboration can be developed, nurtured, and used to benefit adults and children alike in the classroom, crucial to this is ensuring that trainee teachers are fully aware of the range of roles of support staff within the children's workforce – indeed, of 36 roles recently identified by the TDA in schools only six are teacher roles.

THE NEW ROLES OF SUPPORT STAFF IN THE CLASSROOM

Curriculum coordination

The authors of this chapter have increasingly found that many TAs and HLTAs are now in the position of leading curriculum areas, particularly in the primary sector, such as

HLTA Standards 15 & 33

art, modern foreign languages and personal, social and health education. As such, they may also be teaching whole classes (in both primary and secondary phases), planning lessons and recording pupils' progress, leading SEN departments, as well as having responsibility for managing other support staff in their school.

The leadership and management role

It is becoming increasingly evident that TAs and HLTAs are now being integrated into the strategic development plans of many schools, with head teachers seeing the role as fundamental to the provision of effective learning and teaching. Many also include in their vision how TAs and HLTAs may take on management responsibilities which previously would have been carried out by a member of the teaching staff. All the head teachers questioned in Townsend and Parker's (2006) research had given considerable thought to the way that they had implemented the new role. Alistair, a head teacher in a large inner-city primary school is not untypical in expressing the significance that school leaders are now attaching to the role:

> I need people to lead from the centre. I need people like [my HLTA] to lead developments and the management of TAs - she only comes to me when she is unsure ... We've created a more hierarchical structure to the school ... The HLTA is a middle manager, part of a team to enable children to take advantage of being here. We've identified a very clear role for her: lead and support TA, co-ordinate staffing/absence, develop a curriculum role.

New career structures

In the 10 years since Farrell *et al.* (1999) presented their research into the management, role and training of Learning Support Assistants, which identified an almost complete lack of career structure or indeed opportunities for promotion and professional development, a sea-change has occurred, not least in the development of career opportunities which are facilitated by gaining HLTA status.

However, what Wilson *et al.*'s (2007) research also shows is the inconsistency in how schools have defined the role, the financial rewards that HLTAs can expect to receive and the impact, in terms of effectiveness, that they are having in schools. We are now seeing the emergence, however, of career structures and job opportunities for TAs, albeit in an ad hoc manner, which were non-existent just a few years ago. Whilst most TAs are paid on a pro-rata basis, excluding holiday periods, there are now HLTAs on pay-scales which are not dissimilar to those of a Newly Qualified Teacher, with job descriptions which reflect the enhanced responsibilities, notably for managing other staff, and specific aspects of teaching and learning.

THE 'NEW PROFESSIONAL' IN THE CLASSROOM

The importance of the recognition of having attained HLTA status by their colleagues and the state (Parker and Townsend, 2005), has enabled HLTAs to approach new responsibilities not only with confidence and an identified ability but also, as 'professionals', as this head teacher states. 'The two HLTAs [in this school] have grown professionally as a result of undertaking HLTA. One in particular has developed greatly her self-esteem – had low confidence'. (Head teacher, large suburban primary school).

Many other participants interviewed by the authors during their research, cited the word 'professional' when describing the work of their TAs and HLTAs. This is a significant point, and not only reflects the very considerable degree of responsibility and skills now expected of support staff, but how a societal view of what constitutes a 'professional' is changing. Hargreaves (2000) identifies the qualities that used to characterize the 'professional' as being one who has certainly undertaken a long period of training, has acquired a vast body of knowledge, demonstrates a commitment to clients' needs, and operates with a high degree of autonomy. Many now believe that the role of the educator is changing so much that we perhaps should re-define what we consider are the features of the professional, or rather, constitutes the 'new professional' in the classroom. (Furlong, 2005; Lefstein, 2005; Townsend and Parker, 2006) Should we not now also include other qualities which are increasingly important for the professional to demonstrate, such as an ability to work closely with more diverse communities, to be able to communicate effectively with external agencies, and to promote strong partnerships with parents? Hargreaves (2000) also noted the potential that technology can have in terms of helping educators to break down barriers to learning. Should the 'new professional' also be adept at using technology? It is certainly essential today that we are able to access effectively the huge range of guidance and support which is disseminated on the internet by government agencies. Indeed, it can be argued that the modern educator

HLTA
Standards
12 & 28

needs to know how and where to obtain information quickly and accurately (usually through the use of technology), rather than try to develop and hold within themselves an ever increasingly available body of knowledge.

 Activity

Consider the questions below:

- What do you believe are the characteristics that constitute a 'professional'?
- Consider the more traditional definitions of a professional. How do you meet these requirements in your own role within the classroom?
- What do you consider to be important aspects of your role which you also consider to be the qualities needed by the 'new professional' in the classroom?

HLTA
Standards
15, 16 &
20

All educators require a vast body of knowledge that is necessary to support them in their roles, and to make for effective practice – or at least require access to important sources of information and support. On a professional level, this will range from a familiarity with statutory frameworks and school policies to Local Authority guidance. It will also include knowledge of the pupils' individual needs, and any medical conditions where relevant, such as Autistic Spectrum Disorders. On a more practical level, you will need to know about the children you are working with: what are their exact needs; how do they learn most effectively; what can you bring to their learning? You will have acquired a huge and perhaps surprising amount of knowledge in your role, but even more important is how this knowledge is applied to your own practice in the classroom.

What is clearly emerging, as a result of many years of new educational policies and initiatives, is the degree of change which has come about in our perception of the learning environment. The government views education as a central component of its 'modernization' agenda, a key driver of societal change. Data, other than statistical, relating to how these changes have impacted on educators, pupils and parents remains relatively rare. As we have seen in this chapter, TAs and HLTAs have developed roles in many schools which can be surprisingly autonomous and varied. These may involve taking responsibilities for planning and delivering lessons to whole classes without the teacher being present. You, as a key member of the teaching and learning team, will have faced – and will continue to face – challenges which, whilst perhaps viewed with trepidation or scepticism initially, have enabled you to re-think and re-consider your own role and practice, perhaps many times over. This can be seen as an opportunity to really engage with new ideas, to learn innovative ways of approaching problems, and to see outcomes of learning which are quite different to those expected in the (recent) past. The subsequent chapters of this book seek to challenge your own thinking, and present you with opportunities – and hopefully the enthusiasm – for developing your role even more effectively and creatively in the future. Indeed, we are reaching the stage in education where perhaps we need to re-define our own notion of *what is a teacher*? (Arnot and Miles, 2005; Furlong, 2005; Lefstein, 2005).

This chapter asks you to consider your role in both its widest sense and to reflect on your specific skills and expertise. Therefore, you should consider this chapter against all the HLTA standards as it might begin to form a personal audit of your strengths and areas you could develop further.

〰️ Reflective questions

- How do you see your own role developing in terms of helping your school to meet the evolving agenda of education reform?
- What steps do you think you need to take to achieve the effective development of your role?

Further Reading 📖

Edmond, N. (2003) 'School-based Learning for Teaching Assistants', *Journal of Education for Teaching* 29(2): 113–23.

Edmond, N. (2004) 'The Foundation Degree as Evidence of a New Higher Education: A Study of HE Provision for Teaching Assistants', *Higher Education Review* 36(3): 33–53.

Etzioni, A. (ed.) (1969) *The Semi-professions and Their Organizaton.* New York: The Free Press.

Thompson, M. (2006) 'Re-modelling as De-professionalisation', FORUM 48(2): 189–200.

Yarker, P. (2005) 'On Not Being a Teacher: The Professional and Personal Costs of Workforce Remodelling', FORUM 47(2&3): 169–74.

References

Arnot, M. and Miles, P. (2005) 'A Reconstruction of the Gender Agenda: The Contradictory Gender Dimensions in New Labour's Educational and Economic Policy', *Oxford Review of Education* 3(1): 173–89.

Balls, E. (2008) 'The Children's Plan: Building Brighter Futures – Summary', available online at http://www.dfes.gov.uk/publications/childrensplan/downloads/Childrens_Plan_Executive_Summary.pdf (accessed 13 June 2008).

Blair, T. (2005) 'Speech on Education to the City of London Academy', available online at http://www.number-10.gov.uk/output/Page8181.asp (accessed 1 June 2006).

Blatchford, P. (2003) *The Class Size Debate: Is Small Better?* Maidenhead: Open University Press.

Blatchford, P., Bassett, P., Brown, P., Martin, C., Russell, A. and Webster, R. (2006) *Deployment and Impact of Support Staff in Schools. Report on Findings from the Second National Questionnaire Survey of Schools, Support Staff and Teachers* (Strand 1, Wave 2 – 2006), available online at http://www.dfes.gov.uk/research/data/uploadfiles/DCSF-RR005.pdf (accessed 15 May 2008).

Day, C., Sammons, P., Stobart, G., Kingston, A. and Qing, G. (2007) *Teachers Matter: Connecting Lives, Work and Effectiveness.* Maidenhead: University Press.

Department for Education and Skills (2004) *Every Child Matters: the consultation process and summary of questions.* London: The Stationery Office.

Department for Education and Employment (1998) *Teachers: meeting the challenge of change.* London: The Stationery Office.

Department of Education and Skills (2003).

Department for Education and Skills (2007) 'School Workforce in England', available online at: http://www.dfes.gov.uk (accessed: 24 August 2008).

Farrell, P., Balshaw, M. and Polat, F. (1999) *The Management, Role and Training of Learning Support Assistants*. London: DfEE.

Furlong, J. (2005) 'New Labour and Teacher Education: The End of an Era', *Oxford Review of Education* 31(1): 119–34.

Hargreaves, A. (2000) 'Four Ages of Professionalism and Professional Learning', *Teachers and Teaching: History and Practice* 6(2): 151–82.

Lefstein, A. (2005) 'Thinking About the Technical and the Personal in Teaching', *Cambridge Journal of Education* 35(3): 333–56.

Muijis, D. and Reynolds, D. (2003) 'The Effectiveness of the Use of Learning Support Assistants in Improving the Mathematics Achievement of Low Achieving Pupils in Primary School', *Educational Research* 45(3): 219–30.

Ofsted (2007) 'Reforming and Developing the School Workforce', available online at http://www.ofsted.gov.uk/publications/070020 (accessed 10 May 2008).

Parker, M. and Townsend, M. (2005) 'It's What I do Already: Becoming a Higher Level Teaching Assistant', *British Educational Research Association Conference*. University of Glamorgan, September. Glamorgan.

Peddar, D. (2006) 'Are Small Classes Better? Understanding Relationships between Class Size, Classroom Processes and Pupils' Learning', *Oxford Review of Education* 32(2): 213–34.

Quicke, J. (1998) 'Towards a New Professionalism for "New Times": Some Problems and Possibilities', *Teacher Development* 2(3): 323–37.

Rueda, R. and Monzo, D.L. (2002) 'Apprenticeship for Teaching: Professional Development Issues Surrounding the Collaborative Relationship between Teachers and Para-educators', *Teaching and Teacher Education* 18(5): 503–21.

Training and Development Agency for Schools (date unknown (a)) 'Support staff roles', available online at: http://www.tda.gov.uk/support/support_staff_roles/learningsupportstaff.aspx (accessed: 14 August 2008).

Training and Development Agency for Schools (2008) 'Higher Level Teaching Assistants', available on line at: http://www.tda.gov.uk (accessed: 15 August 2008).

Training and Development Agency for Schools (date unknown (b)) 'Definition of Effective Practice', available online at http://www.tda.gov.uk/upload/resources/ppt/sec_role_context08.ppt (accessed: 12 July 2008).

Teachernet (date unknown)' School workforce re-modelling', available online at: http://www.teachernet.gov.uklwholeschool/remodelling (accessed: 15 August 2008).

Townsend, M. and Parker, M. (2006) 'Changing Times, Changing Roles: Evaluating the Impact of Higher Level Teaching Assistants on Learning and Teaching in the Classroom', *British Educational Research Association Conference*, Warwick University, September, Warwick.

Townsend, M. and Parker, M. (2007) 'The Silent Revolution: Higher Level Teaching Assistants and their impact on a contemporary notion of the teacher', *British Educational Research Association Conference*, The London Institute of Education, September, London.

Vincett, K., Cremin, H. and Thomas, G. (2005) Teachers and Teaching Assistants Working Together. Buckingham: Open University Press.

Wilson, V., Schlapp, U. and Davidson, J. (2003) 'An Extra Pair of Hands? Managing Classroom Assistants in Scottish primary schools', *Education Management and Administration* 31(2): 189–205.

Wilson, R., Sharp, C., Shuayb, M., Kendall, L., Wade, P. and Easton, C. (2007) 'Research into the Deployment and Impact of Support Staff who have Achieved HLTA Status: Final Report'. *National Foundation for Educational Research*, available online at http://www.tda.gov.uk/upload/resources/pdf/n/nfer_hlta_report_07.pdf (accessed 31 August 2007).

DISTRIBUTED LEADERSHIP FOR THE TEACHING ASSISTANT

Kitty Heardman

This chapter will:

- Explain why leadership is increasingly a part of the TA role.
- Present leadership models to illustrate how change is facilitated.
- Show how previous experience and skills can be applied to leadership roles.
- Enable TAs to identify which leadership skills and behavioural traits they possess.
- Give practical advice on time management and organizing meetings.

When the decision to introduce the National Agreement (2003a) was taken by the government, it was in the context of recruitment and retention difficulties concerning the teaching profession. It was recognized that issues such as the administrative burden upon teachers and the decline of classroom discipline, combined with the pressures of league tables and regular inspections of schools, with reports being widely publicized, were leading to teachers leaving the profession after relatively short periods of service, and a marked increase in the rate at which experienced teachers were choosing to take early retirement. Thus at the same time the initiative was taken to provide schools with training in a model of change management known as 'Remodelling'. This enabled schools to identify systematically the respective skills and knowledge possessed by each member of staff regardless of qualified teacher status, and, together with legislation that facilitated the delivery of learning activities to whole classes by members of the team other than teachers (DfES 2003b), led to the creation of roles of responsibility for development of areas of the curriculum and school improvement by those who were employed as Teaching Assistants. Over the past five years since the first schools were involved in the Remodelling Process, the number of TAs in schools has increased, and at the same time, the proportion of staff members other than teachers, including Learning Mentors, TAs, HLTAs and Cover Supervisors, holding leadership and management roles has undergone a significant expansion.

HLTA Standard 33

Collarbone (2005 p. 22) states that 'the new demands on schools will require new ways of working, and to make them work will require a greater degree of team working and more widely distributed leadership authority'. But what does this mean in practice for Teaching Assistants?

According to the National College for School Leadership:

> Distributed leadership entails the view that *varieties of expertise are distributed across the many, not the few*. Related to openness of the boundaries of leadership is the idea that numerous, distinct, germane perspectives and capabilities can be found in individuals spread through the group or organisation. If these are brought together it is possible to forge a concertive dynamic which represents more than the sum of the individual contributors. Initiatives may be inaugurated by those with relevant skills in a particular context, but others will then adopt, adapt and improve them within a mutually trusting and supportive culture. (Bennett *et al.*, 2003 p. 7)

HLTA Standard 6

All Teaching Assistants possess skills, knowledge and previous experience that can be shared, adopted and applied by other members of the team, bringing about improvement in a specific area of the curriculum or in an aspect of access to the curriculum as a direct result of this collaborative working. This relies inevitably upon trust, from stakeholders themselves, colleagues, and ultimately the leadership of the school or other educational setting. The case study below demonstrates such trust.

HLTA Standards 4, 5 & 6

Case study

Sasha has been a TA for 10 years and has been a Specialist Teaching Assistant for Speech and Language for five years, supporting pupils from Nursery to Key Stage 2. Since gaining HLTA her level of responsibility has increased involving close liaison and communication with teachers, TAs, parents and other professionals. She notes

> in order for my role to be effective it is vital that I involve other professionals to advise and guide me not only from within school, but from outside agencies too. I have built up a close working relationship with the Speech Therapist and we meet weekly to discuss the pupils and review their programmes. I now have a better awareness of how to support and liaise with parents and can be the difference between them wanting to sign a referral form or not. When I talk to the parents about their child's referral I now assess whether I feel it is a family that would attend clinic or if the assessment is better done in school. This system has worked much better with both the child and parent attending.

HLTA Standards 6, 8, 10 & 19

This case study demonstrates how effective it has been to 'distribute' the leadership of this specialist area from the SENCO to a HLTA with specialized knowledge.

MODELS OF LEADERSHIP

In Chapter 3, Chris Lee states that 'increasingly school leaders are looking to their staff to be innovative and play a major role in school development'. He goes on to list some

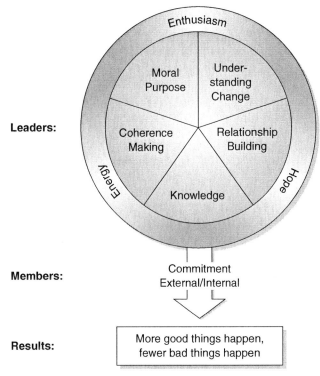

Figure 2.1   A framework for leadership (Fullan, 2004)

principles that might inform your role as a change agent. As a leader of an aspect of school improvement planning, it is inevitable that the TA will need to be aware of models of leadership that facilitate change. This section will consider two such models, starting with Fullan's Framework for Leadership (2004).

Fullan's Framework for Leadership

A diagram of this can be found in Figure 2.1. Fullan puts forward five components for school leadership as follows.

Moral purpose

In an educational context, this would be at the heart of the school's aims or the mission statement. It is reflected in the culture and ethos of the whole establishment. As Collarbone (2005 p. 22) puts it, 'raising standards is important, but if leaders do not treat others well and fairly, they may find they are without followers'. As a TA you are part of creating that culture and ethos.

HLTA
Standards
6 & 33

Understanding change

HLTA
Standards
4, 6,
32 & 33

Although Fullan states that change advice in management books is often contradictory, the Remodelling Process, in which all schools were given the opportunity to receive guidance and training to facilitate school workforce reforms, is flexible, and has enabled many schools to involve their whole staff teams in implementing changes. You may have been asked to implement some aspect of change. Shanta, previously a TA but now a Pupil Services Manager and HLTA, reflected on how this evolved:

> My status in school as Pupil Services Manager was already recognised and going for HLTA seemed an obvious progression. This was the time when the role of HLTA was still unclear: I remember that some staff were unsure if this was something they agreed with. However, the school Change Team of which I was a member discussed it in full and decided to support.

Building relationships

In order to lead successfully the implementation of any project or scheme, it is essential to create positive team dynamics. Within any context we are all part of teams whether as participants or in a leadership role and may have to create new teams when we are invited to develop and run projects. This is more fully explored in Chapter 4. Maria, now an HLTA, describes an example of the range of projects you may able to become involved with and lead a team in implementing:

HLTA
Standards
6, 7, 21,
27 & 28

> one of my greatest achievements has been the development of the international school link at my school with another in South Africa which is proving to be most successful. I have been able to introduce some joint projects between the two schools ... this link has also provided me with the opportunity to become involved in outside agencies that are able to offer support and guidance for international school links.

Creating and sharing knowledge

In order for this to happen, the first three need to be in place. A TA who has been involved in a research project or in gathering information for the compilation of a new policy will be keen to share the resulting knowledge with other members of the team. First of all, however, there is a requirement for positive relationships that foster trust, a basic understanding of the ongoing process of change and a commitment to the moral purpose of the establishment. Siobhan, as part of her Foundation Degree studies, conducted a survey of all the teachers in her school to determine what they felt the role of the TA was in implementing the Behaviour Policy. She observed that:

HLTA
Standards
6, 7 & 16

> whilst it was really interesting I realised that I had to really be aware of ethics and followed the university guidelines in carrying out my survey. All the teachers and TAs who took part needed to know that their answers were not identifiable and what I was going to do with the results. I was asked to join the working party that was reviewing the Behaviour Policy and I wrote the section on the role of the TA which I'm quite proud of!

Making coherence

Education policy is changing all the time, with new initiatives being introduced every academic year, and many existing ones, such as the National Strategies, subject to regular revisions. In order for all of this to be manageable, a high degree of collaboration is required, and this is even more vital with the Every Child Matters agenda. Joe works in a Pupil Referral Unit as a specialist Behaviour HLTA and part of his role involves liaising with all the secondary schools where pupils are partly integrated into the mainstream curriculum and in some instances also involves him linking with the local FE college (Life Long Learning setting) in implementing aspects of the work-related curriculum and being aware of the 14–19 agenda.

> it's an important role and one that I can give perhaps more time to than a teacher, mainly because its not always straightforward with these pupils as what works one day won't the next … the key thing is that I feel I make a difference to both the understanding of the pupils of what my role is for them but also so that teachers and tutors don't get frustrated with them … new inititiaves are all very well but its the pupils we have to think of.

The Five Practices

The second model of leadership we will consider is known as the Five Practices of Leadership. The central focus of this leadership model, constructed by Kouzes and Posner (2003 p. xiii) following detailed consideration of leadership case studies and analysis of 'tens of thousands of leadership assessment instruments', relates to encouragement and feedback. According to Kouzes and Posner, when it comes to getting extraordinary things done, leaders:

1. Model the way.
2. Inspire a shared vision.
3. Challenge the process.
4. Enable others to act.
5. Encourage the heart.

In fact, they felt so strongly about the fifth practice that they went on to break it down into 'Seven essentials of encouraging', creating an 'encouragement index' along the way. The five practices are, by and large, self-explanatory when applied to an educational setting. The first is about demonstrating good practice, the second relates well to the process of school improvement planning, as does the third, whereas the fourth leads to empowerment and delegation. In relation to the fifth practice:

> Leaders create relationships, and one of these relationships is about individuals and their work. Ultimately, we all work for a purpose, and that common purpose has to be served if we are to feel encouraged. Encouraging the heart only works if there is a fit between the person, the work, and the organisation. (Kouzes and Posner, 2003 p. xv)

LEADERSHIP TRAITS

Every role in an educational setting requires a degree of leadership, depending on the size and nature of the organization. In smaller establishments, where teams are restricted in size and people often fulfil multiple roles, this is becoming more and more prevalent. In Chapter 3, on change management, Chris Lee examines how this impacts on the way in which Teaching Assistants' roles have evolved, and outlines a number of strategies for becoming a part of the change process. As a result of applying the Remodelling Process to bring about a more effective deployment of existing workforces, many members of support staff teams in schools and colleges have analysed their personal qualities and career development thus far, going on to apply selected aspects of their previous experience to leadership and management roles that have evolved out of the revised models of leadership. Whilst acknowledging the complex nature of each individual personality and its inevitable uniqueness, owing to differences that can be attributed to social engineering, parental influences, cultural diversity and so on, it is possible to identify and apply specific characteristics that will promote effective leadership.

The following leadership attributes were identified by Gardner (1989 p. 48):

- Physical vitality and stamina.
- Intelligence and judgement-in-action.
- Willingness to accept responsibilities.
- Task competence.
- Understanding of followers/constituents and their needs.
- Skill in dealing with people.
- Need to achieve.
- Capacity to motivate.
- Courage and resolution.
- Capacity to win and hold trust.
- Capacity to manage, decide, set priorities.
- Confidence.
- Ascendance/dominance, assertiveness.
- Adaptability/flexibility of approach.

The above list is extensive, but it leaves room for the addition of further leadership qualities. It might be possible for a leader to recognize within himself or herself a number of these qualities, but not all of them. Similarly, some TAs might display other leadership traits. However, it is appropriate in this context to have a selection of such traits to which TAs can refer, in order to enable them to select a range of personal qualities that they feel they already possess, and seek opportunities to refine, develop and adapt them to their own particular circumstances.

Activity

Go to the *Leadership trait checklist* in Appendix 1 on p. 194. Consider the list of leadership attributes that is presented in the checklist. Identify those which apply to you, and write down three situations in which you might be required to draw upon them whilst fulfilling elements of your own specific role.

Completion of this activity will give you an idea of the direction in which to develop your existing skills, after which it will be possible to consider ways of applying them to a range of leadership roles as these become available within your setting.

LEADERSHIP ROLES

Case study: the team leader

Anna's first job was in retail and she became an assistant manager after a relatively short while. After starting a family, she gained a GCSE in Psychology and worked as a registered Child Minder before starting work in a secondary school as a Teaching Assistant supporting a pupil with Asperger's Syndrome. Eventually, five years later, after securing the post of Senior TA, she became the Team Leader for all the Teaching Assistants in the Year 8 and 9 team, which involved chairing Team Meetings, liaising with parents/carers, other staff and outside agencies, compiling TA timetables for Key Stage 3 SATs, and coordinating provision for pupils with English as an additional language.

HLTA Standards 4, 5, 7, 15, 20, 25 & 33

When Anna took up her role as a TA she already had experience of management in another setting, which had equipped her with some valuable and transferable skills in aspects of management such as establishing relationships with members of a large team, dealing with the public, with parents and dealing with concerns and complaints. She was able to develop these skills further as a result of her work in a secondary school, which also enabled her to build on her existing understanding of specific leadership traits and behaviours. These included chairing meetings, managing her time effectively and other interpersonal skills which will be considered in greater depth later on in the chapter.

Case study: the ICT specialist

Deborah was a full-time mother of three children for eight years, before becoming a Teaching Assistant in a primary school, with responsibility for supporting a pupil with

(Continued)

(Continued)

Prader-Willi Syndrome. After the pupil left, she took up a post as a general TA, and at that point took a Specialist Teaching Assistant course. She went on to complete a Foundation Degree, at the same time gaining her HLTA status. Her interest in ICT had grown significantly and she was now the in-house ICT technician as well as training other members of staff in various aspects of ICT including the use of software, hardware and the internet, coordinating ICT across the school and leading lessons in Year 6. After 13 years she became a TA manager, implementing performance management, delivering booster classes and taking leadership responsibility for a team of 16 TAs.

Deborah's role shares some leadership skills with the one held by Anna, in that they both involve chairing meetings, effective time management and liaison with other groups of professionals. However, Deborah has taken her interest in ICT and expanded her knowledge in order to enable herself to take on the role of a specialist in her field; in Chapter 10 on ICT, Mark Townsend will discuss strategies for utilizing these skills in a range of settings.

Case study: the music coordinator

Robert had always enjoyed playing guitar and singing in the school choir when he was at school himself. He worked in a music shop for a short time before securing a post in a large primary school as a Teaching Assistant. He demonstrated a keen interest in the provision of instrumental music across the school, and very soon took on responsibility for coordination of the peripatetic instrumental teachers who visited the school. This involved timetabling rooms for tuition and liaising with parents regarding the payment for lessons. He has gained HLTA status and now provides PPA time across the school delivering music lessons in both Key Stages 1 and 2, and he also takes responsibility, together with one of the teachers, for organizing school performances and musical productions.

Unlike the other three case studies, Robert has pursued a specific interest in music from childhood, harnessing that particular aspect of his role to bring recognition of his specialist skills and knowledge into a well-defined leadership responsibility. Before working in a school, he worked in a music shop, so he had developed his interpersonal skills, advising customers on their purchases, liaising with a range of suppliers in the acquisition of stock and keeping the accounts for the shop, which involved chasing unpaid invoices and dealing with complaints from dissatisfied customers. The shop also provided music lessons in a suite of rooms that were situated upstairs, and he took responsibility for booking lessons on behalf of the tutors. He therefore acquired the confidence to deal with a range of customers, suppliers and administrative tasks that was to prepare him for the role he now fulfils in school. Furthermore, he was able to build on this experience and progress to preparing learning experiences and communicating with visiting professionals before going on to secure accreditation as an HLTA. This has provided him with the opportunity to apply his skills, knowledge and experience to a role that required leadership qualities and musical ability, together with business acumen.

Case study: the SENCO

Carol was trained and qualified within the nursery/pre-school settings in which she worked for 11 years. She had been the SENCO in two settings for a total of six years, following which she held the post of pre-school deputy manager for four years, then manager for one year.

During this time she had attended numerous training courses to gain a deeper insight into specific learning difficulties, medical conditions and physical impairments. She then transferred to work within a primary school as a 1:1 support for a pupil who had global development delay. She worked with him for two years, providing literacy support for a group of children in the same class. When the head teacher retired and her post was filled by the SENCO, the role was allocated to Carol as 'Assistant Senco', freeing the head to focus on other areas of leadership in her new role.

> HLTA Standards 8, 13, 15, 20, 29 & 30

Until recently, the role of SENCO has been fulfilled by qualified and experienced teachers, but since the Remodelling agenda (2003), when schools were encouraged to audit the skills of their respective workforces and redistribute responsibilities according to expertise, it has been possible for schools to empower TAs, specifically in primary schools, reallocating such duties in the process. It is clear from her work history that Carol has the expertise that will enable her to fulfil the duties of such a role, and so it is entirely appropriate that she should be able to direct her skills into such a leadership role, relieving the head teacher of these duties and enabling her to focus on other aspects of leadership across the school.

In turn, the case studies demonstrate a variety of ways in which Teaching Assistants have drawn upon their specific strengths and established themselves as leaders in their own educational establishments.

> HLTA Standard 7

In order to lead successfully, it is vital that you acknowledge the requirement to refine and develop certain skills, some of the most pertinent of which are time management, running meetings and interpersonal skills. This section will give you the opportunity to reflect on a selection of such skills, relating the respective components of each to your own circumstances and facilitating effective application of these to a range of leadership tasks that form the job description for the type of leadership role that might arise in your own setting.

Time management

An important aspect of any leadership role is that of managing one's time effectively. The implications for this are that the TA is equipped not only to deal with those elements of the role that are clearly defined and set out in the form of an agreed job description, but those which arise unexpectedly due to the somewhat flexible nature of daily events in an educational setting. For example, it might be the case that the school day on a Tuesday usually starts with the TA supervising a group of six pupils for half an hour in a room that is designated for the purpose of providing targeted support, and timetabled accordingly. However, should there arise a situation which requires that the room is utilized for another, unplanned purpose, then the TA will need to have alternative accommodation or methods of delivery identified in advance of such an occurrence, in order to prevent the slippage of curriculum delivery time that arises from the need to make alternative arrangements at the start of the session. If you are responsible for managing the daily timetable it is essential that you are aware of the options, communicating them clearly and effectively so that there are no further misunderstandings, and that you resolve any issues rather than leave them to the TA responsible for the group who will be conscious of the planned session she has to deliver.

An important element of effective time management is the ability to establish which tasks should take priority over the others in a series of tasks that are all perceived by different people to be 'essential'. If you have a leadership role with other TAs it is vital that you recognize that colleagues may be given a number of different tasks to fulfil, and as many TAs do not have autonomy they may rely on you to guide them in prioritizing which tasks to tackle first. Many people spend much of their time tackling an assortment of tasks but at the end of the day may feel frustrated at having achieved less than they had intended. This is because there may be a tension between focusing their attention on those tasks which have the greatest impact on the fulfilment of their roles and those which they are expected to do. Addressing this issue could be considered to be a case of putting tasks in order of importance and then taking them in sequence, one task at a time, and working through each task methodically until it is completed. It is important for effective leaders to master the techniques of personal time management and to guide others towards an understanding of the necessity for such, since the application of these fundamental skills will enable high level functioning, even when the pressure is intense. Furthermore, as a result of developing these skills, you will discover that you take control of your workload, and eliminate, or certainly reduce, the kind of stress that is often a consequence of an unacceptable or unmanageable workload, and an uneven work/ life balance. A crucial element of efficient time management is an essential shift in focus:

Concentrate on outcomes, not on activities

This concept is clearly defined by the Pareto Principle (www.juran.com), also known as the 80:20 rule, which sets out the principle that 80% of unfocused effort gives rise to 20% of results. On the other hand, it takes the remaining 20% of your time, which is a relatively small proportion, to achieve the other 80% of results. Although the ratio is not always 80:20, this pattern of activity can be detected so frequently that it is possible to attribute it to a variety of contexts. Many school leaders will recognize that it is often the first 10% and the last 10% of workload that consume 80% of resources available, particularly where time is concerned. The significance of this for distributed leadership is in reminding TAs to remain focused on the 20% of tasks that will have the greatest impact on outcomes for pupils' attainment and the quality of the educational experience as a whole.

Procrastination

This means putting off something that you should be doing now for some reason or another, and pursuing other tasks that you find more enjoyable and with which you feel more at ease. A lot of people tend to procrastinate, but that does not necessarily lead to them working less diligently than other members of the team; they might work even longer hours than colleagues, but that in itself will not always enable them to accomplish as much as they could if they worked smarter. There are many reasons for this, but three common ones are:

- Failure to distinguish between urgent and important.
- Feeling overwhelmed by the task.
- Poor organization skills.

The first of these can be overcome through the construction of a prioritization matrix (see the **Prioritization Grid** in Appendix 1, p. 195), and the second by breaking down the task into smaller, more manageable steps. In order to make a task more manageable, it is appropriate to construct an action plan. You might find it useful to use the **Action planning template** in Appendix 1, p. 196 to prepare your own action plan when faced with a more time-consuming task such as implementing an intervention programme, for example. In order to address the issue of poor organization skills, you can construct a tick list of things to do and then, over time, become accustomed to crossing off the tasks as they are completed. At times when you find it difficult to motivate yourself to complete certain tasks, you can link each one to an outcome that can either be positive or negative. For example, you might ask someone to check that you have accomplished a certain task, such as making a telephone call that you know will be difficult. An effective way to motivate yourself is to relate a reward to each specific task, such as taking a break on completion of the task, in order to provide yourself with a goal for completion.

Activity

Make a copy of the **Action planning template** in Appendix 1, on p. 196. Select an aspect of your role that requires your leadership in its effective implementation, such as an intervention programme or a specific scheme of work for a target group of pupils. Create an action plan that would assist another TA in future to fulfil the same task.

Setting up a meeting

All types of leadership role, particularly those in educational establishments, require regular, timely and productive meetings. Some meetings are restricted to members of the team that operates within the school organization, but many more involve professionals who, collectively and collaboratively, provide a wider range of children's services. Meetings will often involve pupils, parents and, where appropriate, their legal advisors. The TA will regularly be involved in such meetings, especially if he or she is carrying out the duties of a SENCO or TA team leader.

If the meeting is to fulfil its purpose, it needs to be planned efficiently with an agreed agenda and time frame. Chapter 4 explores meetings in detail in the context of teamwork.

Managing the meeting

Once the need to hold a meeting has been acknowledged, the next step is to ensure that the right people are able to attend e.g. for a pupil with a behaviour difficulty you may invite parents, other TAs, Head of Year, mentor or tutor from within the educational setting and key staff from other agencies within Children's Services. Inviting the right people is essential to the success of any meeting, so it is important to ascertain that all participants will have something to contribute towards the identification of working solutions to any issues for discussion. As the chair, you should try to ascertain that everyone has an opportunity to contribute by guiding the meeting to facilitate a degree of uninterrupted discussion. If you create a timed agenda, when the time agreed for each item is running out, you will be able to stop the discussion, summarize swiftly the debate on that item, then progress to the next item on the agenda. This will prevent the meeting from becoming stuck on a particular issue and leave time for consideration of all the issues listed in the agenda.

When an agenda item is resolved or an action is agreed upon, clarify who in the meeting will be responsible for attending to this matter. To make sure that you avoid confusion and misunderstandings, reiterate the agreed action to be taken and make sure this is included in the minutes.

Minutes are a record of the decisions made during the meeting that highlights the actions agreed. They also provide a point of reference for use at the next meeting so that progress can be monitored. If there is one agency that is constantly failing to complete agreed actions, this can be noted as an issue and referred to your line manager for further discussion with that agency in due course.

The circumstances and purpose of the meeting will be the factors that take precedence when agreeing on the style of the minutes to be issued. In situations of high importance where the minutes serve as an accurate and detailed piece of documentation, the person appointed to take minutes will be required to do so in an appropriate level of detail. If this is not the case, the minutes can consist of a list of bullet points showing decisions made and agreed actions to be taken, identifying the person who is taking responsibility for each respective action. They should be as concise as possible, making certain that all relevant information is provided. Not only does this make them easy to prepare and digest, saving time on their production and distribution, but it means that participants are more likely to have read them when they attend the next meeting.

Whether you are in a leadership role or not, there is a chance that you will find yourself in a position where one or more people disagree with your views, your actions or both. If you are a team leader, for example, you might experience difficulty in securing support for a course of action to be taken to address an issue relating to the way in which the team functions. If you are responsible for leading a facility within a setting that responds to and deals with challenging behaviour, you may find yourself dealing with conflict on a regular basis, whether between pupils themselves, pupils and other members of staff or between members of staff and parents, where the parents do not appreciate a course of action that has been taken. It may not be appropriate for you to address this and it is crucial that you are clear about the boundaries that determine this in your role by consulting your job description or a line manager.

HLTA Standards 4, 5 & 6

However, if this is part of your role, in attempting to resolve the conflict, you will find it useful to follow the steps below:

1. **Listen to both sides**: It is vital that you pay attention to the views and stories of all of those involved in the conflict from the outset. At this point you should try to make a note of the main points being offered by both or all parties concerned. You should also remain calm and unbiased, which means refraining from offering your own opinions about the subject of conflict.
2. **Do your research**: Try to establish the causes of the conflict, and where appropriate and practical, find out whether there are other parties who can enlighten you. Any circumstantial evidence should be kept confidential and the identities of those who have provided further information at this stage should be protected.
3. **Identify the issues**: Having established the facts and separated these from the thoughts and feelings of all of those involved in the conflict, try to tease out the main issues for resolution. They will often be different from those that seemed to be causing the problem in the first instance.
4. **Consider all solutions**: Give everyone involved an opportunity to engage in a degree of exploration of the possible solutions. At this point in the proceedings, it should be acknowledged that no suggestion ought to be ridiculed or rejected as impracticable. Making all parties feel equally valued is part of the process of finding a resolution.
5. **Agree on a course of action**: Take into account all of the suggestions that have arisen from step 4, and then ask all parties to consider the positive and negative aspects of each one. When this has been accomplished, select one solution. If there is time, it is useful at this stage to prepare a simple version of an action plan, in the form of a list of bullet points. Depending upon the age of the pupils, where pupils are involved, it is sometimes effective to ask them to sign the action plan and then provide each pupil with a copy.

It is possible to gain further insight into these and a range of other leadership and management tools by visiting www. Mindtools.com.

〰️ **Reflective questions**

- How often do you receive feedback on your effectiveness as a leader?
- Do you take time on a regular basis to consider your own aims and the purpose of what you are trying to achieve in the context of your school's shared vision?

Further Reading 📖

Dinkmeyer, D. and Eckstein, D. (1996) *Leadership by Encouragement*. Delray Beach, FL: St Lucie Press.

Grint, K. (2000) *The Arts of Leadership*. Oxford: Oxford University Press.

Heller, M.F. and Firestone, W.A. (1995) 'Who's in Charge Here? Sources of Leadership for Change in Eight Schools', *The Elementary School Journal* 96(1): 65–86.

MacBeath, J. (1998) Effective Leadership in a Time of Change. London: Paul Chapman.

Storr, A. (1997) *Feet of Clay: A Study of Gurus*. London: Harper Collins.

References

Bennett, N., Wise, C., Woods, P. and Harvey, J.A. (2003) *Distributed Leadership*. Nottingham: NCSL.

Collarbone, P. (2005) *2010: A World of Educational Difference*. Manchester: MMU.

DfES (2003a) *Raising Standards and Tackling Workload – A National Agreement*. London: DfES.

DfES (2003b) *Time for Standards – Guidance Accompanying the Section 133 Regulations Issued Under the Education Act 2002*. Nottingham: DfES.

Fullan, M. (2004) *Leading in a Culture of Change*. San Francisco: Jossey-Bass.

Gardner, J. (1989) *On Leadership*. New York: The Free Press.

Kouzes, J.M. and Posner, B.Z. (2003) *Encouraging the Heart*. San Francisco: Jossey-Bass.

www.juran.com

www.mindtools.com

3

UNDERSTANDING CHANGE AND BEING PART OF IT

Chris Lee

This chapter will:

- Help you to understand the nature of change and your attitude towards it.
- Evaluate the problems that systems can bring.
- Help you to consider the role of the TA as a leader of change processes.
- Offer some tools that help the change process and help understanding of opposition to changes in schools.

Reading this chapter and undertaking some or all of the tasks provides an opportunity to consider a process, 'change', that might be seen as abstract, but which affects so much, if not all, that we all do in schools. We live in a society of perpetual change which is reflected in the world of education. Within this, the role, responsibilities and status of your professional group, Teaching Assistants (TAs), constantly seems subject to development and change, never more so than through the initiatives restructuring the workforce. Ironically the least changed chapter from the original edition of the *Toolkit* is this chapter but then the one constant of contemporary society may well the change phenomenon. Throughout the chapter there is an attempt to equate change with progress, which is highly problematic. Nonetheless, it assumes we live in a world of rapid change in education and also that we might adopt a positive approach to it, or at least acknowledge that: 'there is a certain relief in change, even though it be from bad to worse ... it is often a comfort to shift one's position and be bruised in a new place' (Washington Irving, Tales of a Traveller, 1824).

The subject of change in education in a library will often be found under the 'management' section in education and, therefore, might be considered more to do with dealing with systems and less to do with the day-to-day work of Teaching Assistants. However, even if not leading change, evolving patterns of work mean that TAs are being drawn into increased involvement and decision making in schools. The developing roles and responsibilities of TAs, mentioned by the authors in Chapter 1, mean that in many cases TAs are not just passive observers and responders, but contributors and innovators in their own right. This chapter is about ideas and practices that might support such new roles but they will also provide ways of thinking about change developed by others both inside and outside the school.

If change is to be effective it must address and have an impact on the values of staff in schools. Unlike practices, values rarely change overnight and that is why it is rare for effective change to take place speedily, especially if it clashes with the values of staff, particularly those in senior positions. To be successful change needs to resonate with a 'critical mass' of both teachers and TAs, sometimes referred to as a 'common mission' which suggests that much 'top-down' change will need to be adapted to fit or blend with the values of particular schools or is likely to be superficially incorporated, even rejected. All change that is badly handled will be damaging, as Fullan states, 'clumsy or superficial attempts at reform, actually decrease commitment – they make matters worse' (1993: 59).

Change in education is continuous, endemic, part of the world of schools. Perhaps this has always been the case but, somehow, in the modern school system, the quantity of change seems to be ever increasing. There are several forces that drive change and they include those which go from worldwide, national and more regional forces to school, group and individual based drivers. Those changes which form part of the latter groups, i.e. school and/or individual based, tend to produce change where there is a feeling of more internal locus of control and ownership, while those which form part of the global and national convey a feeling of external locus on control and ownership. Here the feeling can be of having things 'done to us' and global changes that are made more personal and adapted by the school or individual tend to have more chance of enduring and making a difference.

Global: Two examples here are the rising development and significance of technology and environmental issues on our lives. The computer has revolutionized society and left some feeling remote and disenfranchised, but the digital age marches on under a banner of improving communication and knowledge. While technology promises a better and longer life, the concerns for the environment remind us that mankind's progress may be being bought at a price.

National: Some of the changes are politically determined or some arise from demographic changes that are happening without political control or even influence. For example, education needs to prepare people with flexibility and adaptability for a future which may contain jobs and careers that may not currently exist. The concept of a single, lifelong career is looking increasingly redundant. In addition, there is the potential influence on the education system of a society that has more older than younger people. Other changes are connected to the values and practices that we claim to embrace as a society, nation or group of nations. Such changes are often imposed from above (see Figure 3.1). They are largely determined by the policy makers whose main objectives are to realize promised targets to the electorate, to create

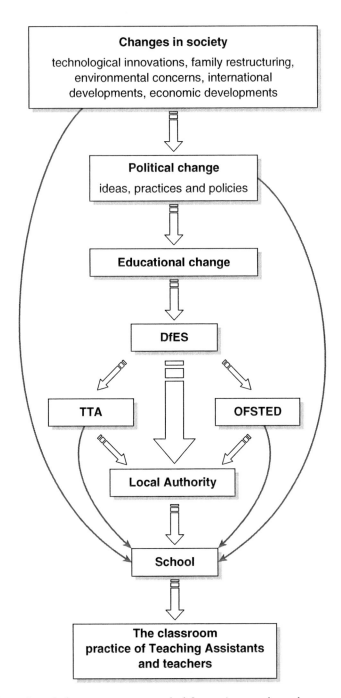

Figure 3.1   Agencies of changes recommended for or imposed on classroom practice

the workforce that will maintain their ideas of an economy, to be better than other countries and to be re-elected! In the UK education system this change is brought about through government organs such as the department for Children, Schools and Families and the Training and Development Agency for Schools who generate reforms – for example Every Child Matters, the 14-19 Curriculum and Revised Standards for HLTAs.

Regional: The growing notion of a regional identity means that public bodies such as local authorities are drawn together and there is growing trend to develop resources and implement initiatives at regional level. Public services such as paramedics and police think in more regional terms. Many initiatives that affect schools used to emanate from local authorities having the temerity to generate initiatives that responded to local needs and some still do, although increasingly they are the agents of delivery of national change agendas rather than the initiators.

School: Schools could also be said to be becoming more the agents of delivery of changes decided elsewhere yet many continue to generate their own initiatives linked to an annual development plan and in response to initiatives and interests of staff and to meeting pupil and parental needs. Sometimes the change driver can be a member of staff such as a new head teacher keen to make a difference to their school.

Individual: Individual personal needs to make a difference and be a change agent can also prove significant. These might include helping children with learning difficulties, or being part of an initiative that we deem as necessary in our school or classroom. While influenced by, and in constant interplay with, the other drivers of change, there are some changes that remain at an individual level. Teaching Assistants undertaking specific research projects as part of their studies will embrace ideas and practices that appear to work for them in improving pupil attainment or behaviour – and have nothing to do with change elsewhere. Sometimes, maybe many times, the idea of the people working in classrooms being pivotal does not appear to be the case, but, to be successful, education still demands personal ideas, skills and philosophies delivered by adults in the school, as Fullan reminds us 'change is too important to leave to the experts' (1993: 39).

The reform agenda seems unremitting and ever prevalent with a focus that often appears to be on what is wrong with schools and instant correction, rather than nurturing sustained positive attitudes and informed ideas towards creating the schools of tomorrow.

This chapter is written with the notion that you, the teaching assistant, are *a significant adult* in the lives of many children and your colleagues and in the working of your school, and that you are an agent for change, either in your own right or alongside others who work with you. This being the case, it seemed that any book looking at the world of the Teaching Assistant should contain a chance to read, stand back and reflect on the phenomenon that we call change. The following activity will help with the reflection process.

HLTA
Standard
7

Activity: reflection on change

Consider a recent change that you were involved in at your school or in your classroom (or a recent school or classroom in which you worked) and record your responses to these questions.

- Was the change generated by global, national, regional, school, personal or other sources?
- Does the origin of a change, i.e. who or what generated it, affect how you view it and your desire to be involved?
- Was there extensive support for the initiative in the school and where did it come from?
- Was there extensive resistance for the initiative in the school and where did it come from?
- What was your stance – were you in favour of it, against it or neutral towards it? (List the good and not so good points that it possessed.)
- What has been the outcome of the change in terms of (a) how people behave differently, and (b) were their attitudes and values changed as well?

THE NATURE OF CHANGE

Before discussing practical matters it is important to look at what change is and reflect on some key features that will apply to most changes. Change is about people behaving differently and, at its most effective, it will also be about changing attitudes and values. Remember too that change means to make different or to alter – it does not necessarily mean to improve or make better. Consider, especially if you are leading change or involved as a 'driver' of the change, that not everyone may think that it is a good idea and they may be right about it or they could fear having to learn or adopt new ways of working which might be theatening. Change is often about making a difference to something that already exists rather than radical reorganization of the fundamentals – it is then more about amending or adjusting and not transforming. The innovation fatigue that schools seem to experience often compels them to amend, rather than reflect on, the fundamentals of what they are doing.

For example, many schools review their behaviour policy in the light of what they perceive to be falling standards in the behaviour of their pupils. The first ports of call are usually sanctions and rewards and how they can be more effective. Rarely do they start by asking:

- **Why do we believe that standards of behaviour are getting worse?** Ways of behaving are constantly changing as are the ways that society responds to that behaviour. One or two key incidents can lead to reaction that demands change when, perhaps, it is not needed or there is a need to look at what is causing a pupil to behave in a certain way and deal with that fundamental problem before resorting to sanctions.

- **What kind of school do we want to create?** All adults will play a part in contributing to the culture of the school, although few are often involved in generating what is often described as the 'vision'. This does not prevent us from having our own vision and ideas about the kind of school we are working towards or want to maintain.
- **What expectations do we have of our pupils?** Do we set high expectations for all pupils, not just concerning learning, but also behaviour? Do we expect problems with pupils rather than compliance from them?
- **How does this link with our behaviour and that of the pupils?** We often forget our role in contributing to pupils' behaviour, not just as a role model, but also in the way that we deal with them. Often Teaching Assistants feel compelled to react differently to pupils, especially ones with whom they work closely, or they develop slightly different relationships with the pupils than the teachers.
- **Why not approach the issue from an alternative position and have a 'positive relationships' policy?** Would not part of the vision that we have for our pupils include helping them to create positive relationships both now and in the future? This approach is inclusive of all pupils, not just those who commit misdemeanours.

The ownership of change is so important and with change imposed on schools from outside forces it often means that staff within them are forced to react without understanding or valuing what has been proposed and, therefore, the implementation lacks a creative element and there is no sense of responding to needs identified from within. In this context change may alter the system, but it has less chance of stirring hearts and minds.

Change comes from small initiatives which work, initiatives which, imitated, become fashion. We cannot wait for great visions from great people, for they are in short supply at the end of history. It is up to us to light our own small fires in the darkness. (Handy, 1994)

Change is, therefore, often incremental and depends upon several small moves forward not giant leaps.

ATTITUDE TO CHANGE

Whatever your own role it is likely that you will encounter different attitudes to a particular change from individuals and, in the case of larger schools, groups. There will be those who are totally against it and will be negative, even aggressive, active resisters. There will also be those who, whilst opposing the change, understand why it is taking place, and may do little to oppose it, passive resisters. Similar to that group are those who are prepared to try everything. They do not care or do not want to be involved in the management of the change, indeed, at times they may appear to be neutral about the whole process. Often this is the case if they are not directly affected by what is happening, but this attitude changes when the full implications are known or they become personally involved. There are those who are followers of most changes and support them, often believing that there is an inevitability about it or that resistance may be a waste of energy. Finally, there is a group that responds positively to change, the change drivers, who do so in the early stages, but become somewhat less enthusiastic during the later stages when it is less innovative and more hard work. All these groups, in themselves, can change in composition and you might recognize yourself in more than one role.

Just as individuals have an approach to change so do schools, and not all schools embrace change and not all are good at it. Those which are good at change have certain characteristics and these can summarized by two words: **communication** and **teamwork**. Those which are not so good, who may well be operating at what Everard and Morris (1996) describe as 'dynamic conservation', which maintains the current structures and familiarity, see change as threatening.

Fullan (1982) discovered four groups amongst teachers in attitude to change:

- A minority who said leave us alone, we will get on with it ourselves.
- A minority who did not want to write policies but were prepared to resource them and be involved in decision making.
- A majority who were prepared to have materials made for them and did not have the time for decision making.
- An equal majority who saw time as a problem but wanted to be involved at all levels and share ideas with fellow professionals.

It would be interesting to find out if such categories also applied to TAs.

Whatever disadvantages there are in people not agreeing with or sharing your enthusiasm for change Fullan (1993) points out that there are also dangers in everyone agreeing with what is happening – **groupthink**.

Collaboration may not always be a positive force and it is important that dissent or differing views are heard. Certainly collaboration does not necessarily bring consensus. How often has practice in the classroom been enhanced by Teaching Assistants questioning and debating the practice of their teacher colleagues – and vice versa! When staff go along with a request from administrative or central bodies, or when there is majority for a certain position, it does not necessarily mean that the decision is wise and will lead to good practice. Positive conflict asks us to question and use professional judgement to determine if there are benefits and/or deficits in a particular idea, without hurting or offending others. Such a process is also a healthy model for pupils.

A second cautionary term, and one whose meaning is often recognized by teaching assistants, is **balkanization**. This is a term often used in the literature and refers to a situation in which members of a group develop loyalties which are so strong that they fail to empathize with other groups, ignore them or even become hostile towards them. In some schools Teaching Assistants are seen as a separate group whose identity is totally distinct from other staff in schools, to the point where they even have their own staffrooms! Mary Pittman, in the chapter on TAs and teachers working together, mentions the negativity felt by some Teaching Assistants who felt like the 'spy in the classroom' and 'overgrown pupils'. Despite the differences between teachers and Teaching Assistants in pay and conditions, they have more in common than separates them.

Meeting the needs of the pupils, fulfilling the aspirations of the school summarized in the development plan and playing an active role in a positive dynamic culture are all common aspirations and far outweigh the differences in the two 'camps'.

PROBLEMS WITH THE 'SYSTEM'

It is not only the willingness or the attitude of your immediate colleagues that will determine whether change can be implemented, but the school itself may have problems within it. This has much to do with how it has been managed, or its history in generating innovation or taking ideas on board, or its relationship with the wider community. These factors might be described as the **system**.

Murgatroyd and Morgan (1993) drew up Senge's 'Archetypes of Systems' and noted that systems can facilitate change or can possess inhibitors to change, and one or more of these might be in your school system. Most TAs will recognize one or two of the following areas, but they become more problematic if they are part of the system and its response to change.

They include:

- The need to **balance the process of change with delay**. Moving too quickly or overreacting with a desire to adopt a specific innovation can create a feeling of dissatisfaction and turbulence from some groups. In the end, the negativity generated causes more problems and takes up more time than the initial problem.
- There may be **limits to growth** and development in the school. A school becomes successful; consequently, pupil numbers and class sizes increase with pressure being brought to expand and employ more TAs, who are not as motivated and as well trained as those already working at the school. The very quality and teamwork of the TAs that made the school successful cannot be sustained and quality is threatened or begins to suffer with a resulting decline in numbers and, as a consequence, few good TAs wanting to work there.
- **Shifting the burden** to a quick fix sudden solution, such as buying a new mathematics scheme to counter poor SATs results or employing three new TAs to deal with behaviour problems, which were a result of poor practice and policy in behaviour management.
- **Shifting the burden to an outside intervenor** by calling in an expert such as the Educational Psychologist and expecting her/him to come up with a magic solution to dealing with a troublesome pupil. Another intervener is the professional development day with an outside speaker who makes an impassioned plea for staff to take on board the 'new' thinking on, say, 'multiple intelligences'. Everyone agrees it was a great session and it is assumed that messages included will happen – just like that! Such ideas need personalizing to the school and its staff and it is that which brings genuine change, however inspiring or amusing the speaker was.
- Schools **erode the goals** and settle for a change that was not as ambitious as the original aspiration. For example, the new mathematics scheme appears to work well, so changes in that area need go no further or plans to employ four new skilled TAs are abandoned despite the preparation work having been undertaken and staff promised increased support.

- Successful change becomes identified with one person, who is perceived as a winner and will receive funding and accolades. By implication there are losers, whose attitude to the laudable innovation is scarred by the process adopted within the system. They adopt a negative stance and the conflict assumes an **escalation**.
- Similar to the above, **more success goes to the successful**. For example, the new reading scheme is a big hit with some staff, therefore it is developed further at the expense of other areas of the curriculum.
- Alternatively there may be **growth and under-investment** and early success is not maintained as a plan for new investment does not materialize. This does not only apply to financial under investment but also to precious staff skills.
- Staff chase resources at the time of announced budget restraint and there is a panic demand, inability to prioritize and the resource allocation becomes unmanageable, leading to everyone feeling disenfranchised and aware that senior managers cannot manage resources. Senge referred to this as a **tragedy of the commons**.
- **Fixes that fail** appear to happen a great deal. The behaviour of a specific pupil has become so antisocial that there is no option but the often used exclusion process. Before long another pupil emerges as the cause of the main behaviour problems, exclusion is considered again without any reflection on behaviour management in the school, resulting in the burden of the school not being lightened.

AS A LEADER OF CHANGE

It may be an expectation that the head teacher is the leader of change, but it would be an unusual role for a Teaching Assistant. However, increasingly school leaders are looking to their staff to be innovative and to play a major role in school development. Aspects of what is referred to as 'distributed leadership' is discussed in Chapter 2. Here are some principles that might help to inform your role as a change agent. They include that:

- You will have little idea how things will work out in the end.
- The culture of the school, including the systems, and the ways that people are treated will be significant.
- There will be numerous approaches to achieving the required change and some of those will bring 'turbulence', which has been defined as: 'change that accelerates faster than our capacity to keep pace with it' (Whitaker, 1998: 13).
- The commitment of others as support may not be necessary at the beginnings of a change project, but you will need support as the process gathers pace and, more importantly, if you are to achieve the desired outcome.
- There will be unexpected support from some people and opposition from those whom you predicted would support the ideas.
- Confliict is likely to form part of the process, and this will be expected by many participants. As mentioned previously, not all conflict is counter-productive.

One caution here is that it is often the case that change leaders are seen charging ahead with change in a solitary manner; they are perceived to be the 'Hero Innovator'. School staff who attend courses, or undertake research, are often greeted with statements such as 'we can tell you have been on a course' when they come to introduce a practical innovation that has fired their interest and they have perceived its relevance to the school. It is vital to recognize that *it is the innovation, not the innovator, that is significant* and it is important to plan and involve others. Identify, consult and work with the supportive forces in the school, the 'critical mass' that will be the sustaining team. They:

- may not always be at the top of an organization, but may be near to it
- may be the people who have the will, resources or freedom to manage operations
- will help you to frequently revisit the issue and check all is going well as monitoring will be essential.

It is highly unlikely that a great deal will be achieved without the consent and support of those near the top of the organization and more will be achieved if they are active in their backing of the process. Fullan (1993, in Everard) suggests that 'neither centralization nor decentralization works' and that both forces that operate 'top-down' and those which operate 'bottom-up' will be required if the change is to be realized.

TOOLS TO AID PLANNING CHANGE

Planning any change allows opportunities to reflect upon change direction and how it will be achieved. The benefits of even limited planning outweigh the small amount of time required and help to identify the likely sources of support and opposition. Innovation brought about by sudden action and little planning has less chance of making a genuine change to practice. One aid to planning is Forcefield Analysis (see below) which is premised on the idea that not everyone thinks an innovation is a good idea, and there will be both support and opposition. It makes explicit that feelings are an important factor in a change. Forcefield Analysis is an aid to planning as it provides a vehicle that:

(a) Compels reflection upon the change that you want to make. We often find that we have been involved in a change or led a change that does not match what we actually wanted to achieve.

(b) Asks you to consider the areas – the 'forces' – that will provide support and facilitate the change. These are important in that allies and supportive systems will help facilitate, motivate and maintain the impetus.

(c) Asks you to consider the 'forces' that will counter the change or, at least, will not facilitate it. On initial identification of these forces it seems that these are nothing more than problems, but they are important for they compel examination of the change and they remind us that problems are inevitable and that we learn from them.

(d) Helps planning by asking you to 'measure' the size of both sets of forces and then consider which will make the best allies and which forces need to be initially countered or confronted.

Case study: Jenny

Jenny has been a Teaching Assistant in her local primary school for 10 years and has developed considerable expertise in issues connected with the promotion of positive behaviour in schools. She has dealt with pupils who have been proved almost impossible to manage in class and she has developed close relationships with many pupils who have had difficulties in conforming to school rules. Because of her skills she has become involved in a group of staff who have agreed to join together in a major review of the promoting positive behaviour policy in the school. One of the areas that Jenny and the team are considering is the way that the reward system operates. When the subject was raised in the team there were clearly two schools of thought. The first group thought that rewarding pupils for good work and behaviour was a mirror of society as this was just what happened in the adult world of work and that obeying the rules, working hard and helping others merited recognition. In opposition to this group were those who felt that children should not be rewarded for good behaviour or work because that was what school (and society) expected from them and that learning and behaving were expectations and therefore rewards were little more than bribes.

The discussion in the group proved to be a heated one and the group who valued reward systems was clearly in the majority but Jenny felt some sympathy for the other school of thought and certainly wanted them to feel that their views had been heard. She decided that she would do two things to help the process. First, she would undertake a 'Forcefield Analysis' of the introduction of a new reward system and asked staff to consider both schools of thought and identify positives and negatives and rank order the issues that their views present. Second, because there was a 'majority' stance in favour of rewards and it had been identified as an expectation of parents, there would an introduction of a new reward system in Year 6 only and it would be evaluated by both the policy group through small scale research and case studies. Jenny appreciated that the introduction of a new approach to rewards depended on a small scale success and if this pilot proved successful it would be embraced further in the extension of the policy.

After a two month 'pilot' and the evaluation she brought her findings to the group. They indicated that the pupils were working well, that there had been fewer incidents of negative behaviour and that the system had met with a positive response from staff and parents. Some pupils, although pleased with the new system, were concerned that quieter and less 'obvious' pupils were not attracting rewards. Jenny brought the findings to the group and it was decided by all that the school should not be dependent on rewards as a means of securing good work and behaviour, extend the pilot to all Key Stage 2 classes and ensure that not only the brightest or most compliant should be rewarded.

Jenny has learned:

1. How important acknowledging the views of the whole group can be.
2. How a small success can underpin a major development.
3. The importance of not rushing such an important change and that real change demands time and support (Fullan, 2007).

Try the activity below to evaluate a change in your own school and reflect on the value of the Forcefield Analysis as an aid to thinking. The idea is to look at your views and the views that might be opposed to your own and consider how change can take place in the light of your views.

Activity

1. This activity is based on Kurt Lewin's Forcefield analysis, examples of which can be found easily by searching on the internet. Consider a change that you are involved in at your school, either as leader, a member of a team or by yourself. Write down *exactly* what change you wish to see at the top of your page, divide the rest into two columns.
2. List the key areas of support – they may be people, but they can also be other forms of resource (time, income, legislation) on one side of your page under the heading 'Supportive Forces'.
3. List the key forces that will prove difficult, obstruct or counter the change on the other side of the page under the heading 'Countering Forces'.
4. Now give each supporting and countering force a number from 1 to 5 in accordance with their significance. For example, the main agent that supports the change will be a 5 and a less significant, but still supportive agent, may be a 1 or 2. Similarly, the main agent that counters the change will be a 5 and a less significant, but still negative agent, may be a 1 or 2.
5. Consider the positive forces and which ones might help in overcoming the barriers – they may have a specific area that they can overcome. How best can they be brought into play?
6. Consider the negative forces and which ones might inhibit the movement of the change. The question that presents itself here is usually should we go for the highest number barrier, hoping that it will influence the lesser forces or should we achieve an initial small success that motivates further movement? It feels a little like a military plan, but it helps to provide the chance to reflect and plan before moving to action. It also will help to identify those things which cannot be changed.

OPPOSITION TO CHANGE

Much of the case study and activity above has been about looking at views other than your own. Sometimes opponents of a specific change raise their objections openly, offering reasons, perhaps excuses, why they cannot sanction what is happening. These include such ideas as:

- The teaching staff will oppose this.
- It does not match the school policy on …
- We don't have the resources (time, skill, money).
- It won't work in this school (too big, too small, specialist role e.g. special school).

- We are drowning in innovation as it is.
- We don't have time for all this stuff you have learned on that course.
- It is just another fad.
- It won't help us overcome our main problems which are …
- It won't help me to do my job better.
- We have done it all before, except last time we called it …
- Please, not before the Ofsted inspection!

If they are reasons rather than excuses, they may be valid and compel you to revisit the plan – but not to abandon the change project itself. Think about the times you have used these yourself and with justification! However, if they are excuses, e.g. Ofsted are not visiting in the near future, and anyway, the changes are in line with the last action plan, then move ahead in the knowledge that you know who will oppose or, at least, not support, and why. The main goal is to ensure that staff express their anxieties and fears to you and share them with each other, rendering subterfuge less likely. The real danger may be those who say they will be behind you and when you look back you cannot see them!

No one likes to think that people oppose their ideas or changes that they see as valuable or necessary, but it is hardly likely that everyone will support you in any idea that you have. The resisters, whether active or passive, force us to ask important questions about the nature of the idea, its value and how we might introduce it. They can be perceived as healthy conflict and part of the change process for which you have planned and on which you will reflect. Controversy sometimes follows innovation and the greater the threat to current practice and to what is seen as the ethos of the school, the more extensive and intensive the opposition is likely to be. They may even be right! An example of what looks at first sight to be quite controversial is not blaming or punishing bullies in school. When explained as not a 'soft option', that it will involve positive approaches to the victim of bullying and that it means the bully has to change their behaviour, rather than make sure they are not caught next time, then it appears less controversial (Bray and Lee, 2007).

Not all opposition is helpful and constructive, indeed, it may be that there is a deliberate attempt to undermine the change by adopting tactics that seek to destroy or deflect or opponents assume a powerless, negative stance that has the same effect – it counters the change. You may well recognize these 'characters' from your experience, they:

- appear reasonable and seem to be approving but then offer a series of 'yes but' statements, which have the effect of closing conversation as they really mean 'no'
- spot a mistake or blemish in the proposal documentation and raise it to undermine the impact of your idea
- demonstrate considerable skill in waiting for the mistake, even misleading or trapping you into making it, and then they pounce

- appear in favour but their presence is more to do with personal aggrandisement and self promotion than genuine support for change
- have far too much to do to be bothered with your ideas and the idea becomes immediately downgraded. Occasionally they take on too much by choice and justify not coping or contributing by saying that they are suffering with over-work
- resort to a problem they have or a lack of status and influence. They don't see that they can make a contribution. It may be nervousness around an issue or perceived lack of training that prevents them joining the team
- set themselves up to fail and appear to be a victim of the challenges presented by the change
- blame your idea for their own inability to manage their time and complete other tasks.

Another aid to planning change is a SWOT analysis. This can be used as a tool to interrogate the value of the change as well as how it will be achieved within a school. It requires a consideration of four aspects: strengths, weaknesses, opportunities and threats. The following Activity provides an opportunity to consider a more abstract change using a SWOT analysis. Consider a change that might be seen as outrageous or impractical: the abolition of exclusion of pupils. While it may seem far-fetched, it is important to consider that many other ideas have seemed outrageous at one time or another but are now part of everyday life in schools, e.g. the abolition of corporal punishment, the use of IT in schools, the National Curriculum, and more pertinently, the extensive deployment of Teaching Assistants, many of whom are studying Foundation degrees and are highly qualified and experienced.

 Activity

The choice of an imposed change is both non-educational and outrageous. The government of the day have announced that from September next year all cars in the UK will be painted bright PINK and this will apply to cars already on the road and to new cars.

Using this extreme, and some might say light-hearted, issue, in small groups or individually, use copies of the *SWOT analysis grid* provided in Appendix 1 on p. 197 to answer the following:

- What are the main strengths of the initiative?
- What are the weaknesses of the idea?
- What opportunities might be presented by such a change?
- What threats does it bring?

If you have worked in a group, reconvene and consider:

(a) Whether there is consensus
(b) If the SWOT analysis has brought about a change in thinking in some people
(c) If it is worth considering.

What usually becomes apparent is that it is possible to see positive and negative features in any change and those pluses and minuses may or may not be apparent and clear.

In the world of rapid development that is the modern school, change, more than ever, should have an aim and a purpose. It is important to avoid an overload of new ideas, but the context of the school development is significant. It therefore needs to be viable in terms of time, as well as considering the disposition and skills of the staff. All too often great ideas become lost in a swamp of innovation.

It is important to reflect on an idea or innovation and begin to plan what will happen and who will be involved. Here are some final ideas designed to help the planning and process of change.

1. During the initial stages avoid organizing too much and getting involved in minutiae. Detailed structures and procedures are likely to be developed during the process and not at the outset.
2. Similarly, avoid simple solutions as they are likely to be limited in their scope, partial in their achievement and probably wrong!
3. Select people who will support you and who will be interested in, but not necessarily in agreement with, what you are doing.
4. Examine the negatives and consider that the forces that run counter to an innovation need to be heard and their contribution considered.
5. By communicating with others at all levels, in all ways, and like never before, uncertainty, fear and rumour are reduced and the perception of threat may turn into opportunity.

In the end, more will be achieved by a planned innovation that proves rewarding for the team involved than by any imposed change led by an individual, especially an outsider. Therefore, before you read about how teams work and how they facilitate good practice in the next chapter, consider the merits of a team approach to change in which decision making is shared work and commitment gained through the early involvement of others. Remember that change is not a single event, even a series of events, it is a journey, with hidden dangers, unknown outcomes and pleasant surprises. We might learn to fear change less, for, as I am told Buddhists say:

> ... all suffering of mankind is produced by attachment to a previous condition of existence. When we eliminate our expectations as to how the future ought to be a continuation of the past, we guarantee ourselves more peace of mind.

〰️ **Reflective questions**

- Should schools have the role of initiating changes in society or responding to changes in society?
- In the growing professional role of the Teaching Assistant, should they be agents of creating change or simply delivering it?
- What is the major change that you would like to bring to (a) your school and (b) schools generally?

References

Bray, L. and Lee, C. (2007) 'Moving Away from a Culture of Blame to that of Support-Based Approaches to Bullying in Schools', *Pastoral Care and Education* 25(4): 4–11.

Everard, K. and Morris, G. (1996) *Effective School Management* (3rd edn). London: Paul Chapman.

Fullan, M. (1982) *The Meaning of Educational Change*. Ontario: OISE Press.

Fullan, M. (1993) *Change Forces: Probing the Depths of Educational Reform*. London: Falmer Press.

Fullan, M. (2007) *The New Meaning of Educational Change* (4th edn). London: Routledge.

Handy, C. (1994) *The Empty Raincoat*. London: Hutchinson.

Murgatroyd, S. and Morgan, C. (1993) *Total Quality Management in Schools*. Bucks: Open University Press.

Whitaker, P. (1998) *Managing Schools*. Oxford: Butterworth.

WORKING TOGETHER

Collaborative and supportive partnerships

Mary Pittman

This chapter will:

- Reflect on the meaning and values of working together.
- Encourage communication within a professional framework.
- Empower the working partnership within positive teamwork structures.

Teachers and Teaching Assistants (TAs) working alongside each other to raise standards and maximize potential is a fundamental aspect of life in most schools. Under the government's 2002 proposals, partnerships between teachers and TAs continued to undergo changes. The introduction of Higher Level Teaching Assistants (HLTAs) brought about further changes to the dynamics of school working partnerships. In addition, the widening expectations of a more integrated service as required by the Every Child Matters (ECM) agenda, presents Teaching Assistants, as it does other professionals, with new communication and teamwork demands.

Collaborative partnerships can be very effective and, as a consequence, be beneficial for pupils, schools and families. However, sometimes the partnership experience between teachers and teaching assistants, as well as with other professionals, can be a frustrating experience for all concerned, as highlighted in the previous chapter in relation to change, and this potentially decreases the positive impact for pupils.

This chapter considers both TAs and HLTAs to be vital members of the school team and the chapter can be read from a number of perspectives. However, for those who want to consider collaborative practice in terms of the HLTA role, this chapter makes reference to a number of Standards which relate to different aspects of working partnerships and teamwork.

HLTA
Standards
4, 6 & 7

DEFINING TEAMWORK AND PARTNERSHIP PRACTICE

What does partnership' or 'teamwork' mean? An existing definition of this relationship states that:

> a team is a group in which the individuals have a common aim and in which the jobs and skills of each member fit in with those of others, as ... in a jigsaw puzzle pieces fit together without distortion and together produce an overall pattern. (Babington *et al.*, 1979, cited in Lacey, 2001: 36)

This chapter asks you to reflect upon your own setting and evaluate how close your working teacher/TA relationship is, to a well-constructed jigsaw, as suggested by Babington *et al.* As you begin to think about this vital partnership, share your thoughts with your colleagues and discuss your underlying beliefs about your working practice.

- What works very well?
- What works satisfactorily?
- What areas could be improved?

It should be recognized that working with other adults in the demanding atmosphere of a classroom can present personal and professional hurdles that need to be **acknowledged**, **addressed** and **overcome**. In any successful relationship, there has to be **understanding**, **compromise** and **empathy**.

The roles and responsibilities of TAs have changed dramatically over the last 15 years. As a result of workforce reform, schools have made and are still making, adjustments to the roles and responsibilities of teachers, HLTAs and TAs.

HLTA Standard 33

In some schools the teacher, is the overall **manager** of teaching and learning, while HLTAs manage teaching and learning in specific lessons, and TAs manage teaching and learning when working with individual pupils or small groups. As you read this chapter consider how the structuring or restructuring of roles and responsibilities is working in your school setting and how this is impacting on you as a team.

As part of their **managerial** responsibility, teachers may need to recognize that both HLTAs and TAs also have increasingly clear and distinct responsibilities which must be realized and effectively coordinated to ensure that roles are complementary and provide the most effective support for pupils.

It is also important to recognize the important role that TAs and HLTAs are already playing and will increasingly play, in supporting the Every Child Matters agenda. Every Child Matters and the Children Act of 2004, recognizes that for children and young people to learn effectively, their health and well being is inextricably linked to their learning, as discussed in detail in Chapter 6. The roles and responsibilities of TAs place them in ideal positions for personalizing learning and enabling pupils to overcome barriers to learning.

In considering the role of TAs in supporting the ECM outcomes for pupils Cheminais (2008) defines the concept of partnership as, 'a group of people joining together, sharing a common problem or issue to be addressed, who take collective responsibility for resolving it' (2008: 24).

TAs and HLTAs, along with teachers and other professionals, are challenged to develop their communication skills and teamwork structures to ensure that they take responsibility collectively for supporting children and young people effectively.

HLTA
Standards
9, 16 &
27

HLTA
Standards
4 & 6

KEY FACTORS THAT REINFORCE THE VALUE OF TAS

During my own research discussions with TAs I have discovered that there appear to be five key factors that continually emerge and which provide TAs with a feeling that they are valued in making a positive contribution to their school and to the classroom environment in which they work.

TAs suggested that, from their perspective, schools, departments or teachers who provided the following conditions were likely to enable TAs to feel part of a productive partnership:

(a) 'Active' systems of providing and accessing information.
(b) Opportunities for 'talk time' between teachers and TAs.
(c) An ethos and commitment to collaboration in planning pupil learning.
(d) A recognition of the part played by TAs in differentiating work for pupils.
(e) Communication systems which encouraged a shared perspective on understanding pupil needs.

(a) 'Active' systems of information

It can be difficult for TAs to get the information they need to feel fully part of a team or to feel valued in a partnership. It can equally be difficult for teachers to have the time to ensure that they have kept their working partners up-to-date with all the factors relating to the school, department, class and individual pupils.

Clearly, schools need to manage information sources and not all information should be, or needs to be, in the public domain; for example certain sensitive information about pupils. However TAs have to receive the information they need to feel fully part of a team and to feel valued in a partnership. A knowledge of confidentiality issues and professional ethics can be an important part of induction training for TAs and enables staff to value the importance of both the information being shared and the role they play in supporting a child or young person.

Activity

For further reflection, use the photocopiable activity, *Collaborative teamwork activity: active systems of information* in Appendix 1 on p. 198. This activity can help you to review what systems of information are already in place, as well as, what systems would be useful to put in place to ensure that TAs and HLTAs are provided with information which enhances their professional judgement.

This activity considers what a TA needs to know in relation to whole school issues, department or Key Stage issues, classroom and individual pupil information, along with access to information from external agencies where this is appropriate to their roles and responsibilities.

In discussion, TAs have teased out various examples of helpful 'active systems' These have included the importance of:

- School induction meetings for new staff.
- A short early morning meeting for all staff on a daily basis.
- A staff information board.
- An intranet site which contains access to programmes of study and planning.
- Time built into employment contracts to jointly review classroom planning or Individual Education Plans.

(b) Opportunities for discussion time between teachers and TAs

A key stressor mentioned by both teachers and teaching assistants is the **lack of time** to meet to discuss roles, pass information, share planning and evaluate educational process and progress.

Teaching assistants often express their concerns that teachers are so busy that they feel it is 'difficult to know *when* to try to speak to them'. Teachers, on the other hand, often feel that the only time they have available is before the pupils arrive or after they leave the classroom. This leaves them with a moral dilemma that: 'given a TA's pay and conditions, it does not seem appropriate to ask them to stay in their own time'. In researching the views of teachers and TAs in relation to **'time to talk'**, a balance of **informal** and **formal** times seemed to be used for different reasons.

Informal time, before or after lessons, or in the staff room, often focused on immediate lesson content, resources and individual pupil needs; these discussions were often spontaneous, acted upon immediately and generally went unrecorded but provided useful liaison.

Formal, scheduled discussion focused on joint planning and evaluation. These involved a much greater depth of communication with planned outcomes which identified pupil progress. Discussion not only centred on what strategies, approaches and resources were in use, but why and how all parties contributed to overall effectiveness and future developments. Significantly, it was also apparent that teachers and TAs felt that they listened more actively to each other during scheduled discussions, providing a platform for positive action. They remarked on a genuine feeling of creativity and collaboration, and a mutual empowerment within this positive work environment to maximize their own potential as well as that of their pupils and the school.

Formal meeting times, which are set up on a regular basis need a clear purpose and a well planned format to ensure that the time is used efficiently. Detailed guidance on organizing, running and managing meetings is given in Chapter 2. Teaching Assistants on the Foundation Degree identified some key points which helped formal meetings to be well managed and effective. These points could be applied to classroom meetings, department or key stage, and whole staff meetings. Positive meetings were those which had:

- Dates given in advance.
- A clear purpose with a pre circulated agenda.
- A focused and achievable start and finish time.
- A specific allocation of time on the agenda which provided a platform for issues of current concern, to be shared, even if briefly, at this point.
- A clear summary period, 10 minutes before the end of the meeting, focusing on what had been agreed, along with which issues required further attention.
- A brief record of the key issues covered, points of action, staff responsible for action etc. These could be recorded during the meeting either handwritten on a form, typed on a laptop or recorded on a Smartboard and printed.

TAs also sometimes need simple, effective alternatives to meetings for some of the ongoing daily communication issues. This is particularly important and relevant where teachers job share, TAs move across the school, TAs are part-time, or supply teachers are utilized. Examples include:

- An agreed system of recording pupil needs.
- An appropriately located bulletin board with key, non-confidential information.
- E-mail updates and contact.

Many TAs on the Foundation Degree, commented that they would prefer to meet and give up their own time, than not to meet at all. They believed that time to talk with teachers made a significant contribution to their job satisfaction. In response, schools who showed their recognition of the additional time given by TAs reinforced their feelings of commitment and value. Positive and creative responses from schools ranged from simple appreciative comments, to providing TAs and teachers with some joint non-contact time, or proposing some flexibility in contact hours, especially if the TA required some time for study when working for a qualification, or providing a TA with access to training opportunities within the school day.

Short, informal chat time and formal meeting arrangements outside of the contact with children, are both essential components in ensuring that teachers, TAs and HLTAs have

HLTA
Standards
4, 5 & 6

strong communication networks. However, because of the complex nature of organizations and people, it should be borne in mind that these will rarely be perfect all of the time, and may need a regular review of whether the meeting times and systems meet current needs.

(c) An ethos and commitment to collaborative planning

A commonly expressed concern from TAs is having advance knowledge of the content and objectives of lessons, or being included in the planning process.

HLTA Standards 17, 18 & 19

TAs can feel frustrated in these circumstances, feeling that they lack the necessary preparation, which makes their impact with pupils less effective. Teachers who give TAs information about lesson content in advance and provide them with opportunities to participate in giving ideas or adapting tasks for specific children, are recognizing that TAs are a very real learning resource. As a consequence of this ethos and involvement, TAs feel they have a specific and targeted role in the teaching and learning process.

Lacey (2001) considers **liaison, cooperation, coordination** and **collaboration** and the differing levels of interaction that these define when we work in a team. Lacey (2001) challenges our perceptions of teamwork by suggesting that:

> it is often argued that the word 'team' is used when 'work group' would more accurately describe the manner in which people are working together. They work alongside each other co-operating and even co-ordinating their work, but they are not a fully fledged collaborative team. (p. 11)

During sessions on teamwork Teaching Assistants from primary, secondary and special schools have been asked to consider the terms used by Lacey in relation to their working partnership with teachers. They immediately recognize these key aspects of teamwork and can provide examples of where these have taken place.

Teaching Assistants suggested that liaison often occurred in a corridor, or over a 'snatched' cup of tea and incorporates brief interchanges of information about pupils' learning or behaviour. Although a vital component of the total communication system, it had limitations when considering more complex or sensitive issues.

Cooperation is what occurs when team members have different opinions about strategies or approaches. Teaching Assistants often identified that cooperation is most readily established when time is clearly set to monitor the action being taken and its effectiveness, along with clear indicators of what would constitute success.

Coordination is what we aim to do in order to reduce unnecessary overlap of resources or roles, so everyone knows their part in the strategy and when and where to carry it out. Teaching Assistants often suggested that it was useful to be clear about when there needed to be overlap and where this was not helpful.

Collaboration involves spending 'quality' time together for planning and evaluating the teaching and learning taking place in the classroom. TAs often considered factors which could affect a positive view of collaborative planning such as the need to blur roles and how this could often be difficult to do because of existing values, attitudes and long held beliefs. For example, both teachers and TAs may hold the belief that teachers are in charge and should do all the planning without any TA involvement. Or both may believe that TAs are not able to give insights about children's learning which are relevant to planning. Both of these beliefs are underpinned by issues such as pay differentials, creating time to talk, a view of the professionalism of teachers, and perhaps the self esteem of both teachers and TAs in relation to their working partnership. It is interesting to consider whether the introduction of the HLTA role and continued changes to the TA role, are challenging perceptions about collaborative planning.

Lacey (2001) suggests that teachers and TAs often recognize that the benefits of collaboration outweigh any of the practical and philosophical difficulties. Many teachers and TAs who work at developing collaborative practice would agree that the process and product can reduce stress. Empathy, creativity and productivity are all increased, resulting in a greater understanding of each others' skills, furthering professional development, and clarifying both collective and individual responsibilities.

The role of senior management should not be underestimated in the introduction and promotion of collaborative practice across the school: for example, the appointment of a senior teacher with responsibility for ensuring that collaborative practice takes place and the introduction of references to collaboration in all job descriptions are important in encouraging collaborative practice.

On the Foundation Degree TAs have shared other ways in which their schools have encouraged an ethos of collaboration and helped to develop it in daily practice. Some schools have:

- used INSET days for joint teacher and TA training in collaborative ways of working
- audited the use of time across the school to identify places in the year, term, week, day or even lessons, where collaborative practice can be supported within school hours.

 Activity

Go to the photocopiable activity, *Collaborative teamwork activity: teamwork processes* in Appendix 1 on p. 199. This provides further opportunity for reflection on where there are barriers or opportunities for collaborative practice in your work setting.

(d) Recognition of the part TAs can play in 'differentiating' work for pupils

Collaborative working practice along with a good understanding of differentiation techniques is vital in developing good inclusive practices and enabling pupils to overcome barriers to learning. Differentiation involves the adult in the 'teacher' role, selecting the most appropriate teaching methods for a pupil to be challenged and yet successful in their learning.

The changing roles of TAs, along with the introduction of HLTAs, now makes differentiation a classroom practice which is a shared by all members of the team

HLTA
Standards
9, 15 & 20

rather than solely the responsibility of the teacher. HLTAs need to know how to differentiate effectively when planning for and teaching specific lessons, while Teaching Assistants need to understand and draw upon differentiation techniques when supporting pupil learning in both one-to-one and small group contexts.

Differentiation and personalized learning are relevant for teachers, TAs and HLTAs to use with *all* learners but differentiation techniques are particularly important when supporting pupils who have particular barriers to learning or who have Special Educational Needs.

The following is a guide to the different types of planned differentiation that teachers, TAs and HLTAs may need to consider to enable a pupil to access learning.

Differentiation of content:

- Individual pupils can be taught in 'smaller steps' than their peers, so the curriculum framework is varied in its structure for some pupils.
- Skills from an earlier Key Stage might be reinforced within the context of a higher level programme of study with careful selection of content and age appropriate resources and approach.
- Pupils follow the same topic but study and develop certain aspects in more depth.
- Different resources may be used to achieve the same learning objective.

Differentiation of task:

- A range of different activities.
- Activities linked to the pupils' interests.
- Recording the activity in a different way, e.g. scribing.

Differentiation of learning outcome:

- Learning outcomes could be differentiated in relation to different performance criteria, e.g. use of 'p' scales in Key Stage assessments, etc.

Differentiation of level of support:

- More individual time given to a pupil by the teacher or teaching assistant.
- Pupil groupings can be arranged to be supportive and varied.
- More support given to preparation and reduced one-to-one support to enable pupil independence.

Differentiation in teaching style:

- A wide range of teaching approaches can be used to suit a wide range of learning styles, e.g. visual approach, VAK – visual, auditory and kinaesthetic, multi sensory, etc.
- Flexibility of approach.
- Adjust the speed of the work task.
- Adjust the speed of the programme of study.

- Provide repetition of concept.
- Pupils work at different rates on the same tasks, so the pace is varied to suit individual needs.

Differentiation of resources:

- Use additional resources, special aids, or modified resources to support learning.
- Use strategies to make curriculum materials relevant, clear, interesting and achievable.

In addition to planned differentiation, TAs often have and want to develop a good knowledge of how to carry out 'on the spot' differentiation.

TAs often learn 'on the spot' differentiation techniques through trial and error, by getting insights into what a particular pupil enjoys or understands, or by watching teachers or other TAs who are experienced in differentiating for pupils. Differentiation, both planned and 'on the spot', is vital for all teaching learning and is particularly important for TAs to use in overcoming barriers to learning. It is important that wherever possible TAs enable pupils to understand which strategies are most helpful to them so that they feel empowered to maximize their own learning potential.

HLTA Standards 8, 9, 22 & 29

Teaching Assistants on the Foundation Degree often find discussing the range of strategies and techniques used by their TA colleagues, as particularly useful to their professional development.

 Activity

The photocopiable activity, ***Collaborative teamwork activity: on the spot differentiation*** in Appendix 1 on p. 200 provides an opportunity for you to reflect further and share ideas with your colleagues.

(e) Communication systems which develop a shared perspective on understanding pupil needs

Sometimes, teachers, HLTAs and Teaching Assistants, do not share a common outlook on children's needs as a result of differences in their personalities, life experiences, beliefs and values. Establishing common goals and putting pupils at the heart of any team or partnership seems to be the key to a successful team. However there are occasions when differences can occur in any working relationship and these differences need not mean that the partnership cannot work.

Katzenbach and Smith (1993) cited in Lacey (1998: p. 39) even suggest that teams or partners who work beyond the natural comfort zones of constant agreement on issues may be able to develop greater success in their working relationships: 'real teams' can be identified by the ability of their members to 'take risks, to use conflict positively, to trust each other and to work interdependently, using mutual accountability' to evaluate their practice.

The following case study focuses on a situation that many teachers and TAs have experienced. Read the case study and reflect on what you would do if you were the TA in this situation.

Case study

Joe, has special education needs and his attention span is considerably shorter than his peers. He especially finds reading and writing difficult. The classroom TA, Mrs Jones, is given a worksheet and asked to work with Joe. Joe quickly loses interest in the activity and starts to misbehave. The teacher approaches Joe and Mrs Jones to find out what the problem is.

Mrs Jones suggests that she and Joe are going to do the worksheet in a new way and that Joe will bring the work to show the teacher when it is finished.

Mrs Jones talks with Joe about ways they could do the work and Joe engages in the activity. Mrs Jones encourages Joe to share his finished work with the teacher.

I have asked TAs to discuss this case study and to consider where or how they can make this situation better or worse and also consider the perspective and frustrations for *all* involved.

TAs often suggest that:

- An immediate, outspoken, negative comment about the handout would imply a criticism of the teacher and make the pupil feel inadequate.
- The issue of TAs not engaging in any alternative strategies and just 'doing what I am told' could slowly make the situation worse for all three participants.
- The TA could make use of some parts of the worksheet or adapt it by using some of the strategies identified in the 'on the spot' activity.
- Breaking the task down and giving genuine, appropriate encouragement and incentives or rewards could be a good way of establishing a positive outcome for the pupil.
- Reviewing the work with the pupil and the teacher alongside the TA was a useful way for longer term changes to practice and greater planned differentiation to be implemented.

In this process of consideration TAs need to concentrate their communications on what *the pupil was enabled to do* rather than an over emphasis on what the *worksheet did not provide*.

Showing the teacher the pupil's finished worksheet can illustrate the pupil's level of access to the work and be a useful starting point for a discussion on what the pupil managed to achieve from the exercise and then what the pupil found difficult.

Sometimes time prevents this level of immediate discussion and so a positive, written comment is an alternative way of communicating the learning that took place and how it was supported.

Describing to the teacher what was done to enable the pupil to take part can lead on to discussions of some of the ways that the teacher would like worksheets or activities differentiated and the information feedback given in the future so that a clear system emerges.

On many occasions, both teachers and TAs speak of the ways in which they avoid any open disagreements and feel that this will maintain harmony, for example: 'I say nothing even when I disagree, I just get on with the job'.

However, when teachers and TAs reflect on their communication levels they realize that their body language, tone of voice, etc. are all part of the communication and these may have given a very different message than the words used.

This case study and the points raised from it show that feedback to the teacher is an essential component of the TA role. But communicating concerns in the right way is something that can prove difficult. Teaching Assistants often agonize over what to say, how to say it and when to say it.

ENHANCING TEAMWORK THROUGH ASSERTIVE COMMUNICATION

Often good communication in teams seems to happen naturally and without effort. However, often partnerships and teams that are the most effective have individual members within them that can assertively communicate. Sometimes, however, team members use non-assertive modes of communication such as passive-aggressive, or aggressive.

Some **passive aggressive** reactions to potential strategies and approaches could be:

- uninterested or dismissive facial responses, e.g. raising eyebrows
- body language, e.g. folding arms and turning slightly away
- remaining quiet, or no vocal response, e.g. staying silent or muttering a reply.

Some **aggressive** reactions to potential strategies and approaches could be:

- negative comments, e.g. 'it will never work, we have already tried that kind of thing before and where did it get us then?'
- negative actions, e.g. placing equipment down forcibly on the table.

Assertive communication, however, means that communication is simply worded, spoken clearly but in a way which accepts the rights of both parties, uses 'I' statements and expresses a person's feelings and difficulties with an issue.

When a team discusses a new strategy to be trialed with a pupil to promote better behaviour or enable greater learning, sometimes staff feel challenged by these changes to practice. Sometimes reservations about an approach need to be aired but in a way that leaves communication channels open. Two examples of assertive communication might be:

HLTA
Standards
17, 18,
22 & 23

- 'I think it is good that we think this through, I am just struggling a bit with the idea ...'
- 'I feel on first hearing this that it will not work but I think that is because I am worried about whether we have the staffing levels to ...'

Another potential challenge may be that TAs want to ask for greater involvement in the classroom planning and workings of the class. Many teachers welcome this and recognize the benefits of sharing some of these roles rather than the TA feeling isolated. However, sometimes TAs do not know how to communicate this in a way which does not imply criticism of their teacher colleague.

Assertive communication involves describing how you feel, a description of the effect of an action or behaviour and a request for what you would like to happen – for example a comment from a TA which says:

> I feel worried when I do not get to discuss the week's planning with you because I feel I am not supporting both you and the children the way that I want to. Is there a time that I could come and talk briefly to you about this each week?

The communication above remains assertively focused within the TA and teacher relationship and roles.

Rose encourages TAs to speak to teachers at the end of a lesson or at the end of a day about situations or problems and seek clarification or advice about any tasks or areas of concern.

> Each participant in a partnership must demonstrate professional respect for the others and this will only be achieved when each partner attempts to see a situation from the point of view of the other. The professional classroom assistant will learn to ask for clarification, and also seek reasoning behind the advice given. Effective teachers will want to provide the most supportive learning environment possible and will welcome an opportunity to ensure that their expectations are clear. (Rose, 2005: 22)

HLTA
Standard
4

Both teachers and TAs need time for training in supportive assertive communication as this is often the key to success within classrooms and is necessary in communication with both colleagues and pupils.

Sometimes teacher and TA partnerships break down. The working relationship can then be difficult to re-establish. It is important to consider what teachers and TAs can do when they cannot find a shared perspective from which to move forward.

The case study below outlines a real situation in which this relationship breakdown had occurred. Often a pupil who displays behaviour challenges can, if teams of teachers and TAs are not careful, be so stressful that maintaining good relationships becomes more difficult than usual. Read the case study and consider what were the barriers in their partnership and what enabled both to gain a shared perspective.

Case study

During a school outreach setting I experienced a teacher and Teaching Assistant who were not speaking a great deal to each other due to a disagreement over the way a pupil with attention deficit and hyperactivity disorder (ADHD) was being taught and supported in the classroom.

After consulting with the teacher the latter expressed her view that the pupil was being over protected by the TA who, she said, allowed the child far too much time and attention instead of being more directive with the pupil and insisting on boundaries. The teacher felt that the pupil was manipulating this TA.

The Teaching Assistant, meanwhile, reported to me that the teacher did not understand the pupil and would never give him any time to focus in the lesson, and that if allowed a little 'off-task time' the pupil would gradually accept redirection without getting angry.

Both staff showed their notes on the child's participation in lessons over the last week in relation to his on-task behaviour. One showed the pupil having had a less than satisfactory week with some lessons in which he was very disruptive; whilst the other showed that the pupil had had some good parts to the week.

It was difficult to get a real picture and the notes, though carefully kept, were written from the perspective taken by the teacher or the perspective taken by the Teaching Assistant and each was measured within their own perspectives.

Drawing on my impartial status as a visitor to the school, we got together around a table and discussed the issues. Subsequently, together, they devised a joint recording system which involved a simple scoring system from 1 to 5 with clear criteria for each score recorded in relation to specifically targeted behaviours.

The next meeting was very positive in that both teacher and TA had similar scores across the week due to the consistency of the system of recording. It was then clear as to which lessons or parts of lessons there had been problems with and which ones were positive for the pupil. The data collection taken using a consistent scoring system meant that the teacher and TA had a shared perspective from which to plan for the pupil.

Over the next few weeks, both teacher and TA began to discuss where they were having success and both developed an understanding of the role they were each playing in helping this pupil. The teacher expressed her understanding of why, when off-task behaviour was minor, the TA sometimes had to give the pupil time to go off-task and then redirect him. The TA expressed her understanding that when the pupil was carrying out more major off-task or disrupted behaviour the teacher needed to ensure that the pupil understood where behaviour was unacceptable.

Sometimes collecting data and establishing facts can help teams to develop a shared perspective rather than base their ideas on their own opinions, or base their opinions on past experience, which may no longer be relevant. Reflect on how you could use data collection, clear recording criteria, etc. to help you make more informed and shared decisions as a team.

WORKING WITH OTHER TEACHING ASSISTANTS

Teaching Assistants need to establish positive working practices between each other. Without such collaboration some pupils may not experience the continuity of provision and learning support that they are entitled to. Teaching Assistants can often provide each other with a very useful source of professional development, provided they are given time and share skills. In some schools there may be more than one TA working in a classroom, or several in one department, and therefore the management of each of the staff member's roles and responsibilities, can become even more complex, with even more collaboration required.

Some of the ways of encouraging reflection on the variety of TA roles within the school, and an understanding of the similarities and differences of various TA roles, can provide valuable evaluative insights, and possibly decrease misunderstandings between TAs carrying out very different responsibilities but all within the wide brief of the TA role.

Teaching Assistants on the Foundation Degree suggested the following ways that TAs could understand each others' roles more effectively:

- **Interchanging roles**: For example, a TA who is one-to-one with a pupil and a TA who is considered to provide general classroom support may have more understanding of each other's roles if they interchange on an agreed and organized pattern, after consultation between the TAs and the teacher.
- **Observations of the roles played by TAs in other classes or departments, or with specific pupils**: This can provide a broader understanding of the needs of the school, the staff, the pupils and the curriculum.
- **Sharing care roles with academic support roles on a rota**: A rota or rolling system organized to ensure that roles are shared can ensure that TAs feel valued and treated equally.
- **Induction and professional development**: Where one TA is an established staff member and another TA is new to the class or department, an induction period to review the expectations of the teacher and the class or lesson routines and to develop confidence may need to be set up and discussed by all the team members. The role of the established TA may also need adjustments in light of new staff and these issues need to be a clear part of any class or team meetings.

Now TAs who have become HLTAs often find themselves working with TA colleagues where it is their role to take the managerial role of teaching and learning for that lesson. Although HLTAs may be concerned at first about how their TA colleagues will respond to this change in roles, often they have had unique insight as TAs as to ways in which TAs can be used effectively to promote learning.

HLTAs can also be concerned about how teachers are viewing their role. A study by the National Federation for Educational Research (NFER), commissioned by the Training and Development Agency for Schools (TDA), published its findings in August 2006. The study reviewed HLTA deployment and impact. The study looked at a number of aspects of HLTA deployment in particular, the additional roles and responsibilities of HLTAs and if the use of this role by schools was raising standards alongside its other aim which was to reduce teacher workload.

The study targeted 1,560 HLTAs and their primary, secondary or special schools. From the 54% response rate, this study revealed a largely positive picture about the deployment and effective working of HLTAs.

UNDERSTANDING GROUP OR TEAM DEVELOPMENT

As TAs work in increasingly diverse teams it is important that they understand not only the processes of teamwork and the practical communication channels and skills but also some of the theories which underpin how groups of people, or teams, establish a working relationship, maintain and develop it and achieve optimal operational working.

Tuckman (1965) provides five key stages of development that 'groups', or teams go through. The stages he identifies are presented below:

- **Forming**: A group or team members are establishing their **rapport, relationships** and **roles**.
- **Storming**: A group or team members are establishing their **differences** in rapport, relationships and roles.
- **Norming**: A group or team members are **settling into a pattern** of rapport, relationships and roles.
- **Performing**: A group or team members are working **at their optimum** within their established rapport, relationship and roles.
- **Mourning**: A group or team members are going to be leaving their group setting and experiencing change and are **evaluating** their rapport, relationships and roles.

Some teams move more quickly through certain stages than others, some teams can also become 'stuck' in a stage.

 Activity

The photocopiable activity, ***Collaborative teamwork activity: Performing as a team*** in Appendix 1 on p. 202 enables further reflection on the developmental sequences that teams or groups go through in establishing, maintaining and completing their working role.

The notion of 'a team' in the school setting is in the process of change. The Code of Practice guidance for working with SEN pupils advocates that pupils themselves, along with parents, are essential members of our school teams. The Every Child Matters agenda is focusing all agencies who support schools on working together more effectively. Hence TAs and HLTAs, as well as teachers, are expected to widen their teamwork practice.

In the busy life of the classroom reflecting on our partnership roles can seem less important than other more pressing issues. However, reflecting on teamwork issues can be vital if the relationship between teachers, TAs and HLTAs is to be positive and their roles are to be complementary in the teaching and learning process.

This chapter has suggested that supportive partnerships and teamwork, whoever this is with, relies upon:

- An understanding of each other's roles and responsibilities.
- Respect for each other's strengths and weaknesses.
- Willingness to use objective criteria for analysing class issues or pupil difficulties.
- An understanding of how *personal* some issues can feel and a willingness to *depersonalize* to ultimately benefit pupils.
- The capacity for telling each other what has gone well and congratulating positives on a regular basis.
- Setting problematic feedback about difficulties with pupils within a generally positive working framework.

The questions below can be used to promote further reflection on partnership and teamwork practice in your setting.

〰️ **Reflective questions**

- How would you evaluate the effectiveness of your communication with teachers, HLTAs, other TAs and other professionals?
- How could you use assertive communication to benefit your teamwork practice?
- Consider what you actively do to develop a shared perspective with colleagues?
- What are your strengths and difficulties in communicating in your team? How could you build on your strengths further and address your difficulties?

Further Reading 📖

Hayward, A. (2006) *Making Inclusion Happen*. London: Sage Publications.

References

Babington Smith, B. and Farrell, B. (1979) *Training in Small Groups*. Oxford: Pergamon Press.
Cheminais, R. (2008) *Every Child Matters. A Practical Guide for Teaching Assistants*. Abingdon: Routledge Group.
Katzenbach and Smith, cited in Lacey, P. (2001) *Support Partnerships. Collaboration in Action*. London: David Fulton.

NFER (2006) *HLTA Development and impact* Research Findings .Training and Development Agency for Schools.

Rose, R. (2005) *Becoming a Primary Higher Level Teaching Assistant.* Exeter: Learning Matters Ltd.

Tuckman, Bruce. W. (1965) Developmental Sequence in Small Groups. Psychological Bulletin 63, 384–399. Reprinted in Group Facilities: A Research Applications Journal Number 3, Spring 2001.

Useful websites

The National Federation for Educational Research
http://www.nfer.ac.uk/index.cfm
Review research into the deployment and impact of support staff who have achieved HLTA status by Rebekah Wilson, Caroline Sharp, Maha Shuayb, Lesley Kendall, Pauline Wade and Claire Easton.
http://www.nfer.ac.uk/research-areas/pims-data/summaries/hlta-status.cfm
Review integrated working and multi disciplinary teamwork at http://www.everychildmatters.gov.uk
Review Training and Development Agency for Schools website, reference to Remodelling and Support staff. http://www.tda.gov.uk

SECTION 2

SUPPORTING PUPILS

SELF ESTEEM

Enhancing the Role of the Teaching Assistant

Maureen Parker

This chapter will:

- Demonstrate the importance of self esteem.
- Explore links to learning; the sense of self.
- Consider the self esteem of the Teaching Assistant (TA) developing a 'professional self'.

UNDERSTANDING THE IMPORTANCE OF SELF ESTEEM

The aim of this chapter is to explore issues relating to self esteem, not only with regard to supporting pupils with self esteem issues, but also for you in your role as a TA and an educator. As adults working in the children's workforce, we are all educators, whatever our title or role, and through our responses to each other, we are subconsciously setting the climate for relationships within the educational setting and also modelling this to pupils who observe and reflect on their observations of our interactions more than we realize. This is a critical concept and one that may be easily overlooked in the fast pace and hubbub of a modern learning environment. A learning environment that is both positive and dynamic can only be sustained by those who create it if all feel valued, have a voice and are heard. It is a crucial development that self esteem is included as one part of The Common Assessment Framework that is directly related to aspects of the Children's Plan (2008) which recognizes the importance of self esteem.

HLTA Standards 1, 2, 3 & 27

As a TA you may actually be part of the primary data gathering for an individual assessment for a pupil or in fact as an HLTA, the Lead Professional. How might the following pages prove useful to you?

You may read this chapter on one occasion when you are focusing on a child you know well and feel has low self esteem from your recent observations and reflections on the pupil's interactions with others. In your search for answers you will be looking to try to understand both your understanding of the concept of 'low self esteem', their

HLTA
Standards
1, 2, 26 &
27

needs and also appropriate strategies to support the development of a more positive sense of self or higher self esteem. The first half of the chapter focuses on this aspect with interwoven case studies of pupils.

On another occasion, however, the focus of your reading may be related to your role and your attempts to gain a greater insight into your own personal and professional development and practice, particularly if your role has changed and evolved as described in Chapter 1. You may be seeking an understanding of why you have begun to react in certain situations differently than before. The second half of the chapter offers some areas to reflect on which are further developed in the subsequent chapter. Responses from research conducted with TAs/HLTAs have been included to illustrate this.

 Activity

Reflect on the following questions:

- How do I support and relate to the pupils I work with? How well do I do this?
- How do my professional relationships make me feel about myself and my role?
- What are the indicators that let me know that I am valued in my role?
- Who are the important people to me within my role?
- What does the term 'self esteem' mean to me?

HLTA
Standards
6 & 7

The responses to the questions above will enable you to begin to consider your place and role within your setting and may guide you to which aspect of self esteem you wish to focus on in the first instance. Self esteem is a complex subject and one that has not perhaps been given the careful attention that it deserves from the perspective of the role of the TA, despite the vast body of knowledge that exists. Popular culture and a perceived perception of an understanding of the term has to some extent 'clouded' the subject. Reading journal papers such as those suggested in the 'Further reading' section will update you with peer reviewed academic views. Developing a shared understanding of self esteem through an exploration of theory and an engagement with and reflection on the key concepts that are thought to define the term are essential if TAs are to effectively support learning and the emotional development of pupils. Understanding your role, the dynamics within the teams you work in and your sense of who you are within the organization is critical in being able to further support pupils within this.

We must also recognize that an educational setting such as a school, like any complex organization, may at times be a challenging environment and thus may not always provide a positive environment for all pupils and staff. As a Teaching Assistant, you are in an ideal position to begin to address this and perhaps mediate the experience for young people through your involvement with pupils, teachers and the curriculum, and your active support of agreed school policies and strategies. Chapter 4 gives an indication of the strategies you can use to develop the skills you need to be able to communicate clearly if you are unsure about any aspect of your roles and responsibilities.

It may be that in your role you only have the opportunity to work with a child for a short period and not to see the outcome of your work in relation to self esteem, but you still have a responsibility as to how you engage and develop your professional relationship with the pupil. The nature of the role you have, and the opportunity you have to develop supportive relationships with pupils compared to other staff, enables you to become alert to pupils sense of self esteem, and their perception of how successful they are at learning new tasks and acquiring new skills, enabling you to plan your approach to meet each individual's needs.

How we, as educators, manage our interactions with pupils is critical if we are to begin to create and reinforce a positive sense of self, both for them as a learner and within the school community and for ourselves in our professional roles. It is vital therefore to focus on what we can do. If we can enable a positive change, no matter how slight, we begin to enhance the development of self concept and an increased sense of self linked to successful learning and social experiences. As educators our sense of self in relation to our professional role may also further develop through the feedback we receive.

A school/education setting as a community of learners offers the opportunity for us to use a systematic and structured approach through, for example, the curriculum, rewards systems and ways of engaging pupils, yet allows roles to be sensitive and to respond to the needs of individuals, pupils and staff. Becoming aware of the fragility of self esteem in some pupils is the first stage in identifying an opportunity to begin to intervene and thus start to enable the pupil to have the confidence to begin to grow and develop in their sense of self in relation to that learning task, adding again to their sense of self.

In this chapter it is not possible to explore this in depth but merely to begin to highlight this aspect of your role. Lawrence's (2006) work is influential in this area. It explores all aspects of self esteem in school and educational settings in some detail and will give you a much more detailed explanation of theoretical aspects of self esteem. Therefore, in this chapter, rather than focus solely on the notion of either low or high self esteem, I would like you to consider the notion of self esteem as a continuum and therefore to begin connect your role with something that is dynamic and potentially in flux.

With this perspective, our main aim could be to enable a pupil to move along that continuum, increasing their self esteem from low towards higher, but being mindful that it is not necessarily 'a good thing' to always seek high self esteem at any cost as we need to take account of other factors such as the age and developmental stage of the pupil. We must bear in mind that the journey along the continuum may take some time and indeed for some, may never be achieved within the school setting, or indeed, as others may judge, life itself. It is important to recognize it is the individual's assessment of themselves that is critical whatever else we think.

Developing an understanding both of the importance of self esteem and the underlying theories and how it links to both achievement and the development and sustainment of positive relationships is crucial.

HLTA
Standards
2, 3 & 6

WHAT DO YOU UNDERSTAND THE TERM SELF ESTEEM TO MEAN?

Previous definitions have included:

Self esteem arises from the discrepancy between the perceived self, or self concept (an objective view of the self) and the ideal self (what the person values, or wants to be like). A large discrepancy results in low self esteem, while a small discrepancy is usually indicative of high self esteem. (Pope *et al.*, 1988: 4)

Self esteem is the individual's evaluation of the discrepancy between self-image and ideal self ... it can be appreciated that the discrepancy between the two is inevitable and so can be regarded as a normal phenomenon (Lawrence, 2006: 5)

Self esteem is the respect and value of the self. It is the concept that there is real importance in what we do, think, feel, and believe. (White, in Bovair and McLaughlin, 1993: 100)

Self esteem is the ability to see oneself as capable and competent, loving, unique and valuable. (Berne and Savary, 1981: xiv)

 Activity

Consider how a child described by others as having low self esteem may present in your class or school.

How would they:

- behave?
- respond to a task or an instruction?
- relate to others?
- respond to change or new situations?

Consider the following case studies, you may recognize some aspects of pupils you know.

Case study: Harry

Harry is 15 and has a Statement of Special Educational Needs. He is described by staff as frustrated and often directs his anger at peers and staff. He will refuse to undertake work which he considers beneath him, but at times gives up when work is set for the whole class that he feels that he cannot complete, yet he is reluctant to accept help.

He has an older sibling who is often in trouble. Staff, particularly cover or supply staff recognize the surname and sometimes assume they have a troublemaker in class, confusing him with his sibling. His behaviour has been described as inconsistent – one day he is pleasant, cheerful and works well, responding positively to encouragement, another day he is rude, disruptive and apparently lazy.

Case study: Amber

Amber is 11, has a Statement of Special Educational Needs for Specific Learning Difficulties (SpLD) and is described as healthy looking and well dressed. She is of average height and build and is described as a quiet, shy and thoughtful child with a kind and caring nature. She is openly friendly with all her classmates yet finds it difficult to form close friendships amongst her peers and so often seems lonely. In the classroom she hides behind her long hair, especially when asked difficult questions. She will avoid tasks at times and can talk out of turn. Attendance is a concern as she has frequent absences from school.

Case study: Jim

Jim is in Year 1. He was 'chatty' last term (summer), but at times is now sullen. He lacks confidence when faced with new tasks and seeks reassurance from his teacher and TA. They describe his behaviour as attention seeking with low-level organizational difficulties and deduce that he is a 'bright child, but lazy'.

At times he interferes with others' work and makes sure staff know that others have made errors in their work.

Staff have observed that there are tensions developing in his friendships. A new baby was born in the summer holidays.

These pupils are different, in age, gender and most specifically their individual needs. Yet to staff they represent three pupils who are not only having a negative experience of school and the process of learning but could all be described as having low self esteem.

Is it possible, therefore, to support the development of a positive sense of self esteem when pupils have such different needs? My experiences as a practitioner suggest it is.

WHAT IS SELF ESTEEM?

Lawrence (1996, 2006) constructed a model that considered self esteem as an embracing term for specific elements in the study of self.

Self image and **ideal self** which combine to give us: our **self concept**.

Self esteem, therefore, can broadly be defined as the inner picture we hold of ourselves.

Self image

This could be considered to be what the person thinks of themself. Lawrence (1996: 3) describes it as: 'the individual's awareness of his/her mental and physical characteristics'. This will have begun to be formed in our earliest days, within the family and our social contacts.

Consider a baby's surprise when biting their toes for the first time, a sensation that lets them know that these feet are a part of them and that they are an individual. Corrie (2003: 99) invites us to pause and reflect on this point, perhaps fundamental to an understanding of self esteem:

> Each small baby is born with its own unique beauty, but how long are they allowed to be perfect just the way they are? For some it is no time at all, they are judged even before they leave the womb: for being the wrong gender, for not being physically perfect, for coming at the wrong time, for having the wrong father and many more. Then as they cry out after they are born, some are not welcomed, some feel rejection in the first moment of life. Is it any wonder that many beautiful, unique beings get lost and hidden behind many layers of negative thoughts and behaviour patterns, and we lose sight of who we really are.

As we grow and develop we may be strongly influenced by both verbal and non-verbal messages we are given from others. Consequently, it is vital that we recognize the importance of the quality of the interpersonal relationships we model and develop and the demand for a high level of communication skills when working with pupils.

Your role as a TA can determine the quality of relationships for a pupil as some will need more structure and nurture in their interactions with other adults within the school setting. For example, pupils with an existing low self image will readily accept and internalize a casual negative remark that will reinforce their existing poor self image. Your role may need you to alert other adults either teaching or supporting the pupil to be aware of the need to choose language carefully when either correcting or explaining a task or activity.

As children enter puberty and adolescence body image often becomes a high priority. The importance of how they perceive themselves to look, or trying to be part of a group, or part of a 'look' can be the source of much anxiety and stress.

By understanding the importance of the elements of self image as part of self esteem, we can be more aware of the difficulties for some pupils despite the positive strategies implemented in school.

Broadly speaking these elements will include consideration of:

- our physical appearance – what we look like
- our skills – what we can/cannot do
- how we relate to others – the ability to maintain and develop relationships
- how we manage ourselves and our emotions.

All of these combine to build our self image. Harry, Jim and Amber all have difficulty relating to others and managing their emotions. Whilst Jim and Harry are more demonstrative in their emotions, Amber is quiet and withdrawn. All indicate they have problems in maintaining and developing relationships with their peers. In some circumstances they indicate a lack of confidence in skills for a task and, as a result, either do not attempt it or sabotage their own success.

Ideal self

This is a consideration of what the person would like to be – their 'ideal'. Over a period of time it may take into account the messages received from other diverse sources. This includes the individual's collected experiences and who they want to be, their own goals, aspirations, expectations and dreams, but with the added complication of considering what they think other people think of them. Clearly, this is a difficult aspect of self esteem for some pupils.

Confusion can arise as we process information from many different sources. How we analyse and act on this information and what part of our ideal self the information relates to will all be taken into consideration. At different times there may be more sensitivity to the development of our ideal self within home, school, or social or other highly influential settings – the importance of what parents, carers, other significant adults and peers think. Inner conflict may be created for the individual because of the influences of these different groups. Pupils may feel that at times they are striving for an image that is unattainable.

–   Jim finds it less threatening to criticize others rather than acknowledge their skills and success.
–   Harry tries to be positive on some days, but is overwhelmed by a negative sense of self and so gives up.
–   Amber is unsure, on the outskirts of the group.

A greater sense of self may enable them all to join in more confidently and acknowledge recognition for themselves.

Self concept

Our self concept is our perception of who we are, our own identity. This links in with our personal map of all our relationships both in our personal lives and in our roles as educators, our understanding of the people around us, our personalities and our individual responses to situations. It is made up of three elements:

•   How we think and connect thoughts – cognitive.
•   How we feel and respond – affective.
•   What we do and how we behave.

Understanding the sense of self

For me the essence of self esteem is defined as a sense of:

- competence
- being valued
- being loved.

By considering self esteem in such a way it is possible to for you to identify and isolate interventions linked to these elements and thus be more aware of the influence you may have.

The starting point for an understanding of the pupil's sense of self is the careful consideration of the potential reasons behind their actions or responses, importantly based on observations and reflections on events rather than your feeling about them (your reflective diary may help).

Harry and Amber, plus other pupils, may believe all or some of the following statements:

- I find it difficult to relate to others, so begin to believe that no one likes me and I have no friends
- no one values me
- I cannot learn and I am stupid
- I find many tasks in school 'high risk' (e.g. learning new skills, completing tasks) and avoid them in whatever way I can
- I am afraid of allowing myself to begin to form attachments or connections with pupils or getting involved in situations that would allow me to grow and develop as a person
- I often feel anxious and seek to please others
- I have strong feelings, but am often either scared of expressing them or unable to manage them
- I don't think much about myself and reinforce my negative perception of myself by making self-disparaging comments – I'm thick!

It is clear, therefore, that pupils with low self esteem do not feel:

- Capable – that they are able to complete tasks. Harry and Amber either avoid tasks by rejecting them or by their behaviour.
- Lovable – that they are unique as a person. Harry is often mistaken by staff for his older sibling who is disruptive, and may not feel recognized for himself and what he can offer.
- Valued – that they can contribute. Amber, whilst friendly with her classmates, is unsure of her place in the group and what she can offer thus tending to isolate herself.

Pope *et al.* (1988) consider self esteem in children in five areas:

- Social – how they feel about themselves and others
- Academic – the child's evaluation of themselves as a student

- Family – his/her sense of place and belonging in the family
- Body image – physical appearance combined with capabilities
- Global – a general appraisal of the self.

If we apply this model to Harry and Amber, then it would indicate the social and academic areas as those in which they may need some support. Harry may also feel that the reputation of his sibling infiuences others' opinions about him and thus he may feel that his sense of place within the family has an impact on the school setting and so he transfers this to his responses and setting. Jim is also affected by this, but his sense of place within the family is in relation to a change in his family setting.

Amber, Harry and Jim may appear to behave or act in ways that would indicate that they have low self esteem, but still try, often with great success, to mask their feelings about:

- competence at the task
- relationship with others
- or their place within the group.

It is important though that we avoid labelling individuals as having 'low self esteem' with limited knowledge of them as individuals because what we perceive may be natural anxiety or fears and not linked to what we think it is linked to. In your role you have the opportunity to influence all of the above primarily by creating positive relationships. However, you may also find that the close proximity of this means that you blur the boundaries of your role and over-identify with the pupil or make judgements based on feelings and responses rather than what has been observed over a period of time. There are a number of 'tests' available that may give some indication of a pupil's disposition and an indicative level of self esteem and offer suggestions for appropriate interventions. (Lawrence 2006).

 Activity

Consider the pupils in your class.
Do they hide behind a mask to avoid a task or new activity that may involve risk or potential failure, e.g. 'class clown', 'Mr/Miss Helpful?'
What are these 'masks' that the pupils you know put on?

Jim is Mr Critical, he may feel that other pupils aren't doing things properly and if he can point this out, he can show that he is not the only one to get things wrong. If he can highlight others' shortcomings he can avoid criticism of his efforts. Very young children are often unsure about their sense of self and try different masks to find out 'Who am I?', 'What am I like?' In this example staff in school felt this was not the case and that he was responding to the change in his home circumstances.

Table 5.1

Competence	Being valued	Being loved
Learn new skills	Have a sense of self	Relates to a significant other
Practise skills	Accept recognition of success	Recognizes feelings
Achieve competence	Reciprocate recognition of success with others	Accepts relationships
Have the confidence to try new activities	Have a sense of their own identity and role in relation to the group they belong to	Knows they are loved

When Amber is asked a question that she does not understand or want to answer she becomes 'Miss Invisible' hiding behind her hair hoping not to be noticed. Contrast that with the attention she draws to herself by talking out of turn, 'Miss Notice-Me'.

Harry at times is 'Mr Superior – this work is beneath me', and at times 'Mr Angry', probably in classrooms where the staff have confused his identity with that of his sibling. He feels angry that they have not noticed him for himself and knows that his sibling presents challenging behaviour in class, so concludes that he might as well act up to the mask he's been given.

Table 5.1 summarizes the elements that make up the elements of self esteem. They are interrelated and each contributes to the growth of the other.

Figure 5.1 further demonstrates the flexibility and creativity we need when supporting the development of self esteem and indicates how as a TA you have the opportunity to begin to intervene to build, even though it may be in small stages, a positive sense of self esteem in pupils. For each pupil the point where you can connect and intervene may be different – you can reverse the arrows or interject at any point in the cycle – but as the model in Figure 5.1 indicates, wherever you enter, it is the beginning of developing a sound sense of self and positive self esteem. I believe we can all begin to connect through the elements of self esteem set out in Table 5.1.

It is not about failing to achieve it is about the response to the failure. We need to teach pupils that we learn through failure and that it is OK to fail as that is how we learn and that we need to take risks to do so. If we are confident to take risks we will learn and begin to build confidence and thus begin to feel more competent.

 Activity

How do you respond when a young person you work with fails to achieve at a task or activity?

Do they receive the message that you expected them to fail or do they feel ready to learn from the experience and try again?

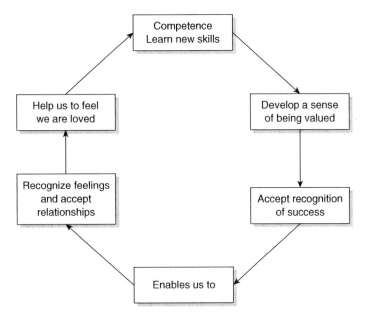

Figure 5.1 Stages for building self esteem

Reflect on your findings, your responses to pupils when they are not successful at tasks is critical. The focus must be on ensuring that the pupil feels confident in tackling the task; a relationship based on mutual respect and trust will enable this to occur. Although some pupils may resist support after they are unsuccessful at a task, you need to ensure that the quality of the relationship is maintained and be sensitive in the way in which you approach this through congruence between your choice of language, tone of voice and body language. If a pupil does not feel competent, this may affect how valued and lovable they feel. Remember too, that how we feel about ourselves at times may make a difference to the way in which we work with pupils. Pupils benefit from contact with staff that project a positive outlook and have empathy and interest in them as individuals, and these parts of our personality will enhance our professional role. However, we must be able to separate our 'self' in times of personal stress or trauma from our professional self and continue to manage our emotions (as the adult) and project this sense of consistency as a role model. There will be times when we may need to acknowledge our own emotions in relation to the role, for if we too feel that in our role as educators we lack competence, are not valued or recognized for who we are and what we can contribute, we will not be effective. We must not only ensure that we are still able to effectively support the learning of the pupils we support, but also that we offer the opportunity for sustained positive emotional growth.

Harry, Amber and Jim (our case studies) have all been supported by TAs who believed in them and who used strategies that enabled them to begin to develop a more positive sense of self concept.

Why is it difficult to change self concept?

As self concept is a personal evaluation, based on our individual interpretation of events, experiences and interactions, it is difficult for another to intervene, even when it is clear to those around us that we are sustaining and reinforcing a negative image of ourselves.

Harry's self concept is determined by what he thinks teachers and his TA think of him. If he feels they do not really know him as a person and value him for himself, but only have 'their perception' of him (which might also be confused with a sibling), then he sees no reason to change. His negative sense of self concept is being reinforced by those around him.

Lawrence (1996) considered this aspect of self esteem theory in the context of his research and identified four characteristics of self concept – shown in Table 5.2. You may recognize these from the pupils you considered in a previous task.

 Activity

Using all the information above consider what strategies you would you use for Harry, Amber and Jim.

Understanding elements of self esteem theory links to effective management of behaviour. The most effective practitioners examine their strategies and endeavour to understand how they react when dealing with difficulties. This knowledge enables us to begin to be aware of the powerful influence that we have over how a young person feels in response to the specific task or activity.

We, as educators, are part of the process of developing self esteem in pupils. Consider the potential negative influences that we can present:

- Emphasis on negative language to describe events with no recognition of what has gone well. For example, a noisy lesson with a group, ignoring the quality of the task and completion that may also have happened.
- Using assemblies and other times when pupils are in large groups to repeatedly stress situations that may only apply to a few, e.g. uniform infringements, litter, movement around the school.

Often there are pressure moments within a school timetable when staff responses to these stressors can culminate, often accidently, in what Canfield and Wells (1976) called 'killer statements'. These manifest themselves as either verbal or non-verbal negative statements that can have the effect of making someone feel worse as a result of an interaction. They undermine an element of an individual's self esteem. They may be in the

Table 5.2

Characteristics of self concept	Some basic points to consider
Avoidance Quiet, shy, may be withdrawn. Will avoid the situation that may expose failure.	Do they appear upright in their posture, using eye contact where appropriate? Do they join in with activities? Are they part of a group? Does the pupil participate or avoid involvement in a task or activity?
Compensation Outgoing, dominant personality. May fight back rather than risk failure.	Do they question either the relevance of activity or their involvement in it? Do they move from group to group? Do they appear to fall out frequently with others? Are they fearful of being put down, tending to criticize first?
Motivation Negative perception of the self illustrated through comments, remarks made.	Do they repeat the same task or activities and appear to fail deliberately? Do they start and restart a task? Do they initiate activities or wait for individual instruction or guidance?
Resistance Rejects any support or guidance offered.	Do they reject any support or guidance even when they have not understood the focus of the task or activity? Do they avoid adult approval during task completion?

Source: adapted from Lawrence, 1996

way we speak, not only to pupils, but also to colleagues, the words we choose, or the emphasis, tone of voice, or accompanying gestures.

 Activity

Be honest – what killer statements do you use?

Are you more likely to use verbal or non verbal statements?

Are there some times of the day or week when you are more likely to use more killer statements?

The language, both verbal and non-verbal, that you use, not only to pupils but about them to other adults in the school setting, can influence the development of the young person's self concept. Skills of communication are vital in underpinning the relationship that exists between staff and pupils. These skills may need to be taught to the pupils, but first consider yourself as Cleo did.

HLTA
Standard 7

Case study

Cleo is studying on our Foundation Degree. As she has been a TA in a primary school for a number of years she decided to take the opportunity to focus on her own behaviour and responses from the pupils for research for an assignment. She was confident that she could demonstrate how her beliefs about a positive approach to behaviour management enhanced her pupils' learning opportunities. Rather than rely solely on feedback from colleagues who observed her, she arranged to be videoed in order that she could analyse her behaviour herself. Cleo thought that she was always positive in her interactions with staff and pupils, indeed she prided herself on being thought of as positive – enthusiastic about her role and ability to build relationships. She always thought about her choice of language and about the words she used to convey praise, affirmation or correction. However, she was not prepared for what the video revealed. She did use positive language, but when the sound was turned down it revealed that her non-verbal language was much more powerful than her verbal language and was not empowering and affirming, but critical and at times judgemental. This enabled Cleo to understand why she did not always get the response from pupils that she wanted. Other staff in the school also chose to be videoed and analysed their own behaviour (including teachers). The outcomes surprised them all and contributed not only to the professional development of all involved, but also strengthened the interpersonal relationships between staff.

THE SELF ESTEEM OF THE TA

Activity

Identify specific times when you felt:

- valued
- acknowledged for your individual commitment and competence at a task or activity.

What did others do or say to give you this feeling?
Reconsider your own earlier definition of self esteem. Is there anything you would add?
How do you believe pupils would respond if you asked them the same questions?

When exploring self esteem we cannot isolate ourselves from this process. How we interact in our work settings with a range of colleagues can also contribute to our development of self esteem. This part of the chapter is intended to introduce the notion of self esteem in relation to developing a professional self and for you to begin to explore aspects of it.

Initial Research with TAs beginning their studies on the Foundation Degree elicited the following responses in relation to how they felt about their roles in the context of self esteem theory. Whilst deconstructing what they were learning about self esteem and applying it to their own perspectives with regard to their role (they had been TAs for varying amounts of time) they offered the following.

Words to describe me as I am now (Self image):	How I would like to be (Ideal self):
Uneasy	Confident
Lacking in confidence	Self assured
Out of touch	Outward going
Tired	Not stuttering
Agitated	Calm
Preoccupied	Happy
Apprehensive	Relaxed
Curious	Even tempered
Excited	Self assured
Tense	Liked
Interested	Tactful

These comments could relate to the self esteem of the TA in their role in relation to two aspects of self esteem theory, self image and ideal self, and therefore may affect how the TA is able to work alongside the teacher to support effective teaching and learning in the classroom. Considering this in relation to the role was a useful exercise as some noted that their lack of positive comments with regard to self image, for example, was linked to a lack of understanding of policies and practice within the school setting and gave them the confidence to realize that this was not a reflection on them as an individual, but an indication of the need to seek greater clarification of expectations and further guidance on expectations from other staff.

Activity

Reflect on the following questions:

- Do you identify with any of the comments in the self image column?
- What can you do to overcome some of the negative feelings and identify with the more assertive comments in the second column?
- Do you need more information from colleagues, for example, or to clarify your role in a specific situation?

Creating the professional self

The concept of a 'professional self' has been recently introduced to students on our programme as a concept to discuss and consider when studying self esteem, as many have observed that there are differences between how they may react in certain situations within their education setting and elsewhere. Many TAs now see their role as being part of a profession, one they have chosen and can see a career path in and not just, as it may have been in the past, to fit in with lifestyle choices for a few years. The range of opportunities for professional development has increased, specialist roles have emerged and a structure for progession both within educational settings and Children's Services has begun to emerge. An agreed national pay structure may soon be in place. Chapter 1 explored 'professionalism' in its widest concept, but what do we mean by a professional self in relation to the role of TA? Teaching Assistants consulted as part of the author unpublished research identified the following key points.

HLTA
Standard 7

Developing the professional self

The role of the TA is becoming increasingly more autonomous in many schools even though the phrase 'under the direction of the teacher' is used in relation to many aspects of it and was a key point that emerged in the development of the HLTA standards. By acknowledging this 'professional self' it is possible to then identify what is critical in sustaining and developing it. Teaching Assistants offered the following:

- Acknowledge the 'me' at work, it can feel different to the 'me' elsewhere, especially when I really know I have made a difference.
- Acknowledge my own skills, especially when I have acquired new ones and there has been a positive effect.
- Recognize boundaries associated with the role and be aware of this even when I am in the local community.
- Seek and give feedback (most of us are not told when we have got something right so we could do it for each other!)
- Recognize that most of the time we 'do a good enough job' and remember that!

When asked about sustaining this 'professional self' they offered:

- Recognize what I need to survive and thrive in my role.
- Be confident and assertive in making sure I am clear about others' expectations and that I can meet them.
- Take responsibility and act on it initiating professional dialogue where I need to.
- Clear communication.

The Johari Window is a model we can apply to looking at self and can encourage us to look at our sense of self with regard to our professional role. It was designed by two psychologists, Joseph Luft and Harry Ingham (cited in White, 1995). It gives the user a template to consider what they know about themselves and what they don't know, in conjunction with what other people know about them and what other people don't know, to create an overall picture of their professional role to reflect upon. Detailed examples can be found by searching for Johari window on the internet.

The use of a window as 'an analogy of a model of self' is apt as it allows us to hide as much, or reveal as much, as we choose. It is apposite in considering the role of the TA as it is evolving and changing not only in response to individual needs but in the wider context of change within schools and the workforce (Chapters 1, 2 and 3).

Briefly the model is shown in Table 5.3. Teaching Assistants on our Foundation Degree completed applied this model to themselves in a module session in the early stages of their studies by beginning to focus on their perception of the role of TA within their own context and setting.

Examples of their comments are included above and indicate how they perceived the role of the TA to change as their confidence increased and acknowledgement from others occurred.

Understanding the importance of the role that you have within a learning organization is the beginning of a process that will hopefully enable you to develop a clear sense of purpose that becomes part of the development of your 'professional self', an identity for your role as a TA. Without that sense of purpose and identity it will be more difficult for you to promote self esteem as part of your practice. The language you use, your non-verbal communication and the types of interactions you display to other adults in the school give an indication of the degree to which you are committed to ensuring that relationships and communication are valued and acknowledged. Pupils are always aware of the quality of relationships they observe.

HLTA
Standards
1, 2, 3, 4,
6 & 7

〰 **Reflective questions**

- Review the method you have chosen to record and reflect on your practice. Do you focus on perceived lack of success and problems?
- Could you more actively acknowledge your 'professional self' noting the skills and personal qualities that enable you to facilitate success for yourself and others every day?

Further Reading 📖

Groom, B. (2006) 'The Teaching Assistant and Behaviour Building Relationships for Learning: The Developing Role of the TA', *Support for Learning* 21 (4): 199–203.

Long, R. and Fogell, J. (1999) 'Self esteem', in *Supporting Pupils with Emotional Difficulties*. London: David Fulton.

Miller, D. and Parker, D. (2006) '"I think it's low self-esteem". Teachers' Judgements: A Cautionary Tale', *Education* 3–13, 34: 1

References

Bovair, K. and McLaughlin, C. (eds) (1993) '*Counselling in Schools: A Reader*. London: David Fulton.

Berne, P. and Savary, L. (1981) *Building Self Esteem in Children*. New York: Crossroad Publishing.

Canfield, J. and Wells, H.C. (1976) *100 ways to enhance self esteem in the classroom: a handbook for teachers and parents*.

Corrie, C. (2003) *Becoming Emotionally Intelligent*. Stafford: Network Educational Press.

Lawrence, D. (1996) *Enhancing Self Esteem in the Classroom*. London: Paul Chapman Publishing.

Lawrence, D. (2006) *Enhancing Self Esteem in the Classroom* (3rd edn). London: Paul Chapman Publishing.

Pope, A., McHale, S. and Whitehead, C. (1988) *Self Enhancement with Children and Adolescents*. Oxford: Pergamon.

White, M. (1995) *Raising Self Esteem: 50 Activities*. Cambridge: Daniels.

6 SUPPORTING EMOTIONAL HEALTH AND WELL BEING
The Role of the TA

Maureen Parker

This chapter will:

- Identify the key aspects of the role of the TA in supporting the development of emotional health and well being.
- Offer suggestions for the development of skills.
- Introduce Transactional Analysis as a tool to aid and enhance your skills in communication.
- Explore the role of the TA in relation to SEAL, Children's Trusts and the Children's Plan.

I have come to a frightening conclusion. I am the decisive element in the classroom. It is my personal approach that creates the climate. It is my daily mood that makes the weather. As a teacher I possess tremendous power to make a child's life miserable or joyous. I can be a tool of torture or an instrument of inspiration. I can humiliate or humour, hurt or heal. In all situations it is my response that decides whether a crisis will be escalated or de-escalated and a child humanized or de-humanized. (Ginott, 1972)

I came across this quote many years ago when I had just moved from teaching in a Special School for pupils with Emotional and Behavioural Difficulties (EBD) to a very large secondary school and I was in the early stages of developing an in-school Centre for pupils at risk of exclusion from school (outcomes evaluated in DfES RR163, 1999). It was displayed on the wall in the Principal's office. Finding this for me was one of the moments I'll always remember in my teaching career, here was a leader of one of the largest secondary schools in the country at the time who was clear in his beliefs and philosophy about how we should be aware of our influence on the experiences of those we teach and support. For me it captured the essence of my own philosophy in evocative words that I take every opportunity to share with others, whenever I am teaching or working in schools. It asks us to pause, stop and think about the choices we can make

HLTA
Standards
1, 2,
3 & 4

in our daily interactions and how powerful our words and actions can be on those we meet with daily in our workplace settings.

The links between understanding and managing emotions (both your own and those of pupils and others) and the development of self esteem are critical in ensuring that the optimum environment is created for learning to be both meaningful and successful for the pupil and educator involved, whether teacher or TA. Both this and the previous chapter represent two parts of a whole and link closely together. As with self esteem the prevalence of the terms 'emotional literacy', 'emotional intelligence' and 'emotional health and well being' in popular culture has led us to believe that we all have a shared understanding of these terms and therefore an understanding of the needs of pupils to support the growth and sustainability of emotional health and well being, if that was the case then perhaps we would have seen less need for some of the initiatives that have developed in recent years.

Day *et al.* recognize that:

> We know that the emotional climate of the school and classroom will affect attitudes to practices of teaching and learning, and that teachers (and their students) experience an array of sometimes contrasting emotions in the classroom. Thus, a significant and ongoing part of being a teacher is the experience and management of strong emotions. (2007: 104)

HLTA
Standards
2 & 4

HLTA
Standards
26 & 27

I would extend this to include TAs also, particularly as you may be the member of staff mediating between the teacher and the student, and carefully, with awareness, modifying your response to other adults to maintain integrity and authenticity with the student.

In developing your practical skills and acquiring knowledge for your role you will be beginning to synthesize and develop your own personal philosophy and beliefs about relationships within schools that enhance learning and also affirm the person. This will be constructed within the context of the culture of your setting as to what is both expected of staff and important to you to convey to the pupils you encounter in your role. This is alluded to in a number of chapters, specifically, those examining the curriculum (aspects of the hidden curriculum) and distributed leadership (see the discussion on moral purpose as well as those considering learning styles, behaviour and teamwork). Understanding your own emotional responses in the context of the needs of individual pupils will enable you to contribute directly to a classroom climate that openly supports the needs of all learners for both educators (adults, whatever the range of roles may be) and pupils.

WHAT STYLE OF EMOTIONAL EDUCATOR ARE YOU?

Children of all ages are very perceptive. They observe, both consciously and unconsciously, and they model the behaviours they see. If as teachers, you are to support the children in your school to become emotionally intelligent, your honesty with your emotions, your care with other's emotions, the words you choose to use and how you follow through commitments are all integral to children's learning. Children do not expect teachers to be perfect and never make mistakes, but they have little tolerance of hypocrisy, so whatever we ask of them, we must be prepared to ask more of ourselves. (Corrie, 2003: 4)

 Activity

Consider how you respond to the following:

It is a busy day in your setting and you had planned the sessions you were to be involved in quite carefully, making sure that you had communicated with all the teachers you were to be working with that day on your specific input. When you arrived at the class to work on your specialist session you discovered that a cover supervisor had replaced the teacher and another session had been planned without, seemingly, a defined role for you. You know you find it difficult to work alongside cover supervisors as the pupils' behaviour seems to change in the class and you feel that no one respects you in this situation. This felt like the last straw as at the first class you attended the teacher was late and whilst you were waiting in the corridor with the class a fight broke out and a senior teacher had to intervene, asking to speak with you about it in the staff room later.

- How would you respond to the enforced changes?
- Would you feel confident to continue with the role you would normally have or would you be able to communicate clearly, for example to ask for clarification of your role?
- Would you be able to maintain the quality of relationships you would normally have in this situation?
- Do you prefer to know the planned sequence of events or is the 'big picture' enough?
- Knowing that you had to speak with a senior teacher later, how would that make you feel?

In the above scenario, it would be easy to feel downhearted and as if you have no control over any part of the situation. The first step is to literally pause and evaluate, firstly on what actually happened and the part you had control over and then recognize that you had no control over certain events or the actions of others. Later, remember to note any key points in your reflective log or journal. Secondly, take time to observe and 'tune in' to the situation: what information do you require to be both effective for the task in hand and affective in your interactions with pupils and others? Can you communicate what you need to perform your role without either undermining yourself or others immediately in an assertive and positive way, or is it more appropriate to speak briefly with the teacher involved at a later time? Is this a situation that is happening with some regularity in the groups or classes you work with and which bothers you? Perhaps you are always anticipating a negative experience and almost without exception that is what you get. Change is necessary and will empower you, for example, could you speak with a member of staff and have a pre-planned strategy agreed that you can use or could your timetable be altered if you are delivering a structured and specialized programme

HLTA Standard 6

HLTA
Standard
7

that needs consistency? Small steps become part of a much bigger solution and most importantly enable you to feel that you are both affective and effective in your practice, a dynamic and positive influence within the groups you work. This contributes to your growing awareness of your potential influence and whilst the next quote refers to teachers it equally applies to the broader support staff role.

> Teachers can only help learners to improve their emotional literacy significantly if they have first addressed their own needs. Emotional literacy is not static or linear, but dynamic and multi-faceted, and emotional literacy needs to be included in 'professional characteristics' and seen as essential to good teaching. (Sharp, 2001: 45)

In the previous chapter you may have begun to explore aspects of self esteem in relation to your emerging professional self and the role(s) that you perform. Whilst reflection on the practical skills you have and the interventions and the support you give daily in your role is critical to your development as a practitioner, it is also vital to consider your emotional style and what you bring individually to the role. Acknowledging this and taking responsibility for it by 'tuning' into this regularly (throughout the day initially until you are more intuitive perhaps) will enable you to begin to identify how your interactions and approach to pupils and others can be improved whether through your choice of words in offering guidance, correction, praise and encouragement or aspects of your body language and tone of voice in implementing behaviour management strategies or instructing other staff. Often we approach such strategies in a simplistic way without taking account of what we bring to any interaction, that is our emotional style and understanding. In my experience as a practitioner not only can approaches to behaviour management be enhanced and become more effective by taking account of this, but the quality of all relationships can improve (aspects of professional relationships are further explored in the chapters considering role, behaviour, leadership, curriculum and collaboration). As a Foundation Degree student you will have encountered approaches to learn-

HLTA
Standard
7

ing that take account of 'learning styles' (as in Chapter 9) and you may have become not only aware of this in relation to the pupils you support but also to yourself as a student in Higher Education. By extending this to consider your emotional style and thus the reactions of others around you to interactions you will be able to see improvements both in the quality of the relationships with pupils and also the effectiveness of various strategies.

As Sharp (2001) suggested, the 'professional characteristics' of good teaching could include 'emotional literacy'. In considering this point, Foundation Degree students suggested that some or all of the following could be characteristics of an emotionally literate educator (TA or teacher):

- An awareness of the influence of their own emotions.
- An ability to manage their emotions despite outside influences or challenges.
- An ability to build strong relationships.
- An ability to demonstrate authentic and congruent behaviour and words.
- An ability to set clear professional boundaries within their role and understand how they link with others.

- A tendency to emotional resilience and not over-personalize experiences.
- An ability to seek and celebrate success in others and themselves.

Case study: Ali

Ali is 15 and described as charming, bright and able. He is not a typical disruptive student in the sense that he is not aggressive. He is not challenging in terms of his behaviour in the classroom. He is not aggressive with his peers. He does not 'up-end' tables and chairs, or swear at teachers or TAs. Ali challenges because he does not always cooperate. He will hold an adult's gaze for too long, which staff find unnerving and they typically can overreact with an escalated inappropriate strategy. He is described as manipulating staff (between teachers and TAs) and does little work at times which staff find frustrating given his ability.

Let us consider the case study above as well as the case studies from the last chapter in this context. Ali is slightly more complex than the others. An HLTA began to work in a number of Ali's classes and quickly became aware of the nature of his interactions with staff and how less experienced TAs and newly qualified teachers found him hard to manage. Although he was not listed as a pupil who would need TA input, his name had been frequently brought up at the TA team meetings she ran and emotions often 'ran high' when colleagues referred to him. Although he had not been abusive or violent, he somehow managed to evoke stronger responses than others who were more outwardly challenging. She quietly communicated this to members of the Senior Management Team and staff development sessions involving elements of Transactional Analysis were instigated to support staff in communicating with and disciplining pupils with more complex and subtle behaviour patterns such as Ali. The HLTA was also attached to an in-school Behaviour Support Centre and spent some time with Ali teaching him strategies using Transactional Analysis in order that he could also understand the relationships within the classroom, his role within them and his response to certain types of teaching styles and personalities. She then had to make sure that key information was distributed and communicated to all staff involved with Ali. One key point that she explored in some detail with her TA team was how in describing Ali's behaviour they all described what they felt about what he did rather than what he actually did. The skill of this HLTA was to recognize that it was as important for her to 'tune' in to the needs of her staff team as of the pupil concerned. Change was enabled at individual pupil, staff and whole school level.

With regard to the case studies in Chapter 5, Harry's TA had to plan carefully as his responses to either the task set, the teacher, or other pupils were so varied and unpredictable. She had to be aware of her own behaviour and how she responded when he was particularly challenging, choose her words carefully and ensure that at all times the focus of her comments remained on his behaviour and actions rather than comments about him. Thus she was able to be mindful of the expectations of the school (including appropriate approaches to discipline) and continue to affirm him as a

HLTA
Standards
1, 3 & 7

person. As with Ali, Amber and Jim needed an approach that was sensitive to their needs yet an understanding from those involved that any intervention may take some time to be seen to be effective.

As a TA you may be the member of the staff team that has this critical relationship, you may be the one that can enable progress to be made towards showing pupils a different way towards stability in relationships with others in their settings and learning. Indeed if you have a role such as Specialist Leader of Behaviour and Attendance, Pupil Services Manager, Learning Mentor or the Lead Professional in CAF you may be both providing some element of support and having a data gathering and monitoring role.

SUPPORTING EMOTIONAL HEALTH AND WELL BEING THROUGH BUILDING SELF ESTEEM

Over time Ali, Harry, Amber and Jim gradually became more confident and began to recognize their own successes as meaningful and worthwhile, not solely through structured photocopiable activities gleaned from a textbook or a programme, but through a combination of the practical (a programme) and the personal – the intuitive, thoughtful, empathetic persistence of their TAs and the teachers who allowed space for this to happen in its own time and to achieve success. To be too rigid in applying a timeframe for a totally positive outcome (as we may judge it) can set the intervention to fail. Regular monitoring is important and is a vital component in any sound intervention, but this may also be an opportunity to continue to affirm the pupil as an individual and to gently remind them what you both are aiming for. It is the point at which the individual pupil begins to acknowledge themselves (internally) as successful that is critical and a point when we can then build on jointly to ensure future success.

> We can use what has already been successful, or as much of it as we can to create more success in a different area. Learners begin to see that they are capable and they can be successful, they can change the way they see themselves and realize they need to create an internal and external environment that is conducive to success. (Corrie, 2003: 25)

Examples of strategies used by TAs to support emotional health and well being through building self esteem are shown in Table 6.1.

HLTA
Standards
9 & 26

In his early writings Abraham Maslow (1970) identified a hierarchy of needs, and within his theory a prominent position was given to self esteem. Maslow proposed that in order to achieve our 'potential' and learn, we must have our needs met as we pass through a series of stages. Training materials developed for the implementation of the Behaviour and Attendance strand of the Key Stage 3 Strategy (DfES, 2004) and Induction programmes for TAs stress the importance of understanding Maslow's stages to underpin

Table 6.1

Strategy	Example	TA
A personal journal or scrap book Giving the pupil ownership over events and the choices they may have made. Encouraging reflection, review and moving forward. Recording events either by pictures, words, using stickers.	Amber was encouraged to use a positive record book.	Amber's TA used this to enable her to record success and reflect on her feelings with weekly sessions to discuss this. Jim's TA used a daily positive statement book and stickers.
You and I messages	Modelling positive language by using I statements and encouraging activities, e.g. circle time, that use I statements: I am worried, I feel happy.	Harry responded well to modelling using positive language. Jim's TA actively adapted her language to I messages. The HLTA gave Ali an insight into and understanding of the effect of his choice of language and responses.
Positive self talk Teach children positive self talk and ways to overcome and bounce off some of the negative messages they perceive are directed back at them.	Allow pupils to visualize scenarios in which previously they have been unsuccessful, provide them with positive statements to overcome their perceived sense of failure and offer ways of achieving real success. Talk them through a different approach to a problem. This is a systematic strategy that works.	Harry needed a 'script' for lessons he found challenging, particularly the first 10 minutes when he found it hard to settle. Amber responded to metaphor, e.g. a curtain coming down for not understanding a task, a staircase for success. Ali needed to understand his own response to others' behaviour and how he was inviting negative interactions.
Affirmations These build on the power of self talk and can be used in many ways.	I am valued in my group. I belong to this class. My skills are valued.	Amber and her TA used daily affirmations. Jim's TA used them to reinforce one-to-one sessions.
Recognition	Can be unconditional (for the person) or linked to tasks. Both must be meaningful and affirming.	TA communicates to teacher. Harry, Amber and Jim's TA all ensured this happened and used smiles, stickers, certificates, comments. The HLTA ensured that Ali's teachers all understood his need for acknowledgement (positively when he was not being challenging). This broke the negative cycle.

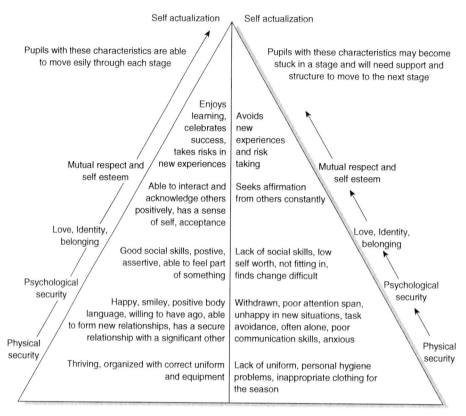

Figure 6.1 Maslow's hierarchy of needs: pupil characteristics identified by TA

the promotion of effective learning opportunities whilst maintaining and developing emotional health and well being. It is important to recognize that an empathetic and structured response to positive behaviour management within a school will promote behaviour advantageous for learning.

As you can see from Figure 6.1 a positive response to pupils who are 'stuck' within a level is crucial if their needs are to be met and an opportunity to reach self actualization (in this context, learning) is to occur. Foundation Degree students deconstructed this model and suggested the points in each stage. Subsequent students working on the same activity noted that some students would perhaps never move up through the model and it may be more relevant to consider each stage as having a continuum from negative to positive, where some progress may be made but that it would be hard perhaps to measure within an academic year.

Clearly links can be made to the inclusion, behaviour and other policies within your school at each stage of this model and it reinforces aspects of self esteem that we have already examined in the previous chapter. Aspects of Maslow's hierarchy of needs are further explored in Chapter 8 in relation to inclusion and ECM.

 Activity

> Do you recognize these stages of development ?
> Assess if you support these stages within your school setting.
> Identify what you do now and what you need to do to ensure that you actively support these stages.
> Identify the links to the school behaviour policy.
> Consider for a moment a pupil you may know well … which of these stages may apply to them? Could this increased awareness of such a model change your approach to the pupil in the future? What could you do differently?

Maslow's model could also be considered in examining the role that a TA could have in supporting systems and structures within school settings and in addressing the needs of individual pupils, by building sensitively stage by stage. Conclusions reached after discussions with TAs are summarized in Table 6.2.

EXPLORING ASPECTS OF TRANSACTIONAL ANALYSIS: SUPPORTING THE DEVELOPMENT OF EMOTIONAL LITERACY

What is Transactional Analysis?

Transactional Analysis (TA) was developed by Eric Berne in the late 1950s. Fundamentally it is:

- A theory of personality – ego state.
- A theory of communication – transactions.
- A theory of child development – life scripts.

Some of the key philosophical assumptions underpinning Transactional Analysis is that everyone is OK, and has the capacity to think, shape their own destiny and is capable of change. On one level this may not seem relevant to educational settings with such a wide range of staff. However, it offers opportunities to understand in greater detail our interactions with others around us and is empowering for those who apply it to both their personal and professional relationships. It also offers opportunities to acquire practical skills in communication and new approaches to relationships that may have a pattern of difficulty. Transactional Analysis may also be successfully taught to pupils enabling them to understand the pattern of relationships and communication that they either attract or invite.

Table 6.2

Maslow stage	TA strategy
Self actualization	Affirm as a person, recognize and acknowledge success.
Mutual respect and self esteem	Praise and encouragement, respond to individual needs, give time.
Love, identity and belonging	Express an interest in the pupil, acknowledge strengths and interests, be a good listener, acknowledge and affirm, use positive non-verbal signals, use reward system.
Pyschological	Acknowledgement of the person, positively reinforce task or behaviour, allow time for interactions between TA and pupil, check pupil's understanding of task or events that have happened, collaborate with teacher over differentiation, use behaviour policy to structure interaction.
Physical	Greet each pupil by name, smile, use school interventions to address physical needs, e.g. ensuring breakfast at breakfast club.

'... it is an approach that can make a serious impact on how schools respond to the complexities of social inclusion. Some of the ways in which Transactional Analysis helpfully contributes to school life are by:

- Promoting discussion and confidence in developing emotional literacy among staff and pupils;
- Providing a framework for managing conflict;
- Presenting an alternative model for understanding and using praise;
- Ensuring effective arrangements for working in partnerships with parents, pupils and other agencies.
- Building pupils' confidence in responding to the challenges of learning;
- Promoting the mental health of both adults and children in schools.' (Barrow *et al.*, 2001: 4)

How can Transactional Analysis be useful to me?

So many times in schools we come across theories and approaches that require a truly whole school approach, and rightly so, SEAL is one such.

It is not an approach that specifically skills and empowers the educator. Although there needs to be a systematic and sound structure linked to policy and outcomes where roles are clearly defined and the actions that each are allowed are clearly understood, there also needs to be both personal skill development and professional development in knowledge of a school system or intervention. Too often, however, a system that is philosophically sound, over time, may evolve into one that is less than respectful of the person. In my experience as a practitioner in a range of settings I have observed many situations that have arisen out of misunderstandings and missed opportunities, and that have failed to be resolved, escalating and this invariably results in pupils becoming more disconnected and disaffected from those around them and TAs feeling like they are responsible for the resulting mess. The role of the TA is unique in that your physical location and presence in the classroom allows you a different perspective both to observe and gather information and then reflect upon it and to intervene. The role of the teacher differs in that the teacher, whilst taking account of individuals, is also mindful of the ethos and climate of the whole class and must focus on this. Using strategies underpinned by Transactional Analysis enables you to choose how you respond to communication both verbal and non-verbal, whether initiated by pupil or another staff member. It is empowering for you as a TA and is a true tool to you based on the theme of this book! It is an integrated approach and enables you to be both congruent in your communication and truly authentic in the personal philosophy and beliefs that you may hold as a TA.

> The hope and optimism of this approach is manifested in its accessibility. Berne said 'If something can't be understood by an intelligent eight year old it isn't worth saying' (Steiner 2001). He opposed professional elitism and the use of complex language. (Barrow *et al.*, 2001: 7)

This section is only an introduction and to become fully conversant I recommend the text Barrow, G. and Newton, T. (2004) as cited in the reference list. Whilst understanding aspects of Transactional Analysis will empower you and improve relationships and communication it is easily taught to pupils. As a practitioner I have had some great success in sharing and teaching Transactional Analysis to both teachers, TAs and pupils. As with any intervention, care must be taken that those teaching it have a sound understanding of the theory that underpins it, this will prevent any potential for confusion or misuse.

At times we all work in environments that may conflict with our beliefs and philosophy in how to relate to pupils and those we work with. Colleagues interpret discipline and sanctions systems in different ways, evidenced by the fact that, while delivery of instructions and choices of words may be consistent, what is conveyed by body language and tone is much more powerful. This may introduce tensions into your professional relationships and whilst you may have successfully 'tuned in', as I suggested earlier, you may need a practical approach that will enable you to manage your emotions and still communicate clearly and effectively. Transactional Analysis will enable you to be calmer, choose your responses and, even if you initially react and choose a more negative interaction, it enables you to pause, reflect and be able to move your position and recover the interaction and maintain the relationship as one of mutual respect. It is about recognizing you have a choice about how you respond and acknowledging the power you do hold as an adult and not manipulating it.

Transactional Analysis enables us to step out of an interaction, observe what has happened and reflect on how it could progress. It is at this point that, with the right choice, change can be effected and a more positive outcome arrived at. It is an approach that can fundamentally enhance self esteem and the development of the self as it provides a structure for choice of language and actions that are positive. At its most simplistic level and one that is critical in any writing connected with understanding and maintaining emotional health and well being, it enables us to acknowledge and separate negative behaviour, words or actions from the person and always offers the opportunity for a more positive solution thus affirming the individuals involved.

> What we do as a society in bringing children and adults together in schools is to give ourselves the opportunity to change the world for tomorrow. It is a massive investment of hope, one that we believe can sometimes be lost sight of in the busy life of the classroom or may be buried in internecine political struggles. (Barrow *et al.*, 2001: 120)

What supports this?

HLTA
Standard
16

With the introduction of Every Child Matters (2004) and subsequent developments such as Social and Emotional Aspects of Learning Primary Materials (2007), it could be said that there is a more structured and consistent framework for schools to work within. This framework was introduced after materials had been trialled and used in secondary schools. It was intended for use in schools who identified that a key element of advancing learning and achievement for individuals and groups was to address and begin to instigate a shared understanding of what other factors could be a barrier to learning as a key focus for their work with children. These include children's difficulties in understanding and managing their feelings, working cooperatively in groups, motivating themselves and demonstrating resilience in the face of setbacks. The focus is on five identified aspects of social and emotional learning: self awareness, managing feelings, motivation, empathy and social skills (DfES 2007). An evaluation of the early stages of this initiative identified that SEAL was most effective where it fitted in with existing PHSE work or circle time and where it complemented the school ethos. This may be your experience. It was also noted that staff were able to be more 'thoughtful' in their approaches and overall staff understanding of social and emotional aspects of learning increased. Ninety per cent of teachers who responded felt that SEAL had been successful, although the results are less clear at the latter stages of Key Stage 2 where there was some negativity, perhaps related to age and gender, which in turn has led to a greater understanding of the needs of pupils. Whilst the involvement of TAs, specifically in small group work, enabled teachers and support workers to become more involved, TAs noted that they would like more formal training on the use of the materials (DfES 2007). If this is your experience of any such initiative then highlighting your concerns and identifying your training needs to your line manager may be appropriate. Whilst you may be a skilled and intuitive practitioner, as I acknowledged earlier, however, it can be emotionally draining and de-skilling for you if you feel that you do not have the correct guidance and support to implement a specialized intervention no matter how good your interpersonal and relationship skills are. If you have knowledge, skills and a specialist role in supporting aspects of behaviour management it may be that you are able to adapt materials and use them accordingly.

Certainly, specific roles have developed in recent years to support aspects of both behaviour and social and emotional facets of learning. Many of you may have additional roles such as Specialist Leader of Behaviour and Attendance, Learning Mentor, Emotional Literacy Support Assistant, Pastoral Support Assistant, Behaviour Support. Further attention to this was given when the government introduced the Children's Plan (2008). This has a number of underpinning principles and set a number of objectives to be achieved by 2020 (to be reviewed 2009).

> We want all young people to enjoy happy, healthy and safe teenage years and to be prepared for adult life. Too often we focus on the problems of a few young people rather than the successes of the many. We want a society where young people feel valued and in which their achievements are recognised and celebrated. (Children's Plan, 2008: 16)

The aim is to ensure that children are 'happy and healthy' with increased funding to Children's Services that has enabled the creation of additional roles such as Parent Support Advisors (PSA), improved outreach from Sure Start Children's Centres and initiated reviews of both Child Health and Mental Health Services. One goal set to be achieved by 2020 is to 'enhance children and young people's wellbeing, particularly at key transition points in their lives' (DCFS, 2008).

What are Children's Trusts?

Chidren's Trusts (2008) are a key development that originate from the Children's Act (2004) and further developed out of the Every Child Matters agenda for a truly multi-agency approach.

> Children's Trusts or equivalent arrangements, are intended to bring together education, health and social services and to promote co-operation with the aim of improving children's well-being. (DfES, 2007: 8)

If you have only recently become employed as a TA your induction will have been to Children's Services rather than solely in education as in the case of your colleagues who have been in post for some years. Children's Trusts place children and young people at the heart giving them a structure for a 'voice' that can be heard and action taken. In planning any intervention, children, young people and their families are now active participants in the process. Children's Trusts have been designed to ensure that at every stage, when dealing with the needs of vulnerable and young people, it is clear who is responsible for what intervention and that the intervention is initiated as quickly as possible transcending any boundaries. This is to ensure that no vulnerable child or young person is left unidentified and unsupported as happened with Victoria Climbié whose experience and story was the inspiration behind ECM. Each Local Authority has created its own Children's Trust and a key strength is that priorities can be determined locally so the needs of children and young people can be clearly met within the provision of local services, e.g. health, education and social services. Children's Trusts have sought to bring together all the agencies that are involved in providing education, health and guidance in the different forms that are available for children and young people under one service. This development is in its early stages but the relationship between schools and the local Children's Trust is fundamental and it may be that it is your role to from a link between elements of the Children's Trust. An evaluation of those involved in the pilot trialling the framework and intervention (Pathfinders) by the University of East Anglia jointly for DfES and the department of Health found that whilst it was early to say,

> there are encouraging signs of reported local improvements based on the work of Children's trust pathfinders, as 25 sites reported specific examples of Children's Trust pathfinder arrangements improving outcomes for children and young people in their area. Several pathfinders reported that they had improved the efficacy of services and some were already working towards re-investing efficiency savings into preventative work. (DfES, 2007: 5)

What are the key features of a Children's Trust?

The first test of a Children Trust is to identify the information that may need to be gathered and by whom and to then be the central point to ensure that it may be shared quickly and efficiently, avoiding replication or a slow and protracted exchange of data with little purpose to it. Strategies and interventions can be identified and prioritized, and staff then allocated to roles with specific responsibilities.

What are the responsibilities of schools?

Schools are just beginning to forge links with their local trusts and these are continuing to develop and strengthen as the pilot projects are evaluated and the outcomes disseminated. Schools are increasingly identifying roles for support staff that place much of the responsibility with them to perform part of the Lead Professional role. Many of you will already be working with the Common Assessment Framework and your awareness of the individual needs of pupils and choice of strategies will be enhanced by this.

⩗ Reflective question

Let us return to the quote at the begin the chapter, reflect on it for a moment. What kind of weather do you bring to the classroom (mostly)? Is there room for some climate change?

Further Reading

Barrow, G., Bradshaw, E. and Newton, T. (2001) *Improving Behaviour and Raising Self-Esteem in the Classroom. A Practical Guide to Using Transactional Analysis in the Classroom.* London: Fulton.

Crow, F. (2008) 'Learning for Well Being: Personal, Social and Health Education and a Changing Curriculum', *Pastoral Care in Education* 26(1): 43–51.

Stewart, I. and Joines, V. (2000) *TA today A New Introduction to Transactional Analysis.* Nottingham: Lifespace.

White, V. and Harris Davies, J. (2005) 'Developing Good Practice in Children's Services', *British Journal of Social Work* 35: 410–12.

References

Barrow, G. and Newton, T. (2004) *Walking the Talk: How Transactional Analysis is Improving Behaviour and Raising Self-Esteem.* London: Fulton.

Corrie, C. (2003) *Becoming Emotionally Intelligent.* Stafford: Network Press.

Day, C., Sammons, P., Stobart, G., Kington, A. and Gu, Q. (2007) *Teachers Matter: Connecting Lives, Work and Effectiveness.* Maidenhead: Open University.

DcSF (2008) Children's Plan.

DfES (1999) *In School Centres for pupils at Risk for Exclusion from School* (RR163).

DfES (2004) Key Stage 3.

Ginott, H. (1972) *Teacher and Child.* New York: Macmillan.

Hallam, S. and Castle, F. (1999) Evaluation of the Behaviour and Discipline Pilot Projects (1996–1999). Supported under the Standards Fund Programme Research Report RR163. London: Department for Education and Employment.

Hallam, S. and Castle, F. (2007) *Children's Trust Pathfinders: Innovative Partnerships for Improving the Well-being of Children and Young People. Findings from the National Evaluation of Children's Trust Pathfinders* (RR717). London: DfES.

Maslow, A.H. (1970) *Motivation and Personality* (2nd edn). New York: Harper and Row.

Sharp, P. (2001) *Nurturing Emotional Literacy.* London: Fulton.

POSITIVE APPROACHES TO BEHAVIOUR MANAGEMENT

Chris Lee

This chapter will:

- Introduce ideas on the highly important and always relevant subject of behaviour management, both in the classroom and in the wider school.
- Consider the importance and power of classroom teams and how members of team can provide mutual support.
- Provide an examination of three fundamental approaches to behaviour management. They are:

  1. **The system with its policy and rules** which illustrates how TAs can effectively use the reward or sanction system.
  2. **Negotiating and contracting** which describes the role that TAs can play in providing pupils with the opportunity to make choices and understand the decisions they make and the consequences of those decisions.
  3. **Relationship and listening** which reflects on the more therapeutic notion of managing classroom difficulties and how TAs can exercise their skills in this area.

HLTA Standards 2, 3 & 26

This chapter is an acknowledgement that Teaching Assistants now find themselves in roles and positions where behaviour management is as much an issue for them as it is for teachers and other adults who work in schools. So much of the writing on behaviour management is designed to help adults to deal with problems after they have happened and they follow a model that suggests 'if this happens then try this'. Although this chapter does include advice on what to do when there are problems, it also places emphasis on the importance of preventing problems. In other words the 'toolkit' comprises what you take out of the box and what you possess yourself or, more significantly, yourselves, for it is all adults functioning as a team that provide a crucial component of any preventative approach.

With new found status through HLTA and with growing recognition that TAs play a key role in determining the classroom climate, behaviour management is a crucial concern.

A simple philosophy underpins all that follows and can be summarized through one question – **what does the Teaching Assistant really have control over in classroom?** The answer can sometimes feel like 'very little' if we are looking at the behaviour of some individual or groups of pupils, but a 'great deal' if the emphasis is placed upon their skills and their approaches to dealing with difficulties. This chapter is then about styles of positive skilful behaviour management and the key stances and techniques that can be adopted. In keeping with one of the key prevailing themes, the 'toolkit', it is not designed to be a prescription but aims to offer a variety of models and approaches that have been found by TAs to be helpful.

MORE THAN SUPPORT

Descriptions of the roles of TAs usually start each line with the word 'support', for example, 'support the plans of the teacher', 'support the assessment policy'. Therefore the role of the teacher was, until recent times, clear in that they were in charge of the learning in the classroom and the behaviour management that secured the climate in which that learning took place. Teaching Assistants were there to support the practices of the teacher and enforce the policies of the school. However, the moden classroom is experiencing turbulence directed by numerous central government initiatives such as Workforce Reform, Extended Schools and Every Child Matters. The concept of the school day, the relationship between educationists and other caring professions and even what it is to be a teacher are all being questioned and maybe redefined. This reform agenda has also changed the landscape for TAs in that they have found new pedagogic responsibilities through the HLTA and with that comes increased expectations of the HLTA as a classroom manager.

HLTA Standard 16

It seems strange, and could be seen as an omission, that there is no mention of **dealing** with difficult or challenging behaviours in the Standards for HLTA, although there is reference to using effective strategies to promote positive behaviour which emphasizes the contemporary notion of promoting positive behaviour. The strategies that would support this might include extensive praise, rewarding good behaviour, work or the avoidance of the temptation to be involved in problematic situations. It would also include being a positive role model and demonstrating tolerance, patience, kindness, consideration and many other virtues. However, the emphasis on 'advancing learning' in Standards 28–31 clearly has implications for being able to manage all aspects of the learning environment including behaviour problems should they arise. In addition the emphasis on keeping learners safe in Standard 32 would include being able to prevent and deal with classroom-based bullying and taunting.

HLTA Standards 28, 29, 30, 31 & 32

TEACHING ASSISTANTS' VIEWS

One useful reflective way to think about good practice is from Teaching Assistants' own experience. When asked what kind of teacher or other adult they have come across, including in their own education, who inspired or did not inspire learning, the answers given have been used to develop the following Activity.

 Activity

Go to the **Rank order sheet** in Appendix 1 on p. 203 and rank order (1–9) the statements shown in relation to your own ideas and viewpoints.

HLTA Standard 3

Observations of each other in a professional context or even our own experience as learners are often the starting point to an approach to behaviour management – 'what worked with us will work for us'. One observation that is consistently made by TAs is the importance of being a good role model and that their pupils are more likely to imitate good behaviour than respond to being told about it.

THE IMPORTANCE OF THE CLASSROOM TEAM

HLTA Standard 6

Whatever the area of work in the classroom, the necessity of teamwork cannot be overstated. The significance of this has been developed by Mary Pittman in Chapter 4. However skilful the TA is, a teacher who lacks the ability to manage the class and who, for example, often turns minor disruption into major conflict, will undermine those skills. The reverse also applies in that TAs who are not operating in line with successful classroom management practice possess the capacity to have a negative impact on the classroom climate and cause disruption rather than resolve it. Talking about his research with two TAs and a class teacher Rix states 'each of them gives way to the other at different times out of respect for their role and because of their different abilities to work with pupils … Rather than clearly designated boundaries between three individuals, theirs is a team endeavour' (Rix, 2005: 198).

However, in discussion with TAs, they reveal that they are not or do not feel that they are always part of a team. One of the many dilemmas they face is that their approaches to behaviour management are often determined elsewhere. It may be the school behaviour policy which sets the climate for reaction to both positive and negative behaviours or it could be the class teacher who may have a specific regime that informs how difficult behaviour is managed. Some schools adopt certain clearly identified behaviour approaches, such as Solution Focused (Rhodes and Ajmal, 1995) or Assertive Discipline (Canter and Canter, 2001). Like any adult working with young people in schools, TAs bring their own values, ideas and skills to any situation and where these match those of other adults the result is consensus and teamwork. Where they do not one of the most likely outcomes is a frustrated and disenchanted TA.

CAUSES OF PROBLEMS

Much has been written about why children misbehave in schools and there is consensus that key factors can be isolated. Included are their:

(a) Emotional well being at the time and how they dealing with what is happening outside the class-room maybe at home or in social or non-classroom based environments such as playgrounds or, journeying to and from school (e.g. bullying).
(b) Family circumstances which could include concern over parents and siblings, parental break-ups, life style at home, for example are they indulged with material goods as a substitute for attention and affection?
(c) Notions of self. As Maureen Parker has suggested in Chapter 5 self image – how they see them-selves – and self esteem – how they perceive the gap between their perceptions of self and their desired self – may influence their behaviour and their achievement.
(d) Stage of development, for example adolescence or educational stage (e.g. transition).
(e) Culture which is not always about, but does include, race and class culture.
(f) Immediate environment such as the classroom, the prevailing weather and the number of pupils in the class.
(g) Physical and mental health and the relationship between the two of them.
(h) Gender, including the need sometimes for boys to demonstrate their 'macho-ness' and girls to feel secure in close relationship with a small group of peers.

This list raises three fundamental questions for understanding pupil behaviour and the TAs capacity to manage it. First, the individual causes are not as separate as they are stated above and such a list renders a complex matter too simple. Second, many pupils experi-ence what some might define as negative experience linked to the factors listed above, and perhaps other negative experiences, but do not misbehave and, alternatively, other pupils appear to have high self esteem, have seemingly excellent relationships with caring par-ents and are not going through a predictably difficult stage in their development, yet still their behaviour is highly disruptive. This can lead to perplexity as we attempt to work out what is causing the problem. Finally, will the level of knowledge about the causes in relation to an individual pupil make any difference in preventing or dealing with any difficulties? The answer is 'maybe' – many of the eight items mentioned above will determine our rela-tionships and reactions to pupils but others will have no impact at all. Fundamentally, skilled practitioners look more at their own values, ideas and skills than the issues that influence the pupils. In the end it amounts to the answer to a single question – what do I have more con-trol over, the child's gender, parenting experiences or culture, or the ability to create a learn-ing environment and deal with any threats to that environment in the form of pupil behaviour? What follows explores are three broad approaches that inform that ability.

HLTA Standards 26 & 27

THE THREE APPROACHES

As an adult working in a school and classroom you bring a variety of skills to the role but you bring much more than that, you bring your ideas, principles and values. It is these that help to begin to inform ideas and skills on behaviour matters. In order to help to begin an exploration of them and how they relate to approaches to behaviour management it is important to engage in reflection on what ideas you possess and how these relate to your principles and values.

 Activity

Reflect upon and describe what skills, understanding and approaches you possess in preventing and dealing with disruption.
  Which works well and why do you think they work?

One method of categorizing intervention approaches considers a specific approach in relationship to the notion of the power of the teacher and Wolfgang (2005) used the teacher's power continuum to construct three main groups. No such equivalent continuum exists for TAs and, given that the TA's role is not one that is as based on the same status in the classroom as the teacher, their differentiated role needs to be taken into account. The continuum is based upon power and independence, with pupils possessing higher levels and determining agendas at one end and at the other end adults and the systems which they create being the prime influence. It is **not** the intention here to advocate a specific place on the continuum for TAs but simply to reflect on their meaning for TAs and what skills TAs bring to the stages along the continuum. This model does not incorporate the most extreme behaviours that result in all adults in school having no choice but to respond radically, for example exclusion for assault. The ability to draw upon various style and approaches, providing they are not incompatible, is a positive feature of behaviour management for all adults (Lee, 2007; Porter, 2000).

The three groups that Wolfgang (2005) isolates are:

1. Rules and consequences

If you undertook the Activity on p. 108 and found that the letter 'S' appeared quite high in your rank order then you might find yourself looking to the authority of the system to support you and your colleagues in the management of individuals, groups and classes. You place emphasis on school policies, rules and structure to secure a framework which supports adults in setting up a climate which aims to ensure compliance and order. The reward system is crucial as is a consistently applied sanction regime.

2. Confronting and contracting

If 'C' tended to occur high in your ranking then you are more likely to value practices which allow pupils to be given the opportunity to make choices and understand the

Table 7.1 Principal theories and power

Process	Power	Authors	Examples
Rules and consequences	Higher adult – lower pupil	Canter	*Assertive Discipline*
		Dobson	*Dare to Discipline*
Confronting and contracting	Power balanced	Dreikurs	*Discipline without Tears*
		Glasser	*Schools without Failure*
Relationship and listening	Lower adult – higher pupil	Gordon	*Teacher Effectiveness Training*
		Harris	*I'm OK– You're OK*

Source: adapted from Wolfgang, 2005

decisions they make and the consequences of those decisions. You see your role as pointing out consequences of actions and to nurture the making of wise choices, and wherever possible to negotiate ways forward. For you there may be several ways forward and varieties of approaches to dealing with difficulties but what is key is that the pupil takes some or all responsibility.

The groups in Table 7.1 are not just categories of behaviour management approaches, they offer a continuum along which power and choice rest more with the adult, **Rules and Consequences**, to pupils determining more and making increased choices, **Relationship and Listening**. One of the key factors that will have an impact on which kind of approach might be predominant will be the values and beliefs of the adult. When consigning the principal theories to a place on a continuum, key factors such as who (pupil or staff) sets the limits, who dictates the agenda, what type of discipline exists or is imposed are considered.

The three groups help classroom practitioners to understand the scope of the approaches and the centrality of adult–pupil relationships. However, this analysis also raises interesting questions for TAs as they do not have the status that accompanies the role of the teacher, although the rise in status of the HLTA and the growing importance of TAs to schools may mean that this is not an accurate proposition. Teaching assistants often have a tendency to build their behaviour management approaches on their ability to relate closely to pupils and their function is not always seen as related to learning but to more pastoral roles. Their role may compel the TAs to function at either extreme of the three groups. For example, a TA whose principal role is to work alongside a pupil for whom communication is difficult and who does not understand the behaviour of others will adopt a natural empathetic and therapeutic stance. On the other hand the TA with a more substantive teaching role in a secondary school may be more reliant on using rules, rewards and sanctions as a basis for their behavioural approach as they provide a scaffold based on decisions and power residing elsewhere. The school behaviour policy will be pivotal here. Even more significant is that any adult in a classroom or school who finds themselves operating in a way that runs counter to their beliefs or values may find that situation very stressful. Recently when working with a mixed group of teachers and TAs in a large secondary school, one particular teacher, a member of a senior management team, talked openly about being compelled to operate within systems, enforce rules and deal with the breaking of them so much that she declared her frustration and her desire to operate 'in a more humane way'. However, not all TAs or teachers align themselves with one approach, some are comfortable with two and some even three.

Even though the role of the HLTA has yet to become fully embedded in the modern school, and there are many ways in which the role of the HLTA is being interpreted (Wilson *et al.*, 2007), the notion of the TA as purely supportive and passive in a planning role looks dated. If TAs are taking on increased direct teaching roles then the demand for effective practice in behaviour management is even greater. This being the case there is a further argument for TAs having knowledge of all forms of behaviour management and their potential for success and they are uniquely placed to draw upon all approaches. Of course some forms will run counter to those which they see as effect and even against their values and application of what feels like an alien approach may produce tension and stress.

HLTA
Standard
7

1. Rules and consequences: pros and cons

As with the other two areas, in this section it is impossible to examine all the attributes of this approach. However, included here are ideas that invite reflection and consideration of work practices. The focus here is upon the 'system', the school policy, the positive side of the system (rules, rewards) and the negative side (punishment).

Schools create behaviour policies that have rules as an integral component and these are linked to the adopted rewards and sanctions. In addition to school rules there are likely to be classroom rules developed by teaching teams or groups of pupils which add a flavour that may be unique to that classroom or subject. These rules say much about the ethos of the school and help pupils and parents understand the aims of the school. Given the increasing number of TAs and other support staff in schools the success of any system of rules would appear to be dependent on their reinforcement through **all** staff and the involvement of **all** staff in their formulation.

Rules help to ensure that punishments or sanctions are not arbitrary but linked to specific agreed ways of working and generating a safe and orderly environment. The Key Stage 3 Strategy (DfES, 2004) suggests that rules should be:

1. developed with pupils
2. clear, positive and enforceable
3. expressed in inclusive language
4. few in number, clearly displayed
5. evaluated, reviewed and changed as necessary.

In the case of younger pupils the language used in the rule is vital and the importance of the verb both in the written rule and in its enforcement cannot be overstated. Young children are helped in their understanding by the reasoning behind the rule so, for example, 'using a quiet voice – helps us to concentrate' Wheeler, (1996) explains the rule and provides a basis for offering rewards for complying with it.

Rewarding pupils for good behaviour is the counter to the more punitive side of behaviour management. Reward systems are more likely to succeed if they are open and endorsed by the whole staff, and while it can be argued that they are little more than bribery they serve to provide pupils with choices, create a climate of celebration and are an expectation of society. Discussing formal rewards used in schools with TAs, their concerns were often that the brightest pupils and those who often behaved badly, but were caught being good, were the most likely to be rewarded not the compliant, quiet, unobtrusive pupil. The other major danger is that pupils conform because of the extrinsic motivation of the reward not because they want to behave or see the purpose in it.

The close relationships between TAs and pupils are often valued by both parties and whilst social rewards (celebrations through assemblies), object rewards (badges and tokens) and privilege rewards (extra computer time) are important, it is often the natural relationship rewards, through acknowledgement or smiles that can matter most. As one special school states in its policy, 'the most effective and enduring rewards that we are able to provide are our attention, affirmation and approval'.

Looking at the negative side, a variety of ways of responding to a behaviour problem is available to the TA. There is the use of *punishments* or alternatively *sanctions* linked to specific behaviours or perhaps pupils making amends for their actions and looking at the *consequences* of their actions. The choice made will have a lot to do with the values of the TAs and their own feelings about what has happened. They do not have the association that historically teachers have had with the punitive side of correcting bad behaviour, but they do possess more of a tradition of working with individual pupils and looking to advise and help them to generate their own solutions. They have little *control over* the classroom but have a potential *influence on* it. It is natural that authority figures, such as teachers, react to defiance and feel threatened by it but for those who have less authority through their role a variety of approaches is useful. Whatever the choice of approach it needs to reflect the approach of the behaviour policy of the school which in turn needs to acknowledge the different role and status that the TA possesses.

While the three terms 'punishment', 'sanctions' and 'consequences' are often used interchangeably, there are distinguishing features that have implications for Teaching Assistants. The first term considered is **punishment**. Working with TAs it has become evident that the forms of negative behaviour that they find most irritating are often the minor ones. 'Rudeness', 'talking out of turn' ('tooting') and 'bad language' feature high in their lists. In common with others within and outside schools they feel that pupils' behaviour has become worse in recent times. They are also aware of the importance of such techniques as labelling the pupils' behaviour but not the pupils themselves. There is a view amongst many that because punishment demands that the pupil is treated in such a way that it is *deliberately unpleasant* they are not always comfortable about it. Wilson (2002) argues that for punishment to be effective pupils should acknowledge that what they have done is wrong, why it was wrong and the impact that they have had on others, plus there should be a feeling of shame or guilt and the punishment should be unpleasant enough to counter the temptation to repeat the act.

The problems with punishment includes that it does not require change in behaviour, can generate resentment, anger or a desire for revenge, and it makes no requirements of pupils to change their behaviour but just to be passive recipients. Significantly for TAs, it can generate emotional distance from those who often need emotional closeness and trusted adult relationship the most. On the other hand **sanctions** are linked with *specific misbehaviours* and the outcomes of non-observance of a rule. They form part of a more formal management policy which means they are predictable and consistent. Power and authority come from the policy and system it supports and, therefore, TAs, as part of the structures and system, can use its authority. Pupils know the outcome of misbehaviour and can see a logic to what happens to them, especially if it supported by reminder of the rule that has been broken. Effective sanctions are judged by whether they match the misdemeanour and if they are designed to bring changes in behaviour. In addition, a sanction policy needs to have an aversive effect for the pupils concerned and the other pupils. They potentially possess many of the negative features of punishment and as Lee (2007) points out:

> Sanctions, when applied harshly have a contradictory nature to approaches to towards learning in that when pupils make errors in their work educators seek to show them where they might have gone wrong, explain matters again maybe using different methods or materials i.e. they seek to help pupils understand what was wrong and how to respond effectively. Behaviour correction based on sanctions lacks these positive elements. (Lee, 2007: 63)

Many schools adopt a scale in which the first offence is approached much like a 'yellow card' in football, as a warning, with a second offence meriting 'red' and the full sanction applying. This means that the 'yellow' one may function as nothing but a warning and is not taken too seriously.

The third choice is **consequences** that are linked directly to the misbehaviour and demand the pupil recognizes that link. They follow *naturally or logically from the behaviour* and, like sanctions, form part of a more formal management policy which means they are predictable and consistent. They offer the opportunity for power and authority to come from the pupil's engagement with their own behaviour and the formal system. They are employed in a reasonable and respectful manner, related to the behaviour not the pupil and underpinned by a desire to teach pupils about their behaviour. The language which results is more reasonable and calm and locates the onus with the pupil. Witness the difference between *Jackie, by throwing the sweet wrapper on the floor you have chosen to tidy the room later* and *Jackie, why are you throwing litter on floor. Pick it up* *now and see me at the end of the lesson.* Ultimately, whatever the approach, punishment, sanctions or consequences, it boils down to a pupil being given a negative experience which results from their own behaviour. Teaching Assistants need to be able to distinguish between the various approaches, relate them to school policy and feel comfortable about their use and their impact on the relationship with the pupil.

2. Confronting and contracting

Any kind of negotiated or contracted view is based upon both parties, adult and pupil, having an influence on the situation. The idea is to secure the needs of the whole group including the teacher and TA and yet also meet the needs of the individual student. One important approach is being assertive. In discussion with a TA, Jenny, she talked about being too aggressive in a situation where a pupil had been disruptive but she did so by referring to her approach as too 'assertive' suggesting a misunderstanding of the term. The alternatives to assertive responses are ones which are aggressive, indirectly aggressive or passive aggressive. Being assertive is then a non-aggressive stance and fits well with the idea of confronting problems and contracting solutions.

An assertive response requires:

- being open and honest in relationships
- recognizing personal needs
- asking that needs should be met
- recognizing the rights and needs of others
- looking for 'win/win' solutions
- taking responsibility for one's own actions
- possessing the capacity to bring resolution to conflict in a way deemed as fair by all parties.

Assertiveness is often a recommended way of behaving for TAs (Vincett *et al.*, 2005) indicating that there is not only a need to be assertive around disruptive behaviour but also that assertiveness results in communication forms that are clear, non-aggressive and consistent. It is indicative of the need for TAs to ensure their professional voice is heard in the classroom or school in what can sometimes feel like a teacher/pupil only environment.

One of the more significant sets of ideas in this area is that behaviour always has a purpose and that a pupil who is misbehaving has goals that they wish to achieve, albeit, as Dreikurs says (Dreikurs *et al.*, 1998), 'mistaken' ones. The argument is that from an early age children seek to find ways of behaving to gain recognition, a feeling of importance and a sense of belonging. This they will do in a way that is positive and constructive or negative and destructive, i.e. 'mistaken goals', and they are:

1. attention seeking
2. demonstrating power
3. seeking revenge
4. inadequacy.

In negotiating or contracting with groups or individuals it is helpful to know about these goals and understand what the pupils is aiming to achieve. One of the ways that TAs can engage with these goals is by analysing their own feelings and reactions to the pupil's behaviour, as impulsive reactions often sustain undesirable behaviour and validate the mistaken goal. This is further explored in Chapter 6 in the context of the role of the TA in supporting emotional health and well being.

> ### Case study: Jackie
>
> Jackie enters the classroom in a way that has become predictable. She generates a loud noise even in the simple act of sitting down and others around her notice her and are distracted by her. Once 'settled' into the lesson, although settled is not perhaps the best description, Jackie starts to seek the attention of the teacher or the teaching assistant – it does not matter which one. First she asks questions, none of them very relevant, then she starts to tap the desk with her new pen, before announcing loudly that she is 'fed up'. She leaves her seat and walks across the room claiming that she needs a piece of equipment that is not really needed for the task she is undertaking. Having exhausted the attention of the staff in the classroom she sets about irritating others and distracting them from their work. Eventually you have to intervene and your response is becoming increasingly impatient and you end up feeling exhausted. Not every lesson sees Jackie in this more disruptive mode as occasionally she appears to be calmer but those lessons are when she is working closely with you or the teacher.
>
> Jackie is obviously seeking attention and achieving her goal in a positive or negative way. In discussion with staff working with pupils who behave in a similar way to Jackie the following ways of working emerged:
>
> 1. Talk to her individually when no other pupils are around.
> 2. Discuss the exact nature of the problem.
> 3. Choose one area to work on at a time, for example, calling out or talking out of turn.
> 4. Give her an explanation about her behaviour, for example, 'When you talk during individual work time you don't finish your work and you stop other pupils from getting on with their work.'
> 5. State the exact expected behaviour from her during a specific activity.
> 6. Check that she has understood the instructions.
> 7. Get her to repeat the behaviour you are expecting.
> 8. Remind her of appropriate behaviour before each activity.
> 9. Reinforce her as soon as she behaves appropriately.

Not all the ideas above will work all the time and this is by no means a comprehensive list but the suggestions offer a clear way forward – Jackie receives attention but not necessarily on her terms. That attention is negotiated with her and forms part of a relationship that ensures all needs are met to some degree.

Experience in schools indicates that 'attention' is the most common goal noted by adults, with 'power' and 'revenge' also recognized, but the fourth goal 'inadequacy', which leads to the child withdrawing, does not always register as a behaviour problem because it does not openly challenge authority. It is, nonetheless, a serious concern and one which sometimes the TA is uniquely placed to observe and engage with.

3. Relationship and listening

As the role of the teacher moves more towards being a manager of learning then there is a danger that their capacity to listen and meet the emotional and pastoral needs of pupils becomes threatened. Teaching Assistants have never possessed such problems, as historically their roles have developed from the role of carer, often of an individual pupil or a small group of pupils. Their role has often meant a close proximity to the personal/social needs of individual pupils and leaves them well positioned to provide support that is driven more by pupil needs and requires high levels of listening skills and empathy.

When working with a group of TAs several years ago it emerged that they were very good listeners, equipped with patience, a relaxed approach and a capacity to engage with the people that they were trying to help. When their skills were itemized they included tone of voice and speech rate, eye contact, facial animation and smiling, appropriate gestures of head and hands and physical proximity. All these are among the helping behaviours that underpin counselling and were described by some TAs as part of their role. As described earlier, teachers can feel frustrated by their lack of opportunity to work with these skills, especially in dealing with children whose behaviour is challenging or difficult. Teaching Assistants are often in a more flexible role and can deploy these skills in supporting pupils in arriving at solutions to their own problems.

One increasingly popular approach to offering pupils the opportunity to deal with their own problems and behaviours, but with support, is Solution Focused Thinking. Unlike others ways of working in the chapter it does require additional training. Nonetheless it has significant potential for those who feel that it is pupils themselves that needs to seek to change their behaviour and it provides a contrast to more punitive, system based solutions. Solution Focused Thinking helps pupils to seek solutions and invites them to 'reframe' their experiences and come up with their own solutions. It places less emphasis on examining past failings and looks to find past successes, i.e. when was their behaviour not a problem? Less time is spent explaining problems, and pinpointing failings and more time is spent on explaining progress, and identifying strengths. The approach is based upon eight stages:

1. **Other people's perspectives**: How others would recognize change in their behaviour.
2. **Exception finding**: When things were better or handled well.
3. **Scaling**: Quantify the problem through asking where their behaviour is now on a scale such as 1–10.
4. **Locating resources**: Working out what skills and strengths they possess that might make things better.
5. **Coping**: Discussing how they are coping and dealing with matters.

6. **Stop things getting worse**: Maybe look to others to provide an initial support.
7. **Constructive feedback**: Highlighting what they are doing well with evidence of improvement in behaviour or attitude.
8. **Ending**: Re-stating goals from the beginning of the session, concluding on time with arrangements for further meetings.

The above stages aim to help pupils take charge of their situation and learn to deal with classroom situations by seeing them differently and reacting in ways that are appropriate not disruptive. This process is not sudden and reactive but is thoughtful and staged and, therefore, time consuming. Teaching Assistants in the context of the classroom team, looking to work with children in ways which give the pupil a leading role in resolving their own problems, are placed to take on the adult role.

CONCLUSION

HLTA
Standards
2 & 7

Contemporary education thinking places increasing emphasis on how classrooms are managed and how positive behaviour is promoted rather than how pupils are disciplined. Given the expanding role of the TA it follows that how they function and interact with the whole classes, groups and individuals will also influence the classroom 'ecology' in which little happens without consequence. Teaching Assistants are now required to possess a range of knowledge, skills and understanding on all forms of behaviour matters. This chapter is designed as an introduction to a breadth of ideas and approaches on which to reflect and some techniques that could prove useful. It was never intended to cover all aspects of the subject but simply to demonstrate that TAs may possess opportunities to influence schools and classrooms in different ways to teachers and this is a force for good that can be embraced.

 Reflective questions

- How important are your values and beliefs in determining how you react to disruptive behaviour?
- What advantages and disadvantages do TAs specifically possess in dealing with difficult and disruptive behaviour?
- Is pupil behaviour getting worse and, if so, how should schools react?

Further Reading

Algozzine, B. and White, R. (2002) 'Preventing Problem Behaviours Using Schoolwide Discipline', in B. Algozzine and P. Kay, *Preventing Problem Behaviours: a Handbook of Successful Prevention Strategies*. Thousand Oaks, CA: Corwin Press.

Behaviour4Learning (2005) *Behaviour and Attendance Materials for Primary Initial Teacher Training Tutors.* Nottingham: (IPRN) for Behaviour.

Behaviour4Learning (2006) *Behaviour and Attendance Materials for Secondary Initial Teacher Training Tutors.* Nottingham: (IPRN) for Behaviour.

Chaplain, R. (2003) *Teaching Without Disruption: A Model for Managing Pupil Behaviour.* London: RoutledgeFalmer.

Department for Education and Science (1989) *Discipline in Schools – Report of the Committee of Enquiry: The Elton Report.* London: HMSO.

Hill, F. and Parsons, L. (2000) *Teamwork in the Management of Emotional and Behavioural Difficulties.* London: David Fulton.

McLean, A. (2003) The *Motivated School.* London: Paul Chapman Publishing.

Rogers, B. (1990) *You Know the Fair Rule: Strategies for Making the Hard Job of Discipline in School Easier.* Harlow: Longman.

Rogers, B. (2004) 'The Language of Behaviour Management', in J. Wearmouth, R. Richmond and T. Glynn, *Addressing Pupils' Behaviour: Responses at District, School and Individual Levels.* London: David Fulton.

Visser, J. (2000) *Managing Behaviour in Classrooms.* London: David Fulton.

References

Canter, L. and Canter, M. (2001) *Assertive Discipline* (3rd edn). Los Angeles: Canter and Associates.

Department for Education and Science (DfES) (2004) *Key Stage 3 National Strategy: Advice on Whole School Behaviour and Attendance Policy.* London: DfES.

Dreikurs, R., Grunwald, B. and Pepper, F. (1998) *Maintaining Sanity in the Classroom: Classroom Management Techniques* (2nd edn). Philadelphia: Taylor and Francis.

Lee (2007) *Resolving Behaviour Problems in Your School.* London: Paul Chapman.

Porter, L. (2000) *Behaviour in Schools: Theory and Practice for Teachers.* Berkshire: Open University Press.

Rix, J. (2005) 'A Balance of Power; Observing a Teaching Assistant' in R. Hancock and J. Collins (2005) *Primary Teaching Assistants: Learners and Learning.* London: David Fulton.

Rhodes, J. and Ajmal, Y. (1995) *Solution Focused Thinking in Schools: Behaviour, Reading and Organisation.* London: BT Press.

Vincett, K., Cremin, H. and Thomas, G. (2005) *Teachers and Teaching Assistants: Working Together.* Berkshire: Open University Press.

Wheeler, S. (1996) 'Behaviour Management: Rewards or Sanctions', *Journal Of Teacher Development* 5 (1): 51–5.

Wilson, J. (2002) 'Punishment and Pastoral Care', *Pastoral Care in Education* 20(1): 25–9.

Wilson, R., Sharp, C., Shuayb, M., Kendall, L., Wade, P. and Easton, C. (2007) *Research into the Deployment and Impact of Support Staff who have Achieved HLTA Status: Final Report.* Berkshire: National Foundation for Educational Research.

Wolfgang, C. (2005) *Solving Discipline and Classroom Management Problems: Methods and Models for Today's Teachers* (6th edn). New Jersey: John Wiley.

INCLUSION

The School as a Community

Rachael Hincks

This chapter will:

- Give an overview of the need for inclusive practice in schools.
- Help you to understand the term 'inclusion' and where it has come from.
- Encourage you to make positive changes to your own practice.

WHAT IS INCLUSION?

> We will know that inclusive education has fully arrived when designations such as the 'inclusion school', the 'inclusion classroom', or the 'inclusion student' are no longer part of our educational vocabulary. (Giangreco, 1997: 194)

As a Teaching Assistant, you may have started your career in school working one-to-one with an individual pupil with special educational needs, and this may still form a major part of your role. Alternatively, you may have one of the increasing wider roles of the TA, perhaps with some responsibility for more than one pupil or for a group of TAs. Whatever your role, you will be involved in providing inclusive education and will have heard this term being used in many contexts.

The agenda for inclusive education has come a long way in the past 30 years or so (see Figure 8.1) since the 1970 Education Act announced that all children were to be deemed as 'educable'. The Warnock Committee's report (1978), concluded that around 2% of school pupils had special educational needs at any one time and that the needs of others could be met within the mainstream classroom, leading to the milestone Education Act in 1981 which laid out new duties for Local Authorities (LAs) to educate disabled children in mainstream classrooms, while ensuring that other children's education is not affected and that there is an efficient use of resources.

Another significant milestone was the 1994 Salamanca Statement of the United Nations Educational, Scientific and Cultural Organization (UNESCO), an agreement by

92 governments and 25 international organizations that pushed inclusive education into the worldwide agenda, stating:

Every child has unique characteristics, interests, abilities and learning needs ...

... Every child has a fundamental right to education, and must be given the opportunity to achieve and maintain an acceptable level of learning ...

Education systems should be designed and educational programmes implemented to take into account the wide diversity of these characteristics.

The 2000 revised National Curriculum for Schools in England (DfEE, 1999) embraced a move towards the inclusive school by giving three principles for inclusion:

- Setting suitable learning challenges.
- Responding to pupils' diverse learning needs.
- Overcoming potential barriers to learning and assessment for individuals and groups of pupils.

(See 'Further reading' for material relating to curricula in Wales, Scotland and Northern Ireland.)

The 2001 Special Educational Needs and Disability Act (SENDA), updating the SEN Code of Practice and 1995 Disability Discrimination Act (DDA), brought further duties to LAs to enable access for disabled children to the curriculum, providing both physical access within the school environment and access to information. It also means it is unlawful for schools to discriminate against disabled pupils in any way, including school admissions policies.

HLTA Standard 15

Every Child Matters, the 2003 Government initiative in response to the Victoria Climbié inquiry, set out five outcomes for children and places a duty on all children's services, not just schools, to provide a better standard of care and to work together locally to achieve this.

More recently, in 2005, the DDA was amended again to include further duties for schools and Local Authorities. This Act, the 2001 SENDA and Every Child Matters will be discussed in more detail later in this chapter.

Activity

What do you understand the term 'inclusion' to mean?

How, in your role, do you promote the inclusion of all pupils?

Who is 'inclusion' for?

So what is inclusion? Much of the legislation implies, or even states, duties towards disabled children, yet even the term 'disabled' can be applied in a wider context than perhaps one might first think. There have been two very different approaches to considering

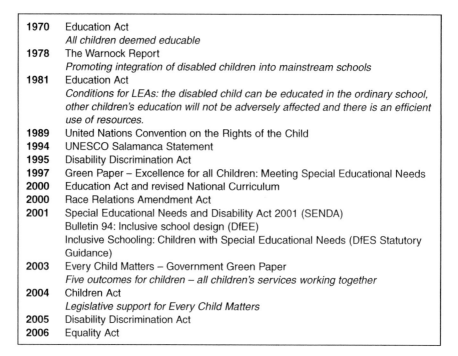

1970	Education Act
	All children deemed educable
1978	The Warnock Report
	Promoting integration of disabled children into mainstream schools
1981	Education Act
	Conditions for LEAs: the disabled child can be educated in the ordinary school, other children's education will not be adversely affected and there is an efficient use of resources.
1989	United Nations Convention on the Rights of the Child
1994	UNESCO Salamanca Statement
1995	Disability Discrimination Act
1997	Green Paper – Excellence for all Children: Meeting Special Educational Needs
2000	Education Act and revised National Curriculum
2000	Race Relations Amendment Act
2001	Special Educational Needs and Disability Act 2001 (SENDA)
	Bulletin 94: Inclusive school design (DfEE)
	Inclusive Schooling: Children with Special Educational Needs (DfES Statutory Guidance)
2003	Every Child Matters – Government Green Paper
	Five outcomes for children – all children's services working together
2004	Children Act
	Legislative support for Every Child Matters
2005	Disability Discrimination Act
2006	Equality Act

Figure 8.1 Key dates in the inclusion agenda

disabled people: the medical model and the social model. The medical or 'within-child' model centres on the disabled person being defined by their disability. It looks for a 'cure' for their 'problem', with the main focus being that the disabled person needs to adapt to society, to 'fit in'. The social model takes a very different view; it was developed by disabled people and considers that disability only exists because of barriers put up in society. For example, a person in a wheelchair has mobility impairment. They are only disabled, that is 'not able', because, for example, buildings they need to enter do not have suitable access. It is this social model that forms the basis for inclusion; that we consider the barriers put up in society, or in this case by schools, that do not allow pupils access to education for any reason.

Inclusion can be viewed simply as being the opposite of exclusion; that if exclusion exists then inclusion has not yet been achieved (Biklen and Knoll, 1987, cited in Giangreco, 1997). Though this definition is an outcome of research that is now over 20 years old, we need to consider whether exclusion still occurs and how much progress has or has not been achieved over this time. It is important to look at the shift from **integration**, a now outdated concept indicating the presence of disabled pupils in the classroom, to **inclusion**, where the needs of **all** pupils are considered and the educational environment is changed in order to meet these needs. Inclusion is about identifying barriers to learning; asking *why* pupils are excluded from education and how these barriers can be broken down.

HLTA Standards 1, 15 & 20

How far have we come? In 2000, Mittler concluded that 'inclusion implies a radical reform of the school in terms of curriculum, assessment, pedagogy and grouping of pupils' (2000: 10). Why radical? It could be argued that whilst many pupils are successfully included in mainstream education, it would take a major re-think in terms of school structures and the curriculum in order to include all pupils and enable them to reach their own individual potential, and that this still holds true today.

Despite Baroness Warnock herself declaring 'there is increasing evidence that the ideal of inclusion ... is not working' (Warnock, 2005: 35), there is much evidence to suggest that, whilst local practice varies (Rusteimer and Vaughan, 2005), inclusive education has been and can be found to be successful:

> The most important factor in determining the best outcomes for pupils with learning difficulties and disabilities (LDD) is not the type but the quality of the provision. Effective provision was distributed equally in the mainstream and special schools visited, but there was more good and outstanding provision in resourced mainstream schools than elsewhere. (Ofsted, 2006)

It is important to remember the role of special schools; the Department for Children, Schools and Families (DCSF, formerly DfES) believes that special schools have an important role in the overall inclusion of pupils with SEN (DfES, 2004b) and that mainstream and special schools need to work together, sharing expertise. As well as being part of a wider structure of including all children, special schools also have to consider the principles of inclusion in the same way that mainstream schools do. Despite all of the pupils within a class having statements of SEN, they are not all working at the same level; differentiation also exists within a special classroom.

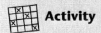 **Activity**

What helps and what hinders you in using inclusive practices in your setting?

REMOVING BARRIERS TO LEARNING

Following the report by the Audit Commission, *Special Educational Needs: A Mainstream Issue* (2002), several issues were highlighted in terms of the challenge faced by schools pupils and families in meeting individual needs. These included:

- Too many children wait for too long to have their needs met.
- Children who should be able to be taught in mainstream settings are sometimes turned away and many staff feel ill equipped to meet the wide range of pupil needs in today's classrooms.
- Many special schools feel uncertain of their future role.
- Families face unacceptable variations in the levels of support available from their school, local authority or local health services.

The government strategy *Removing Barriers to Achievement* (DfES, 2004b) was launched in response to this report, setting a clear agenda for reform in key areas of early intervention, removing barriers to learning, raising expectations and achievement and delivering improvements in partnerships. These targets, along with the Every Child Matters agenda (discussed later in this chapter), will bring significant changes to all schools in order to improve provision and support the inclusion of all children.

If we are to provide effective education for all, it is important to identify potential barriers to learning and seek to remove them, using a social model approach. As a TA, you will most likely be responsible for including an individual or small group of pupils, so it is important that you recognize and understand what constitutes a barrier.

HLTA Standards 1, 15 & 20

Activity

Borys is a six-year-old boy who has been attending his local primary school in the UK since his family moved from Poland four months ago. This is the first time that Borys has been to school, because in Poland they do not start until they are seven. In Borys's class, there is another Polish boy and a girl who has Portuguese as her first language.

Oscar is in Year 6 and has a hearing impairment which requires him to use a hearing aid in one ear. The school does not have any specialist equipment, but the TA linked with the class is experienced in working with pupils with hearing impairments. Oscar finds Maths difficult, which sometimes causes him to become angry and frustrated.

Isobel is in Year 8 at her local secondary school. She has been diagnosed with Attention Deficit Hyperactivity Disorder (ADHD) and has begun taking medication to try to control the symptoms. However, she is trying different medications and sometimes suffers side effects from them.

Go to **Barriers to learning** in Appendix 1 on p. 204, suggest potential barriers faced by each of the pupils in the examples above. See **Barriers to learning: Example**, on p. 205, an example to guide you.

Consider the following:

- What do we know about the pupil?
- What do we need to know?
- What assumptions do we make – are these helpful?

HLTA Standards 1, 8 & 15

When considering barriers to learning, it is important to look at the 'whole child'; for example, Oscar has a hearing impairment and also finds Maths difficult. There is no implication of a link between these facts, so both must be considered individually. One clear barrier might therefore be the awareness of staff regarding his needs; do staff simply cater for his hearing impairment, or are his Maths lessons differentiated appropriately for his ability too? Perhaps the barriers to learning surrounding his hearing impairment have been removed since he has been working with an experienced TA; perhaps his barriers are only related to accessing the Maths curriculum.

In Isobel's case, perhaps it is the side effects of the medication which cause the most significant barrier to learning. If, for example, she is not getting enough sleep, this will have an impact on her ability to take part effectively in lessons.

It is essential to recognize that there might also be attitudinal barriers towards some children, for example Isobel may well be labelled as a problem because she has ADHD. Often it is the label itself which causes a barrier; consider whether you have ever heard a phrase such as 'oh no, not another Jones ... his brothers were such a pain'. In addition, Frederick (2005) reminds us, inclusion 'also means tackling racism, homophobia and bullying'. For some staff and some pupils, it is difficult to challenge prejudice and stereotyped views.

> HLTA Standards 2, 3 & 4

WHO ARE WE INCLUDING?

When considering the question of whom inclusion is for, reflect upon your own education as well as your current role. Has there been a time when you have felt excluded? Did this happen when you were at school? Have you felt this as a TA?

Sometimes it is not only the pupils who might be excluded, but it might also be yourself or other members of staff. Perhaps there are practices within your school which exclude a particular parent/carer or group of parents/carers?

> I don't know why I bother going to Parents Evening ... I don't need to be told by ten different teachers that my boy is no good ... (Mother of a Year 9 boy)

As the CSIE (2000) concluded, 'inclusion in education involves valuing all students and staff equally'. In order to be inclusive in your practice, it is important to consider the needs of everyone. This often poses difficult questions and scenarios, such as what to do when a child's behaviour is affecting the safety of the whole class.

> HLTA Standards 1, 2, 4 & 5

 Activity

Read your school's Inclusion policy

- What is your role within it? Are you mentioned specifically, e.g. 'TAs ...' or less specifically, e.g. 'Support staff ...' or simply 'staff ...'?
- Is your role within the policy clear? How does this relate to the reality in practice?

THE SCHOOL AS A COMMUNITY

If we are considering the need to value all staff and pupils, inclusion can be viewed as an equal opportunities issue and a need to embrace diversity as a positive tool for learning (CSIE, 2000; Jordan, 2008; Mittler, 2000).

Diversity is more than just racial awareness, though this is an important factor. If we look at statistics for diversity in the UK (Office for National Statistics, 2008), we can see:

- The total UK population is approximately 59 million people.
- 48.6% of the population are males and 51.4% are females.
- 22.9% of dependent children live in lone-parent families.
- The majority of dependent children live with both natural parents (65.0%).
- Approximately 149,000 children under 18 provide unpaid care within their family.
- Many children live in 'workless' households with 15.9% in households where there are no adults in work.
- Of the total population 7.9% are minority ethnic.
- In England and Wales, 71.6% of the population describe themselves as Christian, with the next most popular religion being Muslim (2.7%).
- Of the economically active population (aged 16 or over) 3.7% are unemployed.
- Between 5 and 7% of the population are gay, lesbian or bisexual.

HLTA
Standard
9

Inclusion is more than just good practice within the classroom; it is about opening the doors and reaching the whole school and wider community. Ofsted (2001) judged that 'effective schools are educationally inclusive' and that this 'does not mean treating all pupils in the same way … it involves taking account of pupils' varied life experiences and needs.'

Case study: Clover Park Middle School, New Zealand

Clover Park is a multicultural school for pupils aged 11 to 15 years in New Zealand. They have identified that the majority of students have family connections with the Pacific nations of Samoa, Tonga and the Cook Islands. They have aimed to engage families and the wider community, as well as developing pupils' sense of identity by offering three bilingual units/programmes: a Maori–English bilingual unit (now a separate school called Te Whānau o Tupuranga), a Samoan–English bilingual programme and a Tongan–English bilingual class.

The school has received praise from the New Zealand Education Review Office (Education Review Office, 2007), which has a similar role to Ofsted in the UK, for their school practices which involve engaging parents and whānau (a Maori concept of extended family).

The most well developed school practices for engaging parents/whānau are early contact with parents to celebrate students' success or to inform them about behaviour concerns; working with parents and community members to assist in teaching relevant experiences; parents attending performances of cultural significance to each whānau.

The benefits and value of parent/whānau engagement in this school include: parents and whānau feeling comfortable being at the school; being involved in children's cultural and academic education; and being considered as part of the solution to concerns about their children.

The development of a separate Maori bilingual school came as a response to community need and statistics including those which show that Maori students are 2.4 times more likely to be permanently excluded and 3.7 times more likely to be temporarily excluded than white New Zealanders (Education Counts, 2006 cited in Milne, 2007). Milne, the Principal of both schools, believes that academic goals are not enough and that an ethos of a holistic definition of achievement is needed, with a focus on 'the student's relationship to self, their learning, the teacher and other students, the wider world and a reciprocal relationship between home and school' (Milne, 2007).

Whilst it might not be possible, nor advisable, to replicate the Clover Park model in your school, important lessons can be learned which can be applied in individual contexts, for example, considering the needs of pupils with English as an additional language (EAL) regarding identity (to be discussed in a later section), recognizing the traditional career paths for young people in rural communities or in Armed Forces families whilst also expanding their horizons, engaging children in after school clubs and activities run by community members, and recognizing achievement both inside and outside school no matter how small.

 Activity

Reflect on the following questions:

- What strategies does your school have to be inclusive outside of the classroom?
- Where else might there be opportunities to develop this?
- How could you, in your current role, be more involved?

THE DISABILITY DISCRIMINATION ACT

HLTA Standards 9, 13 & 15

The Disability Discrimination Act (DDA) 1995 defined disability and gave disabled people new rights. The SEN and Disability Act 2001 (SENDA) amended the DDA 1995 from September 2002, creating new duties for schools and Local Authorities in addition to those in the 1995 Act, effectively becoming DDA Part 4. These duties are:

- To not treat disabled pupils less favourably under the same circumstances.
- To identify barriers to learning and make reasonable adjustments to ensure disabled pupils are not disadvantaged.
- To develop School Accessibility Plans to demonstrate and plan for these changes.

The Disability Discrimination Act states 'a person has a disability ... if he has a physical or mental impairment which has a substantial and long-term adverse effect on his ability to carry out normal day-to-day activities'. The list is not exhaustive, but some examples include, hearing or visual impairments, dyslexia, learning difficulties, depression and mental illness, Down's syndrome, autistic spectrum disorders, diabetes and epilepsy.

What is a *reasonable adjustment*? The former Disability Rights Commission (now known as the Equality and Human Rights Commission) gives examples of where reasonable adjustments might be made in order for disabled pupils to be treated more favourably.

Case study

A.   A boy with a spinal injury who uses a wheelchair wants to attend his local primary school. The teachers are concerned as they do not know what he should do in PE lessons. The boy might be at a substantial disadvantage if he did not do PE. The physiotherapist is asked to help the school to adjust the PE curriculum appropriately. Amongst other things the school includes:

(a)   an exercise routine to carry out on the mat which other pupils will also do and benefit from;
(b)   ball work sitting on chairs in a circle.

These are likely to be reasonable steps that the school should take.

B.   A large secondary school is opening a special unit for pupils with speech and language impairments. They plan to include the pupils from the unit in mainstream lessons. One of the challenges is how to enable the children from the unit to follow the timetable. They might otherwise be at a substantial disadvantage. The school has an established 'buddy system' as part of its anti-bullying policy. After discussions with pupils, parents and the speech and language specialist teacher, the school extends its buddy system. It provides training for additional volunteer buddies to guide the disabled pupils from class to class. This is likely to be a reasonable step that the school should take.

(Disability Rights Commission, 2002: 59)
Reproduced with kind permission of the DRC; as of 1 October 2007 the function of the DRC is now covered by the EHRC.

 Activity

Consider the examples of Borys, Oscar and Isobel in the Activity in the section 'Removing barriers to learning': what reasonable adjustments could a school make to include those pupils?

The 2001 SENDA did not add any further duties pertaining to pupils with SEN. Schools and Local Authorities are still bound by the duties set out in the 1996 Children

Act, making appropriate provision for pupils with SEN and providing of 'auxiliary aids and services'. You will be more familiar with the SEN Code of Practice, essentially the guidance which is underpinned by the 1996 Act.

In 2005, the Disability Equality Duty was added to the DDA as Part 5A. The Duty for schools comprises:

- A general duty to promote disability equality, eliminating discrimination and harassment, promoting positive images of disability and promoting equality of opportunity.
- A specific duty to prepare and publish a Disability Equality Scheme – a plan to implement the general duty.

The 2001 and 2005 changes to the DDA mean that not only are disabled pupils supported by legislation, schools are duty bound to provide good practice and make every effort to include those pupils identified under the Act.

EVERY CHILD MATTERS …

In 2003, following the inquiry into the death of Victoria Climbié, the Government published the Green Paper entitled *Every Child Matters*. The aim is for every child, whatever their background or their circumstances, to have the support they need to:

HLTA
Standard
13

- be healthy
- be safe
- enjoy and achieve
- make a positive contribution
- achieve economic well being.

The 2004 Children Act provided the legislative support for this paper, outlining the duties for Local Authorities and children's services. From this stemmed the initiative Every Child Matters: Change for Children; a national framework for local change programmes designed to protect children and meet their needs (DfES, 2004a).

The key to Every Child Matters (ECM) is that it is a collaborative long-term project involving all agencies associated with children, including hospitals and community groups. As a TA, you may be involved in enabling and empowering children to meet all five outcomes in school. You might also be involved in the multi-agency aspect of the ECM agenda.

Inclusion in schools and inclusion in society should not be seen as separate issues (CSIE, 2000); the purpose of ECM is to ensure the health and well being of all children, throughout their development, including education in school, and preparing them for living in the wider world. In relation to including all pupils, Every Child Matters draws together all personnel who have a role in removing barriers for all children, barriers faced both inside and outside of school. The Every Child Matters: Change for Children

Table 8.1

ECM Outcome	Link to Maslow
Be healthy	Physiological needs
	(e.g. food, water, warmth)
Be safe	Safety
Enjoy and achieve	Belonging and love
Make a positive contribution	Esteem
Achieve economic well being	Self actualization
	(setting and achieving personal goals)

framework emphasizes the need for collaboration in order to identify individual needs earlier, including SEN, building upon the Removing Barriers to Achievement strategy (DfES, 2004b).

Inclusion is concerned with meeting individual needs; if we link ECM to Maslow's Hierarchy of Needs (1943), we can see that links can be made between each tier of the hierarchy and each ECM outcome (see Table 8.1).

According to Maslow, if physiological needs are being met, then safety needs will dominate and will impact on a person's behaviour. In turn, if these needs are met then needs of belonging and love will come to the fore, and so on until all of the basic needs (the first four listed) are met and self esteem influences behaviour.

Self actualization is concerned with an individual fulfilling his or her own potential; this is the goal that we are aiming towards for each pupil we work with. The links between Maslow and ECM are important; in other words, if a child can meet each of the five outcomes then they are more likely to reach their potential.

Maslow's hierarchy of needs is considered in detail in Chapter 6 in the context of supporting the development of emotional health and well being.

HLTA Standards 6, 13 & 15

For you as a TA, it is important that you are able to identify where, in your role, you can best support children in achieving each of the five ECM outcomes.

Be healthy

In order to promote the health of all pupils, schools are being encouraged to become Healthy Schools (DfES, 2004a). Also, schools will promote health issues through PSHE, Citizenship and other pastoral programmes in the curriculum. Not only are we aiming to improve children's physical health, but their mental, emotional and sexual health, for example by educating children to practice safe sex or to choose to not use illegal drugs. There is also an emphasis on supporting parents and carers in promoting the health of the whole family.

HLTA Standards 1, 2, 3, 4 & 5

There are a number of ways in which you might actively help pupils to achieve this outcome within your role; for example by running or supporting Social Skills groups, through lunchtime clubs, by promoting a balanced diet and a healthy attitude towards food, by greeting children at the door in order to promote emotional well being.

Be safe

Clearly, every school has a responsibility towards the children in their care and each school will have its own Child Protection policy. In addition to protecting children from harm in terms of neglect or mistreatment, schools have a duty to protect against accidental injury, violence, bullying and discrimination. Also, children should be educated to be safe from crime and anti-social behaviour, both as victim and as perpetrator.

HLTA Standard 27

Alongside the construction of mechanisms to keep children safe from harm, we need to make sure that children *feel* safe in all areas of the school. For example, what is the climate in your classroom? If pupils, especially the particularly vulnerable, are exposed to disruption, anger, lack of boundaries and lack of educational challenge, they may not feel safe there. A major part of your role will be in fostering an atmosphere of positivity, nurturing relationships with and between pupils. This is further explained in Chapters 5, 6 and 7.

As a TA, you also need to be clear about your school's policy regarding safety, making sure that you understand, and are able to inform pupils, how, where and who to seek help from or report issues to. Schools may have additional support strategies such as peer mediation and having safe places around school.

HLTA Standards 2, 4, 27 & 32

Enjoy and achieve

All school-age children should be attending school; more than that, they should be attending and *enjoying* school. All pupils should also be achieving academic goals, such as national standards at primary or secondary school, and should be achieving personal goals, such as forming friendships, and enjoying all aspects of life.

You will be working with children who perhaps achieve easily in one of these areas, but not so easily in others and you need to consider how to promote achievement and enjoyment both academically and socially. Success is often solely associated with academic achievement: consider each of the pupils you work with and their own personal goals. Perhaps success is also being able to have some independence, being able to communicate effectively, or being able to self advocate.

HLTA Standards 1, 3, 8, 19 & 21

Make a positive contribution

This outcome could be described as the thinking behind Citizenship programmes in schools; to have a place in society, to know and understand that place and to contribute towards how society works in a positive way. A number of schools achieve this through links with international schools, engaging with the community through organized activities and fundraising for charities, as well as in-house activities such as 'show and tell' lessons between classes or different year groups.

Many schools also have student councils; a democratic group comprising pupils who will have been voted for by their peers and have the role of representing their peers' wishes. These groups can be very effective in engaging pupils in decision-making and demonstrating processes such as elections and voting. A recent study of school councils in London (Davies and Yamashita, 2007) found that 'key achievements occurred when students were accepted as "professionals" who made an adult contribution to the school, with their experience and expertise used on teaching and learning, on behaviour and on school climate' and goes on to recommend a high profile place for councils in all schools.

Learning how to make a positive contribution need not be restricted to timetabled lessons; children learn to do this by observing the interactions of others. As a TA and a role model, you are demonstrating to pupils how to avoid conflict or bullying behaviour and how to form relationships. You will also be promoting pupils' self esteem and helping them to feel confident to put forward their views or ideas without fear of rejection.

HLTA
Standards
1, 2,
3 & 4

Achieve economic well being

This outcome is concerned with getting families out of poverty, supporting them to be economically active, enabling them to live in decent homes and have a good standard of living. Children will be encouraged to engage in further education, employment or training when they leave school, and all schools will have careers programmes in place to support this.

Schools are also encouraged to strengthen links with parents and carers, to promote education as a tool to get out of poverty. In turn, some schools also enable parents to support their children's learning whilst furthering their own education.

HLTA
Standards
1, 2, 3,
4 & 5

To a TA working in an Early Years setting this might sound very distant; however you can begin to encourage pupils to have their own goals. In addition, beginning to teach children about the wider world and helping them to develop life skills is an important step forward.

Activity

Reflect on your role in school

- Can you give specific examples of when you have helped a child to meet one of the ECM outcomes?
- Can you do this for each outcome?
- Revisit Chapter 4 – can you identify when and how you have worked collaboratively in order to promote one or more ECM outcomes?

WORKING WITH PUPILS WITH ENGLISH AS AN ADDITIONAL LANGUAGE (EAL)

In January 2007, 13.5% of pupils in primary schools and 10.5% of pupils in secondary schools were learning English as an additional language (DCSF, 2007). There is no data available which details exactly which languages are spoken in homes across the UK and the number of languages used. Increasingly, TAs working in UK schools are supporting pupils for whom English is an additional language, especially in schools where there is little or no alternative specialist support. This can be a significant challenge for the TA, especially if the child they are supporting understands or speaks little or no English and the TA does not understand or speak the child's home language.

The subject of including EAL learners is discussed here as a separate section because it is all too often assumed that to include a child with EAL is the same as to include a child with SEN, that their lack of English is the same as lacking language. However, EAL is not a special educational need; the 1993 Education Act states 'a child is not to be taken as having a learning difficulty solely because the language in which he/she is, or will be, taught is different from a language which has at any time been spoken in his/her home'.

HLTA
Standard
9

It is important for all staff working with the pupil to have access to information regarding the pupil's background including their educational experience, as many pupils will have been regarded as being gifted or talented when learning in their home language or another language they are fluent in. It might also be the case that, if a child is very young, they will not have ever attended school or that a child has previously been assessed as having special educational needs in their home country. Some pupils with EAL may already be fluent in two or three other languages. If inclusion is concerned with identifying and removing barriers to learning, it is important to also consider other areas of the pupil's background; they may be an asylum seeker or refugee, may have experienced trauma or loss, might be the only English learner or speaker in the family. The pupil is also facing the double challenge of not only learning English, but being taught in it.

HLTA
Standards
1, 2, 8, 9,
10 & 23

We have discussed previously that the process of inclusion is based upon valuing the individual and valuing diversity; in which case, we must make sure that we recognize and positively promote the individual pupil's identity. This means correctly pronouncing their name, rather than giving a nickname or a shortened, anglicized version of their name. This also means acknowledging their home language and making sure there are opportunities for the pupil to speak in the language which they feel most comfortable in. Cable *et al.* (2006) argue that schools and structures placing an emphasis on acquiring English without supporting children's home languages cannot be considered as inclusive.

 Activity

Reflect on the following questions:

- What do you consider your identity to be?
- Is it purely concerned with race, ethnicity or language?

Laubscher and Powell (2003) give an interesting example of the complexities of identity, considering not only ethnicity, but gender, class and the society in which the individual lives:

In this view a Chinese American person can assert her identity as an American, volunteer to serve in the armed forces in the aftermath of the World Trade Center attack, celebrate the

HLTA
Standard
9

Chinese New Year, speak to her children in Mandarin, be a practicing pagan, buy turkey from Wal-Mart with clipped coupons, and serve that turkey with spring rolls at Thanksgiving. (2003: 211)

Though there must be an emphasis of the development of EAL pupils as bilingual (or even multilingual) learners, support needs to be in place to help pupils in acquiring English. Historically, new arrivals would have been placed in language centres or have intensive periods of language tuition. This was found to be unhelpful as children were learning a very structured and rigid version of English which did not bear much resemblance to the way children speak in school and in social settings. Vygotsky's work (see Chapter 9) tells us that language learning has a specific social nature and that children learn from interaction. If this is the case, then EAL learners must, at least, be educated in the mainstream classroom; for these pupils to be truly included, there needs to be a higher level of social interaction within this classroom.

Revisit the Clover Park case study; the emphasis in this school is the development of the whole child, recognizing their heritage and their culture and promoting the use of both their home language and other languages spoken in the country and local community. Here the pupils are actively engaging in learning experiences presented in two languages, so their positive self image can be promoted.

 Activity

The most recent legislation relating to the needs of EAL learners is the Race Relations Amendment Act (2000). All public bodies (including schools) are required to produce a Race Equality Policy and have procedures in place for reporting, monitoring and challenging racial harassment.

Read your school's policy on Racial Equality. What is your role within it?

Can you give examples of when your work has directly supported the implementation of this policy?

INCLUSION FOR ALL?

Imagine that we really valued difference and cared about enabling people to be the best they could become and did not place such a high value on conformity. (Jordan, 2008 p. 14)

HLTA
Standard
7

Throughout this chapter, you will have reflected on your role, how inclusive your practice is, and how inclusive your practice could be. Remember though that inclusion is a process in which all members of the school community need to be involved in order to achieve a situation whereby exclusion is, ideally, eradicated or, perhaps more realistically, minimized.

Reflective questions

- After reading this chapter, what are your understandings of the term 'inclusion'?
- What are the areas for development with your own inclusive practice?
- How could you work together with other staff and/or pupils in your school to improve inclusive practice as a whole?

Further Reading

Ainscow, M., Booth, T. and Dyson, A. (2006) *Improving Schools, Developing Inclusion*. Abingdon: Routledge.

Gibbons, P. (2006) *Bridging Discourses in the ESL Classroom*. London: Continuum.

Jones, P. (2005) 'Inclusion: Lessons from the Children', *British Journal of Special Education* 32(2): 61–6.

Le Métais, J., Andrews, R., Johnson, R. and Spielhofer, T. (2001) *School Curriculum Differences across the UK*, available online at http://www.leeds.ac.uk/educol/documents/00003560.htm

Richards, G. and Armstrong, F. (2008) *Key Issues for Teaching Assistants Working in Diverse and Inclusive Classrooms*. London and New York: Routledge.

References

Audit Commission (2002) *Special Educational Needs: A Mainstream Issue*, available online at http://www.audit-commission.gov.uk

Bicklen, D. and Knoll, J. (1987) 'The Disabled Minority', in Taylor, S. Bicklen, D. and Knoll, J. (Eds) *Community Integration for People with Severe Disabilities*, New York: Teachers College Press.

Cable, C., Eyres, I. and Collins, J. (2006) 'Bilingualism and Inclusion: More Than Just Rhetoric?', *Support for Learning* 21(3): 129–34.

CSIE (2000) *Index for Inclusion: Developing Learning and Participation in Schools*. Bristol: CSIE.

Davies, L. and Yamashita, H. (2007) *School Councils – School Improvement*, available online at http://www.schoolcouncils.org

DCSF (2007) *Statistical First Release: Schools and Pupils in England*, available online at http://www.dfes.gov.uk/rsgateway

Disability Rights Commission (2002) *Code of Practice for Schools*, available online at http://www.equalityhumanrights.com

DfEE (1999) *The National Curriculum – Handbook for Secondary Teachers in England*. London: DfEE.

DfES (2004a) *Every Child Matters: Change for Children*, available online at http://www.everychildmatters.gov.uk

DfES (2004b) *Removing Barriers to Achievement*, available online at http://publications.teachernet.gov.uk/

Education Review Office (2007) *Education Review Report: Clover Park Middle School*, available online at http://www.ero.govt.nz

Frederick, K. (2005) 'Let's Take the Special out of Special Needs', *Times Educational Supplement* 15 July 2007: 19.

Giangreco, M. (1997) 'Key Lessons Learned about Inclusive Education', *International Journal of Disability, Development and Education* 44(3): 193–206.

Jordan, R. (2008) 'Autistic Spectrum Disorders: A Challenge and a Model for Inclusion in Education', *British Journal of Special Education* 35(1): 11–15.

Laubscher, L. and Powell, S. (2003) 'Skinning the Drum: Teaching about Diversity as "Other"', *Harvard Educational Review* 73(2): 203–24.

Maslow, A.H. (1943) '*A Theory of Human Motivation*', Psychological Review 50: 370–96.

Milne, A. (2007) 'The Short End of a Smaller and Smaller Identity Stick', Keynote Address presented at New Zealand Institute Annual Meeting, 25 September 2007, Wellington, New Zealand.

Mittler, P. (2000) *Working Towards Inclusive Education – Social Contexts*. London: David Fulton.

Office for National Statistics (2008) *National Statistics*, available online at http://www.statistics.gov.uk

Ofsted (2001) *Evaluating Educational Inclusion: A Guide for Inspectors and Schools*, available online at http://www.ofsted.gov.uk

Ofsted (2006) *Inclusion: Does it Matter where Pupils are Taught?* London: Ofsted.

Rustemier, S. and Vaughan, M. (2005) *Segregation Trends – LEAs in England* 2002–2004. Bristol: CSIE.

United Nations Educational, Scientific and Cultural Organization (1994) *The Salamanca Statement and Framework for Action on Special Needs Education*. Paris: UNESCO.

Warnock Committee (1978) *Special Educational Needs: The Warnock Report*. London: DES.

Warnock, M. (2005) *Special Educational Needs: A New Look*. London: Philosophy of Education Society of Great Britain.

Useful websites

Centre for Studies on Inclusive Education
http://inclusion.uwe.ac.uk/csi/csiehome. htm

Equality and Human Rights Commission
http://www.equalityhumanrights.com

Every Child Matters
http://www.everychildmatters.gov.uk

Disability Equality in Education
http://www.diseed.org

SECTION 3

SUPPORTING LEARNING

9

TEACHING, LEARNING AND PSYCHOLOGY

Stuart Gunn

This chapter will:

- Examine 'surface' learning and 'deep' learning.
- Define Behaviourism, Social Learning, Constructivism, Social Constructivism.
- Look at Piaget's idea of schemas, assimilation, accommodation and equilibration.
- Highlight different learning styles: reflector, theorist, pragmatist and activist styles, VAK.
- Review Vygotsky's ideas of collaborative learning and ZPD.
- Review Bruner's ideas of scaffolding and mental representations.
- Explore didactic and collaborative styles of teaching and learning.

WHY DO SOME LEARNERS FAIL TO SUCCEED?

Case study

Albert is a curious and inquisitive child. He is 11 years old, on the verge of transferring to secondary school, and whilst on the one hand he appears to be looking forward to it, at times it troubles him. He is aware that he is not successful at many things and finds that hard to understand, especially when he thinks he has understood everything that the teacher or TA has told him. He is often corrected for not concentrating yet his head is always full of ideas and thoughts that seem to spin and tumble and he finds that hard to explain, especially when he thinks he has understood something and then he gets things wrong.

Albert appears to be lacking in success at school, like many young children he appears to have problems concentrating on one thing for any length of time. So let's ask ourselves some questions which could help reveal some answers as to how we might help him cope with school life.

Do the problems lie internally with Albert, for example: his perceived laziness, his lack of motivation, his intelligence or is it just being a boy?

Or are Albert's problems promoted by external factors, for example: being dropped on his head as a child; lack of stimulation at home or poor parental support; perhaps he watches too much TV?

Or is lack of success caused within the environment of the school? Also our own lack of understanding of how a young child like Albert learns.

NATURE V. NURTURE

The big question here might be is it to do with his 'nature' (genes) or the nurturing process he received at home, in his social life with his peers and friends, and at school? This of course is the classic debate of nature v. nurture which so often gets constructed in terms of people being determined by one or other of these factors. I feel it would be much more fruitful if we considered the influence of both. Our home life, schooling and social world influences our social, emotional and cognitive development. Our genes and our biological makeup clearly influence our physical outcome; how much they influence our psychological outcomes is more questionable.

Aspects of nurture

HLTA
Standard
8

In this chapter, the nurturing process which we are most interested in is that of how Albert's teachers and teaching assistants (TAs) might influence him and his learning within the school environment.

Amongst the possible in-school 'roadblocks' to learning could be:

- The lack of an infectious, enthusiastic teaching environment, even boring classes.
- A lack of organization or clarity in the presentation of work which in turn confuses Albert.
- A feeling of being alienated by the culture.
- Individual learning needs are not taken into account and, as a result, appropriately differentiated, stimulating resources are not provided.

HLTA
Standards
6, 10, 17,
18 & 19

These are pretty big questions and they might all be in play at some time for Albert. As TAs you are employed to be part of a team that helps to maximize the potential of each pupil and to make them feel valued as individuals.

CAN WE HELP ALBERT?

HLTA
Standard
22

A good first step would be to grab his attention. We have to remember that we need to engage him as an individual learner and to try to encourage his involvement with the other learners in the group. Teachers and TAs do this through the use of high order inter-personal skills, actively seeking to encourage Albert to offer something about himself, possibly a positive event in his day, or a strongly-held personal interest. On this they build the foundations of a relationship and then tackle his assessed academic needs. This identifies a key principle in effective practice that we **teach people first** and our subject, not as an afterthought, but more as second in order of importance.

How can we help him?

If we get this order of events right we have a better chance of responding more positively alongside pupils like Albert. This means 'feeling the emotional temperature' of the classroom situation. Chapters 6 and 7 consider this in some detail.

HLTA
Standard
16

 Activity

Getting to know your learners:

How do you get to know a new group of learners?

What exercises do you use?

Do you have some really effective methods which have been successful?

What are you trying to achieve by doing this?

Consider the following statement: 'we teach people first and subjects as a secondary activity'.

Does your evaluation of this statement influence your thinking and practice?

Getting to know and relate to our learners is essential, but within the classroom setting helping them to become more effective learners is our central task. Of course we hope that our concern for them as individuals will motivate them to want to achieve higher levels of learning and thus become more confident within the school setting.

HLTA
Standards
22 & 23

As part of this 'press for achievement' in a good school (Chapter 1) the TA has to consider the important structures of the learning process and how these impact on the individual learner. Just as in Maslow's Hierarchy of Needs (1970), learning is most likely to be successful if certain basic conditions are met and the foundations are laid towards 'self actualization'. However, if insufficient attention is paid to assessment, planning, preparation, delivery and evaluation to meet the needs of the individual learner, then, if learning takes place at all, it is likely to be at what Marton *et al.* (1984) described as '**surface**' learning. At this level: 'The student reduces what is to be learned to the status of unconnected facts to be memorized. The task is (merely) to reproduce the subject matter at a later date, e.g. in an exam' (Gibbs, 1992: 2).

HLTA
Standards
17, 18, 20,
21 & 24

THE 'DEPTH OF LEARNING'

Many writers have considered the composition of learning and the impact that such ideas may have on what makes a successful learner. A main aim of education must be to move all learners, including ourselves, from operating at surface level to a much

deeper level. This might be categorized as being attained when: 'The student attempts to make sense of what is to be learned, which consists of ideas and concepts. This involves thinking, seeking integration between components and between tasks and playing with ideas.' (Gibbs, 1992: 2)

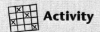 **Activity**

Moving from surface to deep learning:

Think of a time when you felt really comfortable in a learning situation and as a consequence you learnt something at a deep level.

What part do you think the teacher/trainer had in this process?

What were the emotional qualities in this process?

When considering the idea of surface and deep learning we are of course considering different levels of thinking. Bloom (1956) presented a hierarchy, classification or taxonomy which sees the engagement with deeper learning intensify as it moves through knowledge, comprehension, analysis, synthesis and eventually to evaluation. What can be expected at each of these levels is explained in more detail at www.counc.uvic.ca/learn/program/handouts/bloom.html

However, even in the most stimulating of educational settings, it does not necessarily follow that deep, or even deeper than surface, learning will occur. Sotto (1994: 54) quotes Polyani: with regard to some of the factors that are involved in 'trying' to learn.

For deep learning to potentially occur there is still a requirement that over the learning period other **essential contributors** are present. For example:

- Discovery – that in the learning process there will be 'something' that we do not know, but the acquisition of this 'something' would be beneficial and we 'need to know' it.
- Immersion in the problem.
- Puzzlement – the journey will not be simple, there will be 'challenges' and at times uncertainty.
- Active engagement, especially in obtaining information and testing hunches.
- Repeated exposure to the learning situation.
- The presence of an 'expert' who can set up a situation, act as a model of competence, answer questions.
- Periodic insights into the direction of learning and possible outcomes.
- Feeling of pleasure from gaining these insights.
- Doubt that one will ever really understand and a faith that one will finally understand.

Already we have established that creating the environment and opportunities to maximize learning is complex. To try to create optimum conditions for learning you will need, amongst other skills, knowledge and understanding, the capacity to examine how you recognize and develop empowering relationships and how you, yourself, can demonstrate your own 'deep learning' by analysing, synthesizing and evaluating some of the strategies you use to enhance pupil motivation and successful learning engagement.

IDEAS ABOUT LEARNING

Behavioural learning theory

One definition of psychology has been that of the scientific study of behaviour. The **behaviourists'** approach to learning (started by John Watson in 1913) suggested that observing and attempting to change learners' behaviour, as opposed to their internal thoughts, was the most practical way of promoting learning. Pavlov (1849–1936) **conditioned** a dog to salivate at the sound of a bell and the sight of a light. Normally dogs, and other animals, will only salivate when they smell or taste food, which is an automatic response to aid digestion. By conditioning the dog to associate the food (unconditional stimulus) with the conditioned stimulus (the bell or light) Pavlov suggested that the dog **learnt** this associative link and through this, learned to salivate as a conditioned reflex. This **associative learning** is very powerful and is linked to the idea of **associative memory**, which later becomes an unconscious memory.

An example might be that of meeting a new pupil starting a new term. You mention that you will be seeing her in the science block later today but notice that her facial expression has changed. You later find out that at the end of last term she was confronted with an angry response to something she did on that day and in that place. Even the mere mention of entering the science block again has triggered off an associative (unconscious) emotional memory. Of course, there are usually many more positive associative learning experiences.

One of the most famous behaviourists was Skinner (1938) who used the idea of operant conditioning, where the subject has to operate on the environment in order to gain a reward. He taught cats to escape from 'puzzle boxes' and pigeons to peck a correctly coloured disc in order to obtain a reward (either that of escaping from the box or gaining a food pellet) and thus shaped their behaviour towards 'learning' what is the best behaviour. Skinner produced programmed learning materials based on step-by-step conditioned reinforcement, usually through an immediate positive reward, such as praise, for the correct answers. Also incorrect answers are punished in some way. We know that behaviourist' approaches to learning are often effective, as are behavioural therapies. However, there is a strong assumption here that all learning has to be rewarded or even punished.

Behavioural approaches to teaching are also known as 'transmission' models of education where knowledge is offered through the medium of direct instruction. Here learners are often seen as empty vessels where they play a more passive role in the learning process with the teacher being more active. In this model learning consists of successful retention of facts and information through a stimulus (for example, the teacher asking questions) response (the learner responding) connection. Chapter 7 examines in some detail positive approaches to behaviour management.

Social learning theory

As well as direct tuition through reinforcement and reward, children also learn through a more active process of **observation** and **imitation**. Bandura (1963) offered the idea that most learning takes place in a social setting, hence **social learning theory**. He suggested that through observation children learn from an early age to imitate others, particularly adults, and often play games in which they learn to imitate the social rules necessary for them to fit in with their social world. Through imitation a child is able to learn far more than would be possible if it had to be taught all the time. Bentham (2007: 19) notes that:

> Simply put observational learning can be described by the command to watch and learn. This view states that an individual can start to behave in a certain way without previously being rewarded for that behavior ... a person has watched how another person behaves and has observed what has happened to them in terms of being rewarded or punished.

HLTA
Standards
2 & 3

Learning through observation and imitation can quite quickly become internalized so that a child comes to **identify** with that person or that role. This is particularly so with **gender-role** behaviour, although it takes place over a longer time. What is important here is that the child has positive role models to follow so that it can develop an idea of how real people behave in particular social settings. This is particularly important in the imitation of social aggression.

Bandura *et al.* (1963) showed children different scenes of adults either behaving aggressively or non-violently towards a large rubber doll both in real life and on film. The children were then left in a room to play with the doll and other toys. Although an analysis of the results is not entirely conclusive, in general they showed that those exposed to aggressive models performed more aggressive acts than those who had not. Also they were far more likely to imitate those models they saw as similar to themselves. This imitation, and even possible identification process, would appear to have important implications for children's learning and their behaviour.

Activity

Can you think of situations where children might copy negative adult behaviour within particular social settings?

Do children imitate particular gender-role behaviour?

Are boys who watch violent TV and computer games, often portrayed by male figures, more likely to become aggressive?

What positive role models do you see children observing and imitating?

Constructivism

As we have seen, behaviourism suggests that the learner plays a relatively passive role in the learning process. There might even be a suggestion here, in this passive learning process, that children do indeed construct similar understandings in their minds of the new knowledge gained from the teacher. However, if in a science lesson they are asked by the teacher where the water 'went' after it had 'disappeared' from a sheet of paper, we know that there would be many different answers. This is because children construct a sense from their own 'understanding' about new knowledge and concepts. We could go further and say that babies construct their own brains. Current brain-imaging research appears to confirm this. **Constructivism** then is an approach to learning which proposes that models of reality are constructed through an active interaction between innate capacity (what we are born with) and our environment (all those social influences in our daily lives, including, of course, our school experiences). In this model of learning children construct their own view of reality by trying out their ideas in the real world.

Piaget (1896–1980) was one of the most important writers on the ways in which we learn and his constructivist theory of cognitive development has had a major influence in education in Britain over the last 40 years. This has been especially so of children being actively engaged in learning through new experiences.

So, let's return to Albert and his first days at school and consider how Piaget's ideas might begin to explain how Albert feels and thinks in this new setting.

HLTA
Standards
7 & 8

Like us all, Albert's head is full of ideas, thoughts and memories from his past and indeed aspirations for the future. These are ideas he has constructed and accumulated through his experiences, both about himself and of his world, which he has internalized and made his own. This is a process Piaget called **assimilation**.

So, through this process of assimilation, Albert builds up a range of thought patterns (or **schemas**) which guide, and even sometimes control, his behaviour. They could be likened to scripts or prompts which we read in order to remind us about the world and which also help us know what we can expect of it and how we can predict its behaviour. These schemas are very necessary in the process of accumulating our understanding of our world but, equally, can prove problematic if they become fixed and unchanging.

In new situations, Piaget suggested, we need to change them through a process of what he called **accommodation**.

For example, when Albert finds himself at his new, large secondary school for the first time he might have to change some of his ideas (the existing schemas in his head). In his comparatively small primary he had been used to being the first in the queue for lunch. However, today he is in a different environment, but still with the same schemas and scripts about the world and therefore the same expectations. In this new environment there are many more people who also want their lunch at the same time as him. He quickly finds that getting what he wants is more problematic. 'For Piaget, cognitive development was due to an interaction between the developing child and the child's experience within the environment' Bentham (2007: 15).

Now Albert, and possibly many of the others who may also not have learnt the art of waiting and sharing, has at least two choices here. Through some rather quick learning he could **assimilate** the new environment and its conditions, **accommodate** these with his existing schemas, adapt and change his behaviour and wait his turn. Alternatively he can leave his existing schemas intact without any accommodation. In this case he will soon find that the world is rather less accommodating and that at some time he will have to learn to change his behaviour or live with the pain of having to fight the world single-handedly, a potentially painful process, but one which we know many children go through.

Activity

Trying to change our schemas and our behaviour:

Can you think of a time when you, as a TA, did or did not, change your ideas (your schemas) about a new working environment that you were in?

Can you remember the outcomes of that piece of thinking and possible behaviour?

How might these ideas relate to, and explain, the behaviour of some of your learners?

As a biologist, Piaget had observed plants and animals needing to achieve a level of homeostasis (a need to maintain the same state of being), usually with regard to keeping warm and having enough nutrition and water. This physiological state of balance is also necessary for human beings but is equally necessary in terms of their thinking and feeling about the world, their **psychological state**. Piaget came to believe that there has to be accommodation because most people feel most uncomfortable when 'out of balance with the world'. Piaget called this **equilibration**, a process where one strikes a balance between changing one's schemas to adjust to one's environment. If this is so then Albert needs to balance his original schema about always getting his lunch first with the reality of his new environment and the equally demanding presence of others. He requires a more equal balance between his thoughts and his new world; he needs to learn a new set of schemas.

These reflections on changing thinking lead on to one of the most important issues educators have to recognize – that in the learning process, there is a great deal of **unlearning and relearning** to do if we are to accept new ideas about the world.

Unlearning some of our most cherished ideas and concepts about ourselves and our world is often quite difficult. Many of these ideas come to us either through our direct observations about the world or through being told by others of their 'truths'. Thus we gain a store of common sense, or at least sense which is commonly held by many others.

ALTERNATIVE IDEAS

Over the years there has not always been agreement about the definition of learning, especially in educational circles. Woolhouse suggests: 'Learning occurs whenever a

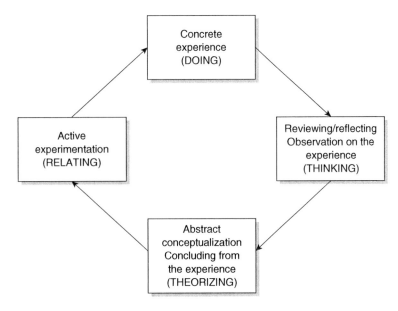

Figure 9.1   Adapted from Kolb (1984)

person adopts new, or modifies existing patterns of behaviour in a way which has some influence on future performance or attitudes' (Woolhouse *et al.*, 2001: 12).

This process is possibly something like the concept described by Kolb (1983) in his Cycle of Experiential Learning which starts with real experiences and, through a reflexive, thinking process leads to new learning (see Figure 9.1).

Is this how we see Albert changing his view of his new school environment where he starts with a new concrete experience of the world, 'having to wait for his lunch', then reflecting on the situation, thinking about what it means for him and then deciding what to do about it?

If he changes his behaviour we can assume that some new learning has taken place and that he has adopted some new ideas or modified them, thus changing his old schemas.

Certainly that's what we hope, and schools expect, he will do to get back to a state of balance in terms of his thoughts and behaviour in regard to his new experience at school.

We can see from this model the need to provide real, concrete experiences, but in order to learn from them we need to promote reflection on our values, attitudes, beliefs and behaviour and consider how this affects us and other people.

These ideas fit quite well with Honey and Mumford's (1986) notions of the possible ways in which people learn through **doing, thinking, theorizing** and **relating to the real world in a pragmatic manner**. They suggest that we all experience these four learning processes, though not necessarily in the order suggested in Figure 9.1, nor with equal intensity, or to equal levels.

If, after a lesson, we ask pupils how they have learnt we often get some interesting responses:

I like to have a go and see what happens even if it goes wrong and I wanted to ask lots of questions about it before anyone else did.

(Activist)

I like to gather information and mull things over. I was trying to work out what it has to do with what I already know about the subject.

(Reflector)

I like to tidy up and reach some conclusions. I asked questions to see how these new ideas fitted with my own ideas. Also I was trying to work out if I could think of a logical way of solving the problem posed in the session.

(Theorist)

I like tried and tested techniques that are relevant to my problem.

(Pragmatist)

Honey and Mumford's concern is to observe how people learn within this 'framework'. We all use 'theories' to help us understand our world and so that we might also be 'reflective' about our actions. In addition we often need to know how things 'work in practice' and may often just need to jump in and 'have a go' at things, often on a trial and error basis without too much thought. There may however be one or more of these elements which are dominant and we have our preferred style(s) in our approach to learning and some style(s) in which we are less comfortable and in which we may need to become more adept.

We all know about people who act before thinking and who may also not reflect on the consequences of their behaviour or its affect on others. Conversely some people do too much thinking and reflection and this may mean that they never try things out in practice or may never volunteer knowledge in a whole class setting.

HLTA Standards 8, 10, 13, 17 & 18

Work on learning styles offers guidance on how we prefer to learn and is an important part of our toolkit in assessing how our pupils are engaging in learning. If, for example, you as teacher have a preferred learning style and always approach your teaching from this perspective, then there is a possibility that your teaching may not be engaging with potentially 75% of the group of pupils who do not share this style.

They will also have quickly detected this one-dimensional approach and potentially lost motivation to be part of the learning experience.

Activity

Consider the ideas below. Can you identify some preferred learning styles amongst your pupils?

If so are you potentially teaching to their perceived strengths?

PRAGMATIST	The learner might demonstrate this preferred style through being: ordered; structured; practical; accurate; organized; hands on; detailed; exact.
	They may learn best through: checklists; outlines; charts; summaries; data; use of laboratories; use of computers; practical reading; short lectures.
REFLECTOR	The learner might demonstrate this preferred style through being: sensitive; emotional; imaginative; colourful; motivated by deep feelings; flexible. They may learn best through: group discussion; media and music; peer group; role play; use of fantasy and imagination; themes; arts; humour; short lectures.
ACTIVIST	The learner might demonstrate this preferred style through being: independent; creative; risk-taking; inventive; problem solving; curious; investigative; intuitive.
	They may learn best through: games and simulations; problem solving; creating products; independent study; experiments; opportunity to demonstrate unusual solutions; options; open-ended work; few restrictions.
THEORIST	The learner might demonstrate this preferred style through being: logical; academic; structured; intellectual; a reader; a researcher; evaluative; a thinker; a debater; studious.
	They may learn best through: reading; lectures; working alone; term papers; library work; note-taking; essays; research.

So, as a simplistic example, if your own preferred learning style is Activist and you make this your main teaching style, then you will probably be keen to promote independent study and offer opportunities for pupils to learn with few restrictions. However if a quarter of your group are Reflectors, who essentially prefer humour, imagination and engagement, then they might find the whole experience frustrating and pointless.

Peter Honey's Learning Styles Questionnaire is, quite correctly, protected by copyright. However, when offered the chance to complete it people quickly recognize themselves and their preferred learning style. Should you wish to investigate this further refer to Peter Honey's website (NB: the Learning Styles Questionnaire can be completed online for a fee at www.peterhoney.co.uk).

Complementary to preferred learning styles is the concept of preferred methods of receiving and perceiving information. This recognizes the fact that we take in information via a range of senses:

- Visually through our eyes.
- Through auditory stimuli.
- Kinaesthetically, through our sense of touch, by feel and physically engaging with the world. This is encapsulated in the familiar VAK (visual, auditory and kinaesthetic) ideas about learning styles or preferences.

Research suggests (Smith, 1998) we prefer to learn predominately through a specific stimulus. So, **visual learners** will 'see' concepts in their minds and be able to recall them more readily. For them graphs, charts, posters, keywords displayed and mapped out will help their learning. Also they may tend to talk in visual images, 'I see what you mean'; 'I can't quite picture it'.

Those for whom an **auditory** stimulus is important will enjoy the engagement of discussion, hearing stories, and will prefer to receive instructions verbally. They might be relied on to remember verbal classroom direction given out by the teacher more readily than non-auditory learners.

Kinaesthetic learners may prefer to learn through doing and will certainly benefit from physical activity and concrete reinforcers. For them bodily movements, dance, PE and gestures are important when recalling events and describing ideas and concepts.

So, to try to maximize potential we need to ensure, where possible, that all senses are stimulated.

Learning and management of effective teaching is, therefore, clearly not straightforward. It should be noted here that recently, Coffield *et al.* (2004) have questioned the assessment and value of learning styles. Their findings can be accessed at the Learning and Skills Research Centre website at www.lsrc.ac.uk. Not only does it appear that people have differing preferred learning styles, we also know that children's and young people's understanding of their world is often quite different from that of adults. Depending on their age, they do not have the same range of contexts in which to set new ideas and thus very often misunderstand what they hear from adults. Their 'commonsense' understanding of the world is often quite different from ours and we know this sometimes to our cost, and especially if we do attempt to get into their 'field of knowing'.

An example is that of the movement of the sun in relation to the earth. Clearly, by every day observation we can see that the sun circles the earth. It is usually only by the 'authority' of others that we come first to accept, and then possibly later to understand, that the reverse is true. Even in the face of Galileo's evidence, the Pope could not accept this truth and was thus unlikely ever to begin to understand it.

Some adults are like that about new ideas, but for children the problem might be different, they may not be ready, in terms of cognitive development, to accept such abstract ideas and thus not be able to explain how they happen.

HLTA
Standard
8

Activity

Checking for understanding:

Ask some of your learners about their understanding of some scientific concept.

For instance, how do clouds form? Where does water go when a wet piece of paper dries?

Why does it get dark at night? Why do some heavy things float and some light things sink?

In response to these questions ask them how they came to know some of these things, who told them and when did they learn them?

HLTA
Standard
8

An example of an HLTA Standard relevant to this theme is Standard 8. Within the HLTA standards (Appendix 2) there are other examples that relate to teaching and learning.

Social Constructivism

For Lev Vygotsky (1896–1934) the place of the teacher and initiator of knowledge was central in this learning process. However, he also suggested the idea of collaborative learning where teacher and pupils could exchange ideas in an interactive manner. This process of **joint learning** – in this case pairing the more 'knowledgeable' with the less 'knowledgeable' – and placing the 'teacher' at the centre of helping children understand themselves and their world both as an educational and social process was essential. These ideas represented a radical alternative to Piaget's ideas since Vygotsky wished to emphasize the social dimension of learning, suggesting that even the youngest child is a social being and that all learning is social. Vygotsky did accept Piaget's idea of children constructing their own understanding of their world and being active organizers of their own knowledge. However, he moved away from Piaget's idea of this being a mostly solitary experience and suggested that the social and cultural world of the child with its special sign systems, speech, writing and number, for instance, influenced the child's cognitive development, particularly after the age of two when language use was dominant. Thus this socially dominated learning environment became known as a **social constructivist** learning approach.

Vygotsky suggested that in this social world gaining and making personal sense of new knowledge was a two-level process: firstly, at an **interpersonal level**, between people and then, later, **intrapersonal** as the new idea or concept is internalized. This process is one of mixing new ideas with an existing understanding of the world. Since these ideas come partly from our personal understanding of the world and partly from other people's new ideas and we actively construct them for ourselves, rather then passively accept them, they are of course very personal 'constructs'.

> Vygotsky and Piaget had different views in regard to maturational readiness, that is, at what age, or stage of development, a child would be ready to learn new knowledge ... Piaget would say that the student would need to discover the concept for themselves ... Vygotsky, however, believed that thinking and understanding was developed through communication and dialogue. (Bentham, 2007: 17)

 Activity

Seeing the world from others' points of view:

Can you recall a time when you were exposed to a new concept and managed to misunderstand it because you saw it from your own egocentric view point?

(The example that springs to mind for me is that of Laurie Lee's first day at school when the teacher told him to, 'sit there for the present'. On his return home his mother asked him how he got on. 'Oh, it was quite good, but I never got the present.' The teacher had clearly not de-centred thus not seeing the idea of present from the point of view of a child.)

Can you think of a similar example from your experience of working as a TA with young children?

This process of internalizing new ideas can be problematic since all of our individual understanding of the world will tend to differ to some extent. This is particularly the case where ideas about people's behaviour, values and cultural norms are concerned. In this process of aiding understanding of new ideas it is important to know what the learner already knows.

Vygotsky anticipated this process by suggesting that we can help people to move to another, 'deeper' level, or 'zone' of knowledge through what he called the **Zone of Proximal Development (ZPD).**

This process of moving children to a new zone of knowledge and understanding starts by assessing what the child already knows. From there it attempts to build new knowledge on top of that existing knowledge and as near to it (in close proximity) as possible. In this way, the child is taken on to a new zone of knowledge which is commensurate with their ability to gain and understand new ideas.

This newly acquired knowledge and understanding will be different for each child, not only because their starting point of knowledge will be different, but also their individual learning capacity at any one moment will be different for many reasons.

Helping children to connect with knowledge they already have is an appropriate way to commence teaching, but also a way of helping them to integrate existing knowledge with new knowledge thus deepening their understanding of new ideas.

My experience also tells me that people know more than they think they do and helping them to find this '**unconscious**' knowledge is an important way of promoting self esteem. Through the use of questions aimed at learners' existing level of knowing we can indeed tap into this knowledge and then move them to higher levels. This can be achieved by carefully structuring and guiding a particular sequence of learning experiences. Jerome Bruner (1983) offered the idea of a **scaffold**, which adults and older siblings provide, supporting the child whilst he or she is trying out new knowledge, thus helping them towards higher levels of knowledge and understanding than he or she would achieve if worked alone. As the child becomes more confident the scaffold can be removed or used again when needed.

These ideas from Bruner fit well with Vygotsky's idea of **joint learning**, with the more 'advanced or accomplished' learner helping the less knowledgeable person to a new zone of learning. This is central to the whole process of the acquisition of knowledge and its understanding. The process could be facilitated by an adult or a more knowledgeable pupil and offers an ideal of mixed ability teaching. In such a situation anyone could be both a teacher and learner with the teaching child moving possibly from 'simply knowing about a new idea' to 'understanding it' merely because s/he has articulated their ideas to someone else.

As teachers ourselves we know that often the best way to learn and understand new ideas is to teach them to others. Vygotsky offered us the rationale for doing this. He also suggested that this was positive socially, as it has the essential hallmarks of **collaborative learning** as opposed to a competitive striving for new knowledge.

Essential to this idea of collaborative learning for Vygotsky was that of the place and value of language: firstly, using language so that communication is at the child's level of understanding and secondly exposing the learner to richer and more complex language thus developing deeper cognitive thoughts. For Vygotsky it is language, in its broadest sense, that is the essential component in this cognitive process. The richer the language which a child is exposed to the greater will be its cognitive development and the greater will be its thinking capacity.

Bruner (1975) agreed that thinking is enriched and facilitated by language and that language is used for communicating the processes by which we learn to think. This thinking process helps to develop mental representations of our environment rather like Piaget's mental schemas. For Bruner there are three stages to this development of our learning.

- **Enactive representation** which consists of the actions we make or the memory traces of the feelings of those actions. For instance, riding a bicycle, making a cake, performing some dance steps each get 'represented' as muscle memories. This learning through doing can also be seen as a kinaesthetic process in which there is a feedback to our brains so that we have an internalized model of this activity. This can be used to both represent that activity when we wish talk about it to others and when we wish to repeat the same action. Here the child is limited to remembering only those things which it has actively done. It would not, for instance, be able to recall films or TV programmes it had seen or even words it had read.
- **Iconic representation** is where information is stored in the brain in the form of sensory images, usually visual but they could also be in the form of other senses, taste, smell, etc. Thus the range of things which can be stored in the child's memory is extended, e.g. familiar faces.
- **Symbolic representation** is the third and most important, since through this process we can store abstract concepts like 'love', 'hate' and 'peace'. This is possible because we can use symbols (cat, dog, 1,88) which do not have to look like the thing we are thinking of. The range of things we can think and talk about thus become almost infinite since we can also read and remember other languages and even music. The important function here is that of memory, but essential for the communication of this stored knowledge is language.

Since language is so important in the learning process it is essential that we use it carefully in our teaching, for example asking appropriate questions in order for pupils to make connections with their existing knowledge and to move them to deeper levels of understanding. Also we need to develop a dialogue with our learners so that they can articulate their ideas and thus understand them, and themselves, better. Socrates, over 2,400 years ago, recognized that learning was a two-way process and that rather than lecturing people it was better to enter into a dialogue. This approach also recognizes that people may know more than they think they do and that through an even-handed discussion there could be a 'journey of discovery', not only of new ideas but of existing knowledge as well.

By asking the right questions at an appropriate learning level and listening carefully to the responses Socrates taught his untutored slave about trigonometry.

Thoughtful, sensitive responding is useful in terms of connecting and reassuring people about their own practice, the value of any learning experience and their self esteem. For example, a group of TAs when asked how they had internalized the main points from a session on how they taught the Additional Literacy Strategy (ALS) gave the following responses:

Considering, asking questions, usually with a follow-up question, to see how their ideas fit with mine.

(Theorist)

Having a feeling of empathy with others helps me to recall and thus learn. For example, when there was a general misunderstanding about a feature of the ALS programme it made me think if I was fully aware of all the implications of that point.

(Reflector)

Matching what I got from others with my own knowledge helped and finding out how they operate in their own practice confirmed some of my ideas.

(Pragmatist)

Just getting in there and asking questions, not waiting for others to come to me.

(Activist)

I have linked these responses to learning styles (see Honey and Mumford (1986) above) to illustrate the 'circular' nature of transmitting knowledge, and that there is often a connection with the way in which we engage with new knowledge and thus possibly remember it.

IMPACT ON TEACHING

HLTA Standard 7

Reflecting on our own learning and learning styles might suggest specific areas of strength and weakness and that there could be scope for improvement in our teaching styles, methods and approaches. We should be striving, to the best of our ability, to maximize the learning of all pupils by constantly examining our own teaching. When it comes to the issue of teaching style you should be very knowledgeable, since, as Teaching Assistants, you have observed more teaching and teaching styles than most people. Only one group of people have seen more and that is your learners, the young people in your classrooms who sit day by day being exposed to many different teachers and their teaching methods and styles.

To examine some possible teaching approaches and styles let's start with your experiences and ask you to recall both early and more recent experiences of teaching from the point of view of you as learners.

 Activity

Remembering some significant learning moments:

Recall your experiences of being taught –

1. As a child in a primary school setting (5–11).
2. As a young adolescent in secondary school (11–16).
3. As a post-16 student either at a sixth form or FE college (16–18) or as a professional (16–60).

Consider the style of teaching and its human approach and also how you felt in those different settings.

What emotions did you have then and now recall?

A traditional concept of pedagogy (teaching of children) suggests that learners were quite passive in the learning process, likened to empty 'mugs' to be filled from the full 'jugs' of knowledge by their teachers. Alternatively, other schools of thought suggest that there is a greater recognition of people's prior experience and knowledge and a concern to use that knowledge within the learning situation and to promote a more collaborative learning environment.

In this way they are engaging learners in three essential learning roles:

- they are the 'learner' receiving information;
- they are also a 'supporter' helping others in the group, and
- they themselves are a teacher/facilitator offering ideas to others.

In this second model there is a more even-handed sharing of knowledge and a more democratic level of power between teacher and pupil/student, both in terms of teaching styles and knowledge ownership. In addition the line between teacher and learner, which was often well defined in the pedagogic model, is less clearly drawn or needed.

In your work with your pupils/students you will use an eclectic mix of models of teaching.

Articulating ideas between individuals, particularly in paired work where a more intimate dialogue may be had, usually helps to provide clarity about issues and often moves people from merely knowing something to understanding it. So this more personal and intimate process can help prepare people for sharing their ideas in the more 'public' forum of the group and, in the process, makes for a deeper understanding of their own ideas. Also, for the many children who do not have the opportunity to express their ideas and to be listened to by others this process is vital in encouraging their motivation and self esteem. Many of you will know how valuable this has been through the use of Circle Time.

> HLTA Standards 14, 15, 17, 18, 19 & 20

Matthew Lipman (2003) in his work with young children over 20 years, shows clearly how this process of dialogue develops thinking skills and general cognitive development. He offers children the opportunity to engage in philosophical debate, getting them to question ideas just as Socrates did in his Greek city state. Ideas such as:

'If I am dreaming am I still alive?'
'If I did not have a brain could I still think?'
'Is it my body which thinks or is it me?'

The aim is to make children think and to challenge some conventional ideas. They are also encouraged to challenge each others' ideas and that of the teacher in a collaborative quest for a deeper understanding of their own ideas and thoughts. An essential part of this process is that they learn to listen to other people's ideas and, very importantly, to be listened to by others. As Lipman says it can be: 'an intoxicating experience for children to have their peers listen to and respect their ideas'. It is clearly a process involving a range of social skills, particularly those of waiting, listening and accepting the ideas of others, even when they disagree with yours.

> HLTA Standard 4

Lipman used his methods to help 'slow learners' to improve their learning and demonstrates how a group of children who are 12 months behind their peers can make up this 'deficit' in one term.

One important current idea appears to have close links both with learning styles and teaching approaches. This is the idea that individuals might have different 'intelligences'. Gardner (1983) suggests that there could be at least seven realms of knowledge or intelligences: linguistic, mathematical/logical, visual/spatial, musical, interpersonal, intrapersonal and kinaesthetic, and is even considering three further areas. Also he suggests that different cultures value these realms of knowledge in different ways. David Wood (1998) offers the idea that: 'different societies selectively develop the latent talents of their children in ways that reflect their collective values' (Wood, 1998: 281).

HLTA Standards 6, 19, 20, 22, 23 & 24
An important implication for us here is that if we want to develop children's full potential we need to find out what their strengths are and build upon these. We also need to widen our view of what intelligence is. In Western cultures we have valued linguistic and mathematical and logical abilities but other cultures have placed a greater value on kinaesthetic intelligence, considering dance and appreciation of graceful movement as important. The importance of interpersonal skills is also of great value in education but in today's schooling environment may not be regarded as highly as the ability to demonstrate competence in literacy or numeracy.

 Activity

Recognizing different domains of ability:

Do you recognize children with different domains of ability (intelligence?) who have sometimes gone unacknowledged?

Also, does the idea of effort and ability have any meaning for you in the way you respond to children's success in school?

One of the ideas I like to emphasize in this whole educational debate is something that might appear rather obvious, and that is the distinction between teaching and learning. My years of both teaching and observing others in that activity, suggest that we appear to know more about the processes of teaching and focus on them more than we do on what learning is and how it occurs. I feel strongly that today, with the increase in classroom technology, which clearly enhances our teaching methods, there may be a danger of losing sight of what our learners are learning and how they are developing their thinking skills.

WHAT KIND OF TA ARE YOU?

To conclude this chapter I would like to offer you the opportunity to create a framework that enables you to informally consider your own values, attitudes and practice. (See Appendix 1, page 206).

The framework is based on an original questionnaire by McGregor (1982). Although the questions may appear somewhat stark and a little polarized they can raise some important issues about values and attitudes and approaches to teaching which you may wish to reflect on and discuss with colleagues. The range of questions encompasses ideas from previous chapters within this book, but which are vital in a holistic consideration of professionalism and teaching.

〰 **Reflective questions**

- Can you think of any of the issues you have read about in this chapter which might have particular relevance to your current practice?
- How might you implement some of these ideas in your practice; which might have particular importance for you at present?
- What help might you need from your institution in order to be able to implement any new ideas?

Further Reading 📖

Donaldson, M.A. (1984) *Children's Minds*. London: Flamingo.
Eysenck, M.W. (2002) *Simply Psychology*. East Sussex: Psychology Press Ltd.
Gilbert, I. (2002) *Essential Motivation in the Classroom*. Abingdon: RoutledgeFalmer.
Haynes, J. (2002) *Children as Philosophers*. Abingdon: RoutledgeFalmer.
Hayes, N. and Orrell, S. (1998) *Psychology: An Introduction* (3rd edn). Furlow Longman Group.
Smith, A. (1998) *Accelerated Learning in Practice*. London: Network Educational Press.

References

Bandura, A. (1977) *Social Learning Theory*. New York: General Learning Press.
Bentham, S. (2007) *A Teaching Assistant's Guide to Child Development and Psychology in the Classroom*. Abingdon: RoutledgeFalmer.
Bloom, B. S. (ed.) (1956) *Taxonomy of Educational Objectives: The Classification of Educational Goals: Handbook 1, Cognitive Domain*. New York and Toronto: Longmans.
Bruner, J. S. (1975) 'From Communication to Language: A Psychological Perspective', *Cognition* 3: 255–87.
Coffield, F., Moseley, D., Hall, E. and Ecclestone, K. (2004) *Should We Be Using Learning Styles? What Research Says to Practice*. London: Learning and Skills Research Centre.
Gibbs, G. (1992) *Improving the Quality of Student Learning*. Bristol: Technical and Educational Services.
Honey, P. and Mumford, A. (1986) *The Manual of Learning Styles* (2nd edn). Maidenhead: Peter Honey Publications.
Kolb, D. (1983) *Experiential Learning: Experience as the Source of Learning and Development*. New Jersey: Prentice Hall.
Lipman, M. (2003) *Thinking in Education* (2nd edn). New York: Cambridge University Press.
McGregor, D. (1982) *The Human Side of Enterprise*. New York: McGraw-Hill.
Marton, F. Hounsell, D. and Entwhistle, N. (1984) *Experience of Learning*. Edinburgh: Scottish Academic Press.
Maslow, A. (1970) *Motivation and Personality* (2nd edn). New York: Harper and Row.
Skinner, B.F. (1938) *The Behaviour of Organisms*. New York: Appleton-Century-Crofts.
Sotto, E. (1994) *When Teaching Becomes Learning: A Theory and Practice of Teaching*. London: Cassell.
Wood, D. (1998) *How Children Think and Learn: The Social Context of Cognitive Development* (2nd edn). Oxford: Blackwell.

PROMOTING LEARNING THROUGH THE USE OF ICT

Mark Townsend

This chapter will:

- Capture the essence of how ICT is moving forward very rapidly, with an emphasis on understanding how our pupils are using technology.
- Identify the barriers that we, as educators, face in developing our use of technology, and provide examples of how practitioners in the classroom have overcome them.
- Explore the intrinsic qualities of technology and how they can be harnessed to support effective and dynamic learning opportunities.
- Engender a sense of enthusiasm for how the new technologies can support all areas of learning and teaching.
- Identify a selection of useful resources which can support TAs in the classroom.

> The simple truth is that the emerging technologies will revolutionise teaching and learning. And it will happen not in some comfortingly distant future of tinfoil jumpsuits and jetpacks, but during the next 15, 10, or even 5 years: the school days of the children currently in our infant classes. (Futurelab, 2007)

Since this chapter was originally written in 2004, the world of Information and Communications Technology (ICT), or rather, the way that our pupils engage with technology, has changed dramatically. I have therefore taken the opportunity to completely re-write this chapter to acknowledge these changes, and to share an understanding of how educators in the classroom can perhaps develop learning experiences in ways which meet the needs and challenges of an evolving educational system (as alluded to by a group of leading educational thinkers in the opening quote).

In a relatively short period of time, ICT has become a ubiquitous and essential tool for the educator, offering challenging new choices and a wide portfolio of possibilities (Heppell, 2000: xiii), and is continuing to evolve at a rapid pace. I have adopted an approach here which will seek to exemplify both how the intrinsic qualities of the new technologies can benefit the learner and educator, and offer examples of good practice through the use of a series of 'real-life' case studies.

THE RISE AND RISE OF THE NEW TECHNOLOGIES

The significance that the government attaches to technology in schools is exemplified by both the level of investment in computer technology for schools – some £552 million was spent in the year 2005–6 on ICT products and services (excluding curriculum software) in UK schools (BESA, 2007: 11) – and in the voices of successive government ministers of state and their advisers. As far back as 2003, Professor Stephen Molyneux predicted that in five years time, individually we would be 'consuming 30 gigabytes of digital information per day', whilst employment opportunities for those entering the workforce would be very different to those of their parents: '50% of workers will be employed in industries that produce or are intensive users of information technology', and, 'most new jobs will occur in computer related fields … 80% of these jobs do not even exist yet'.

Charles Clarke in 2003, then Minister of State for Education, was similarly 'bullish' in his belief that ICT was rapidly evolving in its significance to the economy, and that its implications for the workforce, and clearly the employees of the future were very great indeed, reporting that '97% of all current job vacancies in the UK [required] some element of ICT skills'.

Whilst Molyneux's predictions about our 'digital diet' may have largely come true – many of us are indeed consuming huge amounts of digital information, primarily in the form of music and video downloaded from the internet – his and Clarke's assertions on the impact of ICT on the workforce are rather less easy to evaluate. Certainly, many employees are spending increasing amounts of time working on the computer and communicating with colleagues via an intranet, but are the real benefits this can offer under-exposed and under-developed? For example, many administrative duties can be performed from home using secure access to files stored on secure corporate intranets, and do we always need to be travelling to meet face-to-face with colleagues? Software exists, some freely available, which enables users to perform all the rituals and functions required of meetings, but replicated 'virtually' with participants based in their own homes (Townsend and Parker, 2007).

The implications of this for the educator are enormous: almost everyone must be equipped to meet the technological demands for the future if society, and therefore the individual, are able to work and prosper. Educators are now in the position where they have an opportunity to make real shifts in their own pedagogical vision and philosophy about the new technologies, their place in schools, and their wider cultural importance (Snyder, 2001). Whatever one believes about the future of technology, it is clear that it is impacting on all our roles in the classroom in very significant ways. A TA in North Devon, reported in a recent Foundation Degree Seminar how her own role has evolved:

HLTA Standard 28

> The advances in software and hardware technology, the internet, and the ease of their use have had a profound effect on the way teachers view ICT. As confidence and enthusiasm [for ICT] have grown, my job has become vastly more varied.

The British Educational Communications and Technology Agency's (Becta) annual review, *Harnessing Technology: Schools Survey, 2007*, reports in detail on the 'state' of technology within schools. In the five years up to 2007, most significantly, has been the growth in the provision of interactive whiteboards (IWBs), with primary schools now having on average eight per school, and secondary schools, 22 (Becta, 2007). During that same period the number of educational laptops available to pupils has risen by over 300%. Does this reflect two key attributes which are driving the phenomenal growth of technology forward: interactivity and mobility?

 Activity

Go to *The impact of ICT* in Appendix 1 on p. 208. Consider how the evolving use of ICT has impacted, firstly on your school, secondly, on your pupils, and thirdly, on your own role as a TA. Discuss this also with your ICT coordinator and other colleagues.

Increasingly, there is a divergence between the way that ICT is taught in schools, and the way that pupils are using their computers once at home (District Administration, 2007). Educators are now part of a 'new communicative order' (Street, 1998) in which they have had to quickly adapt to new methods to support learning and teaching if they are to continue engaging a generation of learners brought up on digital technology. Schools have access to new technologies which go far beyond the traditional PC: Interactive Whiteboards, hand-held devices, tablet PCs, geo-satellite navigational systems, data-loggers, programmable robots, digital cameras (still and video), MP3 recorders and players, and in some cases, video-conferencing facilities.

HLTA Standards 12 & 28

Whilst the two key government agencies concerned with education, the Department for Children, Schools and Families (DfCSF) and the Qualifications and Curriculum Authority (QCA), along with BECTA, offer guidance on every aspect of learning and teaching using ICT, pupils will have their own agenda in the use of technology which is enabling them to transform physical, social and cultural boundaries with high degrees of dexterity, speed and confidence; and they have also evolved their own language: txt.

It seems highly likely that the future role for many TAs will involve the increased use of ICT, whether this is preparing teaching materials, taking individual pupils for one-to-one teaching, leading whole class sessions, or even managing ICT resources for the whole school. How can TAs move their own confidence and skills forward in the use of technology, particularly when faced with a young generation of learners who are very likely to be more adept at using computers than most adults (Veen and Vrakking, 2006). By taking an individual example, we can look at the barriers which may confront the TA, and identify ways in which these potentially can be addressed.

HLTA Standards 20, 27, 30 & 31

Case study

Jo, a TA working with Year 5 pupils, identified herself as a reluctant user of technology – an 'analogue' as Prensky (2001) would describe her. Her role in school did not involve her in the active use of technology, and at home she avoided using the family's computer, except for making the occasional purchase from an online bookshop – for which she often enlisted the help of her teenage daughter. After attending an ICT course designed for TAs, she reflected upon her own relationship with technology, and concluded that 'consciously or unconsciously' she had adopted an avoidance strategy where technology was concerned, reliant on the pupils' skills if she did have to use the computer for teaching and learning. She also now realizes that ICT has the potential to really transform learning for her pupils. Should she strive to become, using Prensky's terminology, an intuitive, and *indigenous* user of technology, a *'digital native'*, or at the very least, a 'digital immigrant – those who were not born into the digital world but have become fascinated by, and adopters of the new technologies?'

Recently, Jo had been involved in her school's own evaluation of their use of ICT, using Becta's *Self Review Framework* (see 'Useful websites' section at the end of the chapter). This enabled her senior managers to:

- see what 'good' use of ICT looks like
- benchmark the school's progress against other schools
- identify the school's strengths
- produce action plans for improvement.
  (Becta, 2008)

However, from observing how her pupils, and indeed her own children, were using the computer, she decided that other criteria may be more relevant to the development of her own role and practice, and completed the review adapted from Cox *et al.* (2000) and John and Wheeler (2008, Appendix 2). From this activity, Jo realized that she was beginning to empathize more strongly with the positive factors of ICT, and began to identify ways, in collaboration with the school's ICT coordinator, in which she could certainly address issues around providing lesson diversity, differentiation and creative delivery and overcome difficulties with her perceived ICT skills and confidence.

HLTA
Standards
6, 7, 9,
12, 20,
27 & 28

Barriers to the effective use of educational technology are well documented (John and Wheeler 2008). Becta (2004) identifies the following key areas of difficulty confronting educators:

- **Lack of confidence**: TAs will frequently say that their pupils know more than they do about computers, and may be reliant on pupils for assistance when they encounter difficulties with ICT use. The prospect of using the IWB in front of a large class can initially be daunting for anyone.
- **Lack of competence**: The majority of ICT skills acquired by TAs, and educators in general, have been self-taught, with limited opportunities for attending school-based training sessions available. Ofsted (2005) continue to report on the variation in levels of educators' skills, and the quality of in-school ICT training.

- **Lack of technical support**: Many problems which occur with technology are usually small-scale and readily overcome. However, certain levels of technical literacy are required if operators of technology are able to develop an intuitive, on-the-spot approach to solving problems.
- **Lack of time**: Teaching Assistants are busy people; they regularly cite difficulties with accessing their school's network during non-teaching time, and will often find that other family members take priority with the use of home PCs in the evenings.

OVERCOMING BARRIERS TO USING ICT

> Most computer-based activities do not require high levels of skill ... rather, an understanding of a few basic principles and the time to explore and play is key to the successful use of ICT. (Tyrer *et al.*, 2004: 151)

HLTA
Standards
12, 19,
21 & 28

Sime and Priestley (2005) identify the tensions emerging between the 'idealized' vision for ICT use in schools, as determined by policy makers, both at national and local levels, and the 'harsher realities faced by educators'. Barriers identified by TAs to their use of ICT certainly fall into the categories outlined by Becta above, although interviews with support staff indicated very specific examples which exemplified the difficulties that they themselves encountered. One TA worked with a teacher who saw ICT as a 'distraction from teaching literacy and numeracy', whilst many reported that access by pupils to computers was mainly limited to the weekly sessions in the school's computer suite. Other factors, including basic practicalities such as slow internet access, incompatibility between laptop and network-based software, and printer failure, were reported as being commonplace, and in one TA's words, a 'terrible waste of resources'. Sime and Priestley (2005) also report that, whilst confidence and competence in ICT are fundamental to the effective use of technology, there are certain factors which need to be considered if users are to move their own professional development forward, which can be categorized as:

Philosophical

An ethos held by educators that through the use of technology they are more likely to achieve a higher-level goal than through other means. They must also believe that the use of ICT will not detract from other high level objectives, and demonstrate criticality in its use.

Experience

Educators need to identify what they need to know, and how they will obtain the necessary support to overcome difficulties. They should feel 'in control of the technology', and be able to cope with technical failure, perhaps in front of a potentially large audience, who may not always be empathetic.

Resources

Access to 'reliable' hardware and software both at school and home, is essential, enabling TAs to play with and explore the different modes of technology. Human resources should be considered: what are the attitudes of colleagues towards their use of technology, how helpful – and available – are colleagues who can offer technical support?

HLTA
Standard
28

Community

Who is out there to help or empathize with me? Whilst there will undoubtedly be colleagues who share commonality with their ICT experiences, what other opportunities exist for meeting others outside school? The concept of learning communities is not a new one, but the significance of their role in germinating and sustaining groups of individuals coming together 'in pursuit of a shared experience' is potentially very great (John and Wheeler, 2008). With a move in recent years towards developing school 'hubs' and clusters, there may well be opportunities for TAs to set up their own communities with a particular focus. Jim, a TA in an Early Years setting, had sought to improve his own professional development in ICT, but wanted to involve colleagues from other schools. Appreciating that out-of-school meetings may be difficult for some staff to attend, he decided to set up an online discussion forum, using a freely available platform. Starting with a small group of enthusiastic users, posting ideas for using ICT with the Foundation Stage classroom, along with technical tips, the virtual forum evolved quickly, and now involves a large number of regular contributors from a wide geographical area.

Back to Jo...

Jo had been able to move her own skills forward remarkably quickly once she had evaluated her personal needs, and decided what she actually waned to 'do' with the technology. She observed how pupils were apparently highly motivated to see their work published on the internet, and had an idea for supporting pupils in a collaborative, online, learning activity which seemed to serve as an ideal framework for developing her ICT skills. Identifying a group of pupils who were reluctant writers of poetry, she set up a web-based text-processor, freely available from a large internet search engine. This enabled any users, with a password, to access the same interactive text pages and edit them simultaneously, from any location using the internet. The pupils were asked to collaboratively develop a poem, verse-by-verse, incorporate images, and even correct each other's spellings and grammar. Jo had, without attending any formal training, but with some assistance from the ICT coordinator, learned how to set up an online shared documents account, edit web-based resources, including adding hyperlinks to other websites, navigate a text-processor menu, edit image files, and monitor electronically the use of the resource by her pupils.

HLTA
Standards
20, 21,
22 & 28

MAKING LEARNING COOL: HOW OUR PUPILS ARE USING TECHNOLOGY

> There needs to be an interplay between an understanding of the goals of the activity and the variety of ways in which pupils learn, through exploration, consultation, collaboration, guidance, questioning and explanation (Loveless, 2003a: x)

HLTA Standards 18, 19, 20, 21, 30 & 31

The new technologies are clearly offering opportunities for developing learning in ways which are not only innovative and dynamic, but the functionality and qualities of the internet, known as 'Web 2.0', are also driving forward the pervasive sub-culture for which technology is clearly the key vehicle (John and Wheeler, 2008). Can we harness these in order that we may draw upon pedagogies which are empathetic with our learners? The case study pupil illustrated below demonstrates not only typical use of ICT by the younger generation, but importantly how his approach comes from a very different cultural experience to that of Jo's.

Case study

John, a Year 7 pupil, leaves school at 3.30pm. Half an hour later he is at home in his bedroom, and switching his computer on. Within another minute, he is connected to his *Facebook* social networking site. There are 5 new messages from friends on it, and an invitation to a party at one of their houses on Saturday night. He keeps *Facebook* running but now logs into his *YouTube* account. At lunchtime he had filmed, using his mobile phone, several friends re-enacting an Eminem music video. Using an infra-red connection, he transferred in seconds the video onto his computer, and swiftly uploaded it to *YouTube*. He copies the video's web address (URL), and sends it to his friends via his *Facebook* account. John then settles down for lengthy session with Grand Theft Auto (IV), during which time this evening he will also simultaneously 'chat' to other users located around the world about how to negotiate the various 'traps' that game-players are presented with.

This scenario may seem quite alien to those who have not been brought up with technology; however, if we, as educators, are to engage pupils in their learning through the use of technology, do we not need to understand the principles inherent to ICT which are apparently so attractive to the younger generation? Prensky (2001), has quantified how the 'IT Generation' access media; it is worth noting how this may have been at the expense of time spent reading.

Most young people in the UK by the time they are 21 will have:

- sent over 200,000 text messages
- played 10,000 hours of videogames

- watched over 20,000 hours of TV
- talked for 10,000 hours on mobile phones
- seen over 500,000 TV adverts
- spent less than 5,000 hours reading.

 Activity

How are your pupils using the internet inside and outside the classroom? From non-intrusive conversations with pupils consider:

- What they are using the internet for when not directed by the educator.
- What skills they have developed for negotiating the world-wide web.
- Which of these skills have been formally taught in school.
- Which of these skills they have acquired for themselves (or from their peers).
- How much time do they actually spend accessing the internet?

Their answers may, or may not, be a surprise to you, but it is very likely that their use and experiences of the internet is very likely to concur with Byron's (2008) highly detailed findings, drawn from a large number of key research sources, that identified the ways that children were using technology, and the associated risks:

- 'Some 99% of children aged 8–17 access the internet.'
- 'As children mature, they begin to use the internet in increasingly sophisticated ways: 8–11 year olds are more likely to say they are going online for gaming purposes, whilst 12–15 year olds are using it as an educational tool as well as for downloading music/movies/videos and watching video clips. The oldest age group (16–17 year olds) are most likely to be sending email, visiting social networking sites, uploading photos/videos and either maintaining or contributing to other people's 'blogs' or websites.'
- '57% of 9–19 year-olds have come into contact with online pornography.'
- '25% of children and young people have met someone offline that they first made contact with online.' (Byron, 2008)

Looking in closer detail at the attributes, we can begin to identify exactly what the inherent qualities or characteristics of technology are which are making it so attractive to pupils, and therefore potentially such an effective tool for supporting learning and teaching. The DfEE (1998), Hardy (2000) and Sharp *et al.* (2002), below identify the key characteristics of technology:

- **Speed**: fast access to many varied sources of information.
- **Capacity**: access, store, and manipulate a huge amount of information.

- **Automaticity**: emphasis on outcomes, rather than processes.
- **Communicability**: send/receive/gather information easily and quickly.
- **Provisionality**: change/revisit/re-sort/re-present information easily and quickly.
- **Interactivity**: deciding how to access/sort/present information.
- **Non-linearity**: decide sequence of accessing/sorting/presenting information.
- **Multi-modality**: access/sort/present information using a variety of media.

To these we can also add the qualities of:

- **'Chat'**, or **synchronicity**: the potential for users to access others' computer screens simultaneously, most often seen in the ubiquitous 'chatroom' environments. This same technology has also been responsible for the development of social networking sites and collaboratively-built web-pages, epitomizing the opportunities for interactive working that ICT can offer.
- **The computer as impartial educator**: Ulicsak *et al.* (2001) noted that children often see computers as being 'non-judgemental', and even if judgements were made by the computer, ('that's the wrong answer, try again') they did not see these as negatively as when made by an adult.
- **'Coolness'**: ICT, without doubt, has certain degree of 'street cred' about it. Many students are stimulated by the fast moving and responsive nature of technology, its culture and language, the ability to personalize interfaces, and rapid accessibility to an ever-growing virtual library of online resources.

A NEW PEDAGOGY FOR THE CLASSROOM: *'TECHNOLOGY DOESN'T CHANGE PRACTICE – PEOPLE DO'*
(Loveless *et al.*, 2001: 73)

How can we now consider these attributes in the context of learning and teaching, and their application in the classroom? Loveless *et al.* (2001: 63) pose the question: 'What are teachers for in the Information Society?' This is set within the context of not only re-defining the use of technology in practical terms, but also asks us to examine the intrinsic role that ICT will play in our own understanding of pedagogy. They argue that we have now moved into a phase where a re-evaluation of teaching strategies and how children learn is required. Professor Stephen Heppell (2007) eloquently sums up the very positive impact of technology on today's children, enabling them to help 'make the world a little better', a world in which they can,

HLTA
Standard
28

'compose and perform music without acquiring any ability to play an instrument, shoot, edit stream digital video without any media training ... swap ideas with scientists online about volcanic activity ... follow webcam images of ospreys hatching ... and generally push boundaries of what might be possible ... Little of this was easily achievable in the classroom ten years ago.'

A tool for collaboration

Case study

Jenna and two friends from her Year 8 class, have been working on recording a music video in free time at school. They have been using a piece of music software, which a TA who had enhanced responsibility for ICT had brought to their attention. It enables them create, mix and manage music. Jenna plays the bass-guitar and has been uploading a series of tracks to the software, whilst her friends, who are unable to read music or play an instrument, have been adding vocals (theirs), drum beats and brass (computer-generated). This is a substantial project: they hope to have around 20 minutes of original material available after a month's intensive work. Without realizing it, they have demonstrated learning collaboratively through the active exchange of ideas (Gokhale, 1995) and taken responsibility for their own learning (Totten *et al.*, 1991). ICT used within the collaborative learning context has the potential to move the role of the educator from leader to that of facilitator, or informed guide. The intrinsic qualities of ICT which have also helped to promote the success of this activity are:

HLTA Standards 18, 23, 24, 26 & 28

- Provisionality: it is quick and straightforward to edit work on the screen. The software readily enabled the pupils to change musical elements as well as erase and add tracks as desired.
- The production of high-quality outcomes: the resulting music was professionally presented, with the created audio files possessing the clarity and definition of a purchased CD.

The TA who had supported them with the project considered the key learning points for herself from this activity:

HLTA Standard 12

- The importance of being able to allow pupils to lead and manage their own learning in terms of producing a creative outcome.
- That the learning scenario here would have been very difficult to prepare for using traditional teaching methods, resources and planning.
- The range of skills and attributes necessary to produce the outcome was facilitated through primarily self-directed exploration, play, investigation, evaluation and re-formatting of ideas.
- That her role, as a TA, was primarily here that of a facilitator – any other role adopted may well have interfered with the originality of the outcome.

Stimulating creativity

Case study

Jane, A TA in a secondary school has recently started an after-school computer club, in line with the DfCSF's policy on Extended Schools, and ensuring the availability of ICT for pupils

(Continued)

(Continued)

who have limited or no access to computers at home. Having recently carried out a study on gender and ICT, Jane's class teacher perceived a need for a club which would attract girls; national (ComputerWeekly.com, 2007) and school data indicated that only one-fifth of pupils who eventually took up a career in IT were girls. Jane signed the school up to Computer Clubs for Girls, set up by e-Skills UK, which offered access to a range of resources designed to engage girls in the use of technology. A series of activities, including making animated videos using Plasticine models, and creating digital photographs based on the styles of modern artists produced enthusiastically received results. So successful has the club been that within a term there was actually a waiting list to join it. Jane reflected on the definition of creativity provided by NACCCE, (1999: 28) and considered how she had used technology to encourage the pupils to generate ideas, fashion and refine their thinking, be purposefully motivated, and offer opportunities for genuine originality in their outcomes.

HLTA
Standard
12

Communication

> For most people, technology makes things easier. For people with disabilities, however, technology makes things POSSIBLE. (Radabaugh, 1988)

ICT as a tool to present, publish and communicate ideas is well established in schools, with the technology itself being the motivational factor (Loveless, 2003a). Pupils can readily edit their work, integrate their own designs and formats, add images, print outcomes in colour, or publish to a wider audience using the internet. For pupils with learning difficulties, the inherent qualities of ICT may offer even more opportunities to support learning and teaching.

Case study

Jamilla, a TA working with pupils who have Severe Learning Difficulties in a community special school, developed an interest in using software which could help develop literacy skills. Few of her pupils could write or type independently, but were at the stage of recognizing words by their pattern or initial letter sound. She also identified the need for pupils to be able to record 'on paper' their thoughts, ideas, responses and experiences as independently as possible.

Recognizing the importance of identifying individual pupil's needs, recording skill developments, and the importance of planning for progression (Townsend, 2005), with the support of her class teacher, Jamilla implemented a series of computer-based activities for the pupils. These activities used proprietary software which allowed for the educator to set up word, picture or symbol banks on the screen (In this case the software used was Clicker 5, for more information please visit www.cricksoft.com), which were then selected to create a phrase or

HLTA
Standard
12

HLTA
Standards
22, 23,
24, 25 &
28

sentence within a document. Each task was differentiated to meet individual needs, and offered the potential for developing very specific literacy skills. Several pupils were unable to recognize words and for them Jamilla incorporated digital photographs and Makaton® symbols into their 'word banks'. Stuart Gunn, in Chapter 9 identifies the importance of evaluating and understanding children's preferred learning styles. Taking this into account, Jamilla had also been able to design formats for her activities which reflected her own assessment of how the pupils learn most effectively: she was able to incorporate audio, video and animated features to engage pupils at an individualized level.

Whilst the pupils each had their own individual tasks on the computers, Jamilla recognized the importance of being able to communicate their achievements to the group. She loaded their completed outcomes onto the interactive whiteboard, enabling them, in the plenary sessions, to report to their peers, and indeed adults, with surprisingly positive results: they were able to present their work clearly, and lead others through their presentations.

Jamilla was particularly impressed at the confidence demonstrated by individual pupils when using the IWB. Pimley and Bowen (2006) identify the importance of providing children with learning difficulties with opportunities to exercise choice and control, and report also on the raising of self esteem, supporting Hall and Higgins' (2005) findings that children gained a boost in confidence from work which is shared on the IWB.

HLTA Standard 20

HLTA Standard 1

If we are to embed these pedagogical strands in our thinking and practice, we also need to develop an understanding of the new skills and concepts that will be required to support them (information literacies), a new view of how we construct knowledge, and an analysis of a more complex understanding of pedagogical processes (Mortimore *et al.*, 1999, cited in Loveless, A. and Ellis, V., 2001). What do these mean for the TA? Certainly, the scenarios above provide examples of how technology can be used with originality and offer a real impact on learning.

These qualities may be most effectively examined from a comparative viewpoint. Below is an activity in which examples of 'old' and 'new' pedagogies (the list is by no means exhaustive) are identified, illustrating how our approach to learning and teaching may potentially be evolving in line with the qualities which are offered by ICT.

There is now emerging a new set of learning parameters, or 'literacies' which will equip pupils – and their educators – with the skills to engage with new technology:

- **Technological literacy**: developing the skills for accessing technology.
- **Information literacy**: the ability to gather, organize and evaluate web-based data.
- **Media literacy**: creating and distributing resources which meet the needs of various audiences.
- **Global literacy:** understanding interdependence and collaboration processes offered by the world-wide web.
- **Literacy with responsibility**: social consequences of communicating with an unseen and unknown audience. This would also include the deliberate misuse of technology, particularly in the context of cyber-bullying, accessing unsuitable materials, and breaching academic protocols (such as plagiarism, or pupils 'copying and pasting' large sections of text from the internet into work without necessarily reading and understanding the content).

HLTA
Standards
, 9, 10,
2, 14,
9, 20,
1 & 28

 Activity

Consider the 'old pedagogies' listed below. Has your own practice changed in any of these areas as a result of using ICT? If so, how, and have they had a positive or negative impact on learning for your pupils?

Old pedagogy	New pedagogy
Know as much as there is in the book and as much as a teacher says.	Use strategies to decide what is worth knowing in the head and what needs to be stored: not all information should be learned.
TA uses books, worksheets and notes on paper to pass on his or her knowledge to the pupil.	TA helps pupils access, select, evaluate, organize, and store information coming from a wide range of sources.
Students put information on paper for TA to see.	Student writes directly to the web for parents, family and friends to view.
Books are the main source of knowledge.	The world-wide web is the main source of knowledge.
Learning goals using technology are not integrated or present.	Classroom goals are integrated with the power of technology.
Outcomes are neatly handwritten and look as though they have been produced by children.	Products have a 'professional' appearance, produced using colour and attention to design.
Information is presented to groups through speech, OHPs, pictures.	Presentations use a range of multi-sensory resources, including animations, video, web-pages.
Pupils do their homework on paper or in books. They hand these in to the teacher for marking the following day.	Pupils access their homework folder on the s school's Virtual Learning Environment (VLE). They upload their completed homework tasks to their folders from home. The teacher marks the electronic documents and sends feedback via the VLE.
Pupils obtain information in a linear fashion.	Using the web, pupils become highly skilled at using a hyperlinked, non-linear, dynamic environment.
TAs record their activities with pupils in notebooks. They pass them to the teacher at the end of the lesson.	TAs access their class's assessment folder on the VLE. They enter comments on pupils' progress at the end of the lesson into electronic forms and upload them to the assessment folder.

Adapted, with permission, from Loveless *et al.*, 2001: 80.

How will these be taught or acquired, and what now is the place in the curriculum for the more traditional literacies?

INTEGRATING ATTRIBUTES: DEVELOPING A MODEL FOR THE 'NEW PEDAGOGIES'

An understanding of the individual concepts listed in Table 10.1, and importantly, the potential for making the links between them lie at the heart of effective pedagogical practice using technology. There is still strong evidence, however, to support the view that ICT is not always used as effectively as it might be in the classroom (Ofsted, 2005; Tondeur *et al.*, 2007).

CHANGES AHEAD: WHAT MIGHT THE 'DIGITAL FUTURE' LOOK LIKE, AND HOW CAN WE MANAGE TO KEEP UP WITH THE CHANGES?

> None of us can predict what the world will look like in the future, but one thing is certain: technology will play a major role in its shaping. We can also be certain that those who learn how to harness technology effectively will be the best prepared to meet its challenges. (John and Wheeler, 2008: 129)

Making predictions about the future evolution of technology is always going to be difficult, although mobility and ubiquity are clearly key words underpinning its development. Back in 1962, Marshall McLuhan envisaged technology metaphorically shrinking

Table 10.1

Inherent characteristics of ICT	Attributes of learning and teaching ICT can facilitate	The 'new literacies'	National Curriculum statutory requirements
Speed	Collaboration	Technological	Finding things out.
Capacity	Creativity	information	Developing ideas and
Automaticity	Communication	Media	making things happen.
Communicability	Independence	Global	Exchanging and sharing
Provisionality	Problem-solving	Literacy with	information.
Interactivity	Investigation and	responsibility	
Non-linearity	exploration		Reviewing, modifying
Multi-modality	Motivation and fun		and evaluating work as it
Synchronicity	Differentiation		progresses.
'Coolness'	Personalization		
	Higher order thinking skills		P-Scales for pupils with
	Assessment		Severe and Profound and
			Multiple Learning
			Difficulties.

the world to that of a *global village* in which we have abolished the concepts of *space and time*. Nine years later, Illich (1973), in his polemic against traditional education systems, developed his argument for the establishment of *learning webs*, providing all those with a desire to learn access to resources at any time. He believed that it should be possible for all to be able to share knowledge, and that opportunities should exist for everyone to make public their concerns, issues and arguments. The 'invention' of the internet by Tim Berners-Lee in 1989 has turned these ideas into reality, with the concept of the traditional classroom now being seriously challenged as the most suitable learning environment of the future.

Certainly, all the new technologies are now taking their place in the curriculum, although schools vary tremendously in the rate of their introduction, and use. Indeed, recent research (Sime and Priestley, 2005) indicates that although educators in schools show great interest and motivation to learn about the potential of ICT, in practice, use of ICT can remain focused on a narrow range of applications. The current 'push' towards the use of Virtual Learning Environments is a potentially defining stage in the development of the digital classroom – using such platforms will potentially have a very great impact on our educational use of technology, possibly bringing an end to paper-based learning.

HLTA Standards 20 & 28

For the digital classroom to be a success, it is clear that educators need to have an understanding of both the pedagogy underpinning its use, but they also require a certain level of skill, competence and confidence. A useful tool for identifying levels of skills, and barriers to achievement is provided in this Activity (adapted from Cox *et al.*, 1999 and John and Wheeler, 2008).

Activity

Go to *The positive and negative factors which can influence my use of ICT* in Appendix 1 on p. 209. Identify and reflect upon those factors which can affect the way we perceive the use of ICT. What are the specific skills I need to develop, and also how do I turn the negative factors into positive ones?

HLTA Standards 7, 9, 20 & 28

It is always important to 'keep up' with all developments which impact on practice, but as John and Wheeler (2008) argue, digital technology has a particularly powerful role to play in supporting this objective. Whilst the management of ICT – technology and curriculum – may well be in the hands of teachers and senior managers, TAs are intrinsic to the successful use of technology. They frequently have a real insight into individual pupils' learning needs (which are not just academic), bring with them ideas and innovations from their own experiences and are frequently working with pupils in a focused context (such as when leading intervention strategies for groups of pupils). Given the speed with which technology is moving forward, how can we hope to keep pace? Firstly, it is important to map a pathway for your professional development, and consider these maxims:

- Be inspired and motivated by the potential that even straightforward applications can offer given an imaginative and confident approach to their use.
- Avoid being 'seduced by the technology', and feeling you have to always use the latest software application or gadget (John and Wheeler, 2008).
- If your school cannot afford to buy an application you think would be suitable to support a particular learning scenario, is there a substitute freely downloadable from the internet?
- Share your experiences with others.
- Do not worry that students know more than you – learn from them, and be prepared to play with technology.
- Do not fear failure. An unwillingness to participate in experimentation (therefore increasing the possibility of failure) may stop us from fulfilling our potential with ICT, and, according to Papert (1993), errors allow us to analyse, and learn from our mistakes, fixing what went wrong from an acquired understanding.

 Reflective questions

What might the learning environment of the future look like?

How might my pupils be using technology in five years' time?

Now visit Professor Stephen Heppell's photo-tour of the Thailand Knowledge Park, Bangkok at: http://rubble.heppell.net/heppell/tk_park/default.html. How does this environment compare to your own school, and what are the features here which could promote learning in the 'digital age'?

How might you manage your own learning to meet the requirements of the new learning environments?

The best way to predict the future is to invent it yourself. (Molyneux, 2003)

Further Reading

Heppell, S. (2007) Professor Stephen Heppell's weblog, available online at http://www.heppell.net/weblog/stephen/ (accessed 13 April 2008).

Livingstone, S., Bober, M. and Helsper, E.J. (2005) 'Active Participation or Just More Information? Young People's Take Up of Opportunities to Act and Interact on the Internet', *Information, Communication and Society* 8 (3): 287–314.

Loveless, A. and Ellis, V. (2001) *ICT, Pedagogy and the Curriculum*. Abingdon: RoutledgeFalmer.

Veen, W. and Vrakking, B. (2006) *Homo Zappiens. Growing Up in a Digital Age*. London: Network Continuum Education.

Wheeler, S. (ed.) (2005) *Transforming Primary ICT*. Exeter: Learning Matters.

References

Becta (2004) *A Review of the Research Literature on Barriers to the Uptake of ICT by Teachers*, available online at http://partners.becta.org.uk/upload-dir/downloads/page_documents/research/barriers.pdf (accessed 5 May 2008).

Becta (2007) 'Harnessing Technology: Schools Survey ', available online at http://schools.becta.org.uk/upload-dir/downloads/page_documents/research/harnessing_technology_schools_survey07.pdf (accessed 11 May 2008).

Becta (2008) *Self-review Framework*, available online at http://schools.becta.org.uk/index.php?section=srf (accessed 10 May 2008).

BESA (2007) *Information and Communication Technology in UK State Schools: Summary Report*, available online at http://www.besanet.org.uk/besa/documents/grab/ICT2007_SUM.pdf?item=993&file=1 (accessed 10 May 2008).

Byron, T. (2008*) Safer Children in a Digital World: The Report of the Byron Review, Commissioned and Supported by Officials from the Department for Children, Schools and Families, and the Department for Culture, Media and Sport*, available online at http://www.dcsf.gov.uk/byronreview/pdfs/Final%20Report%20Bookmarked.pdf (accessed 15 May 2008).

Clarke, C. (2003) 'Keynote Speech to KS3 and ICT Conference', London, November.

ComputerWeekly.com. (2007) 'Schools Running IT clubs for girls', available online at http://www.computerweekly.com/Articles/2007/07/19/225659/schools-running-it-clubs-for-girls.htm (accessed 19 May 2008).

Cox, M.J., Preston, C. and Cox, K. (1999) 'What Factors Support or Prevent Teachers from Using ICT in their Classrooms?', paper presented at the British Educational Research Association Annual Conference, University of Sussex at Brighton, 2–5 September.

DfEE (1998) 'Annex B: Initial Teacher Training Curriculum for the Use of Information and Communications Technology in Subject Teaching', available online at http://www.dfes.gov.uk/publications/guidanceonthelaw/4_98/annexb.htm (accessed 12 May 2008).

District Administration (2007) 'The New Literacies', available online at http://www.districtadministration.com/viewarticle.aspx?articleid=1292 (accessed 12 May 2008).

Futurelab (2007) *The Future's Bright, The Future is...*, available online at http://www.futurelab.org.uk/resources/publications_reports_articles/vision_magazine/VISION_Article604 (accessed 12 July 2008).

Gokhale, A. (1995) 'Collaborative learning enhances critical thinking', *Journal of Technology Education* 7(1): 22–30, available online at http://scholar.lib.vt.edu/ejournals/JTE/v7n1/pdf/gokhale.pdf (accessed 23 April 2008).

Hall, I. and Higgins, S. (2005) 'Primary School Pupils' Perceptions of IWBs', *Journal of Computer Assisted Learning* 21: 102–17, available online at www.blackwell-synergy.com (accessed 12 May 2008).

Hardy, C. (2000) *Information and Communications Technology for All*. London: David Fulton.

Heppell, S. (2000) 'Foreword', in N. Gamble and N. Easingwood (eds) *ICT and Literacy*. London and New York: Continuum.

Heppell, S. (2007) Stephen Heppell's weblog (29 January): *'Assessment and New Technology: New Straightjackets or New Opportunities?'*, available online at http://www.heppell.net/weblog/stephen/ (accessed 13 April 2008).

Illich, I. (1973) *De-schooling Society*. London: Penguin.

John, P. and Wheeler, S. (2008) *The Digital Classroom. Harnessing Technology for the Future*. Abingdon: Routledge.

Loveless, A. and Ellis, V. (eds) (2001) *ICT, Pedagogy and the Curriculum*. Abingdon: Routledge Falmer.

Loveless, A., DeVoogd, G. and Bohlin, M. (2001) 'Something Old, Something New...Is Pedagogy Affected by ICT', in A. Loveless and V. Ellis, *ICT, Pedagogy and the Curriculum*. Abingdon: RoutledgeFalmer.

Loveless, A. (2003a) *The Role of ICT*. London: Continuum International Publishing Group Ltd.

Loveless, A. (2003b) 'Creating Spaces in the Primary Curriculum: ICT in Creative Subjects', *The Curriculum Journal* 14 (1): 5–21.

McLuhan, M. (1962) *The Gutenberg Galaxy*. Toronto: University of Toronto Press.

Molyneux, S. (2003) 'Keynote Speech to the Plymouth e-learning Conference', University of Plymouth, November 23.

Mortimore, P. (ed.) (1999) *Understanding Pedagogy and its Impact on Learning*. London: Paul Chapman Publishing.

National Advisory Committee on Creative and Cultural Education (NACCCE) (1999) *'All Our Futures: Creativity, Culture and Education'*, Report to the Secretary of State for Education and Employment and the Secretary of State for Culture, Media and Sport, available online at http://www.cypni.org.uk/downloads/allourfutures.pdf (accessed 9 May 2008).

Ofsted (2005) 'Embedding ICT in Schools. A Dual Evaluation Exercise', available online at http://www.ofsted.gov.uk/assets/4128.pdf (accessed 10 May 2008).

Papert, S. (1993) *Mindstorms: Children, Computers and Powerful Ideas*. New York: Perseus Publishing.

Pimley, L. and Bowen, M. (2006) *Supporting Pupils with ASD*. London: Paul Chapman Publishing.

Prensky, M. (2001) 'Digital Natives, Digital Immigrants', available online at http:// www.marcprensky.com/writing/Prensky%20%20Digital%20Natives,%20Digital%20Immigrants%20-%20Part1.pdf (accessed 12 May 2008).

Radabaugh, M. (1988) cited in 'National Council on Disability (1993) Study on the Financing of Assistive Technology Devices and Services for Individuals with Disabilities', available online at http://www.ncd.gov/newsroom/publications/1993/assistive.htm#6 (accessed 31 January 2008).

Sharp, J., Potter, J., Allen, J. and Loveless, A. (2002) *Achieving QTS. Primary ICT – Knowledge, Understanding and Practice*. Exeter: Learning Matters.

Sime, D. and Priestley, M. (2005) Student Teachers' First Reflections on Information and Communications Technology and Classroom Learning: Implications for Initial Teacher Education, *Journal of Computer Assisted Learning* 21(2): 130–42.

Snyder, I. (2001) 'Hybrid Vigour. Recording the Verbal and the Visual in Electronic Communication', in A. Loveless and V. Ellis (eds) *ICT, Pedagogy and the Curriculum*. Abingdon: RoutledgeFalmer.

Street, B. (1998) 'New Literacies in Theory and Practice: What are the Implications for Language in Education?', *Linguistics and Education* 10(3): 1–24.

Tondeur, J., van Braak, J. and Valcke, M. (2007) 'Curricula and the Use of ICT in Education: Two Worlds Apart?', *British Journal of Educational Technology* 38(6): 962–76.

Totten, S., Sills, T., Digby, A. and Russ, P. (1991) *Cooperative Learning: A Guide to Research*. New York: Garland.

Townsend, M. (2005) 'Meeting Individual Differences: Using ICT to Support Communication Skills for Children with Learning Difficulties', in S. Wheeler (ed.) *Transforming Primary ICT*. Exeter: Learning Matters.

Townsend, M. and Parker, M. (2007) 'Test Driving Turbo-charged Technology: An Evaluation of a Web-based Platform for Tutor Evaluation', *Proceedings of International Conference of Distance Learning (ICODL)*, Athens, pp. 232–7.

Tyrer, R., Gunn, S., Lee, C., Parker, M., Pittman, M. and Townsend, M. (2004) *A Toolkit for the Effective Teaching Assistant*. London: Paul Chapman Publishing.

Ulicsak, M., Daniels, H. and Sharples, M. (2001) '*Raising Awareness in Children of Group Skills using and Expert System*', *Proceedings of World Conference on Artificial Intelligence and Education* (AI-ED 2001) San Antonio, pp. 607–9.

Veen, W. and Vrakking, B. (2006) *Homo Zappiens. Growing Up in a Digital Age*. London: Network Continuum Education.

Useful websites

Support and guidance in the educational use of ICT

Becta Schools: the British Educational Communication and Technology Agency disseminates formal advice on the use the use of ICT in the classroom to all educatiors. This advice ranges from the strategic management of technology, though to the evaluation and use of specific resources.
http://schools.becta.org.uk

Teachernet: Useful ICT guidance for teachers at all Key stages, and includes how ICT can be integrated into the curriculum, examples of good practice, lesson plans and a number of discussion groups.
http: www.teachernet.gov.uk/teachingandlearning/subjects/ict

Curriculum online: Offers advice, guidance and examples of ICT resources which can be purchased online (some resources are free).
http://www.curriculmonline.gov.uk/Default htm

Kidsmart: a practical internet safety programme website for schools, young people, parents, and agencies, produced by the children's internet charity Childnet International.
http://www.kidsmart.org.uk/

Teaching ideas for using ICT in the classroom

KentEd: aims to support both teachers and pupils in the use of ICT across the curriculum by providing pages of resources, lesson ideas and links to 'safe' websites on the internet.
http://www.kented.org.uk/ngfl/index.htm

SUPPORTING THE CURRICULUM

Rachael Hincks

This chapter will:

- Help you to develop and understanding of the term 'curriculum'.
- Examine changes in the curriculum in schools and why it needed to change.
- Give practical case studies relating to supporting learners in the core curriculum.

WHAT IS THE 'CURRICULUM'?

When talking to TAs and other staff in school, there is often an assumption that the curriculum is something which is structured and government driven, in essence being the National Curriculum; however, it is actually much wider than this. As a TA, you will be involved in supporting the curriculum and in delivering the curriculum, so it is important that you have a good understanding of its meaning and implications.

HLTA Standards 13, 14 & 15

Think about the aims that your school has: this may be available as a printed document, perhaps at the beginning of the school's prospectus for parents. Some of the aims might relate to helping children achieve their potential, meeting academic goals, promoting their emotional and spiritual well being and giving them guidance and behavioural boundaries.

Activity

Read your school's Aims document and/or the Mission Statement.

What is your school aiming to do for each child?

What areas of a child's development does your school aim to promote?

Bearing this is mind, what do you believe the term 'curriculum' to mean?

In order to develop a working definition of curriculum, it is important to consider where learning takes place. Learning will happen whenever children are in social situations (Chapter 9), which could apply to the corridors, playground or dining hall, as well as learning, hopefully, taking place in the classroom! Even before the introduction of a National Curriculum, it had been recognized that the curriculum in schools encompasses the wider experiences of pupils which the school plans, some of which may take place outside of school (Stenhouse, 1975; Kerr, 1968). Skilbeck (1984 p. 21) considered the curriculum to be 'the learning experiences of students', and referred to these experiences as being 'expressed or anticipated in educational goals and objectives, plans and designs for learning'. Within each of these definitions, there is a need to look beyond what is planned. Walker (2003 p. 5) divided his definition of curriculum into two parts, considering 'content and purposes'. 'Content' can be viewed as the National Curriculum part, the list of what is to be covered; 'purposes' are the reasons why the content is being taught, for example 'to transmit the culture, to improve society or to realise the potential of individual students'.

In order to decipher what is meant by the term 'curriculum', it is important to consider what it is we are aiming for. If the outcomes of a child's time at school are for them to be successful, we need to consider what a child needs for that to be the case. What do we mean by success? Of course, we wish to prepare children for the world of work or further study, so academic achievement is encouraged; for some pupils the development of social skills or learning how to be independent is paramount. The 'curriculum' in school needs to reflect its aims.

Newby takes a somewhat cynical view when he writes:

> Today's curriculum is disjointed. At primary school, we struggle to reconcile a ... child-centred, progressive curriculum and a National Curriculum emphasising (some would say, fixating upon) literacy and numeracy. In the secondary school, we teach young people an amalgamation of the subjects of a content-based curriculum ... and an instrumental, vocational curriculum focused on the world of work. (2005: 297)

Newby's description of a child-centred, progressive curriculum reflects the need for the school curriculum and its aims to be one and the same. He further emphasizes the issues he has raised when he states 'however the world changes and so must the curriculum'. Many schools now are, successfully, moving towards a much more cross-curricular and holistic approach to the curriculum.

HLTA Standards 13 & 16 We will discuss curriculsm change and the National Curriculum later, but it is important to note here that the curriculum in schools is changing and is being encouraged to change. The National Curriculum was revised again for 2008 and new aims devised, the purpose of which is to embed the outcomes of Every Child Matters (Chapter 8).

The curriculum should enable all young people to become:

- successful learners who enjoy learning, make progress and achieve
- confident individuals who are able to live safe, healthy and fulfilling lives
- responsible citizens who make a positive contribution to society. (QCA, 2008)

In addition to the structure of a National Curriculum, schemes of work in school must take account of individual pupil learning needs, including pupils with SEN and those who are identified as being Gifted or Talented. These individual needs also extend further than purely academic goals, and this is finally being recognized through the new National Curriculum aims. The school curriculum should be inclusive, flexible and based on a framework of values which nurture and encourage the individual.

HLTA Standards 9, 10 & 15

In our discussion of curriculum, we have considered that it is more than just a government directive, more than a written plan, and encompasses all learning opportunities. Indeed, there is a further element to the curriculum, one which is referred to as the 'hidden curriculum'.

Think about the colleagues you work with whom you consider to be good practitioners: what makes them good? A good teacher or TA is able to engage and motivate children, a skill which is often attributed to an individual's personality. A good teacher or TA will use positive body language, speak clearly and calmly, maintain eye contact and be enthusiastic. These unintentional messages are an aspect of the hidden curriculum. Skelton (1997 p. 188) describes the hidden curriculum as 'that set of implicit messages relating to knowledge, values, norms of behaviour and attitudes that learners experience in and through educational processes.'

HLTA Standards 1, 2, 3, 4 & 6

 Activity

Considering our discussion of the curriculum so far, try to write your own definition of the term 'curriculum'.
You might wish to separate this into two parts: the overt curriculum and the hidden curriculum.

CURRICULUM CHANGE

The written curriculum in schools has not always been directed by the government; before 1988 there was no National Curriculum in schools and the choice of subjects taught was decided by the schools themselves, despite schooling up to age 10 having been compulsory since 1880 and up to age 14 since 1918 (the leaving age was again raised several times, until finally to 16 in 1972).

The National Curriculum, introduced in 1998, has undergone two significant cycles of change in the past 20 years; one in 2000 with the addition of overarching aims and inclusion statements, and one in 2008 to align expectations with the outcomes of Every Child Matters (QCA, 2008). The introduction of the National Curriculum was in response to calls for a structure in schools which addressed issues of entitlement for all pupils, with an aim to raise standards and to give accountability (Wyse *et al.*, 2008). Whilst setting out a syllabus for schools to cover, in the 1988 version there was little direction in terms of how each subject was to be delivered, leaving interpretation down to individual schools and individual teachers. This resulted in differences in

HLTA Standards 13 & 16

achievements between similar schools and disagreements about how specific subjects, especially English and Maths, should be taught.

In 1997, the National Literacy Strategy for Primary Schools in England was introduced in response to a number of factors, one of which was the results of the 1995 Key Stage 2 tests, in which only 48% reached the expected Level 4. Though the National Curriculum had already divided English into three parts: Speaking and Listening, Reading and Writing, the National Literacy Strategy went further and subdivided content into three levels: word, sentence and text level. Teachers were given the content to be taught term by term, with directions on how it should be taught in the daily literacy lesson, or 'the literacy hour'.

HLTA Standards 14, 17, 18, 19 & 21

The National Literacy Strategy resulted in a number of changes in classrooms, including the organization of the day, how reading is taught, the use of phonics and how TAs are deployed. You will, no doubt, have felt the significant impact the National Literacy Strategy has had on the role of the TA; for example, many TAs now have a responsibility for the delivery of part of the Literacy Strategy such as Wave 2 and 3 interventions. We will look at the changes to reading later in this chapter.

In September 1996 the then Department for Education and Employment set up the National Numeracy project with an aim to raise standards in Maths. Initially it was purely a research project, but following the response to the National Literacy Strategy, it became an approach to the delivery of Maths, and the National Numeracy Strategy was launched in 1999.

HLTA Standards 13, 14 & 16

The National Literacy and Numeracy Strategies were deemed to be having a positive effect on standards in schools (Ofsted, 2002a, 2002b) so were introduced into Secondary schools in 2001 and core guidance spread into other key subject areas in both phases. These strategies have since been repackaged as the Primary Strategy and the Secondary Strategy to be used across all Key Stages.

The study by Wyse *et al.* (2008) drew some negative conclusions about the increasing governmental control over school curricula since 1988; that whilst there is evidence of some improvement in educational standards achieved by some Primary pupils, there is an overall decline in the quality of Primary education due to the over-emphasis on literacy and numeracy at the expense of other subjects.

HLTA Standards 9 & 10

With the picture in Primary looking somewhat less flexible, perhaps the future for Secondary is getting better; for 2008, the National Curriculum for Key Stages 3 and 4 has been changed in a number of very significant ways (QCA, 2008). The overall aims now relate to the Every Child Matters agenda, with much more concise Programmes of Study allowing for more flexible, personalized, tailored learning. Schools are now able to offer languages at KS3 which might be more relevant to the community or for future careers, e.g. Mandarin, and the KS3 citizenship curriculum will now contain a focus on national identity and diversity in the UK.

Perhaps these revisions allow McFarlane's vision to be able to say 'yes, we may still be covering 10 subject areas, but within each of those subject areas we're only going to cover a small number of big ideas and we're going to cover them in depth' (McFarlane, cited in QCA, 2005). The 2008 National Curriculum changes seem to go some way to address issues raised following the last change in 2000. For example, White (2005 cited in QCA, 2005) believed that:

> the greatest change that's required in the curriculum now is for us to see it as a whole and not as a series of pieces. For too long we've seen it as simply various blocks; various subjects; various chunks, as it were. Now we've got to see it as a whole.

The overarching aims concerning the development of the whole child along with shorter and flexible Programmes of Study should allow for greater cross-curricular amalgamation, but this remains to be seen.

 Activity

How have the changes which have taken place over the years impacted upon your role in the classroom?
Can you identify areas where these changes are still having a significant impact?

There have been major changes in the curriculum across the other parts of the UK. Despite the original National Curriculum of 1988 being intended for England, Wales and Northern Ireland, a Curriculum for Northern Ireland was implemented in 1996 and in 2000 the Welsh Assembly Government took over the National Curriculum for Wales. The Welsh National Curriculum remains broadly similar to that of England, with the exception of Welsh being a compulsory subject as either a first or second language.

Pupils begin school at age four in Northern Ireland, whereas it is generally at age five in the rest of the UK. Pupils in Scotland and Northern Ireland have seven years of Primary education before transfer to Secondary, whereas this is only six years in England and Wales.

One major reason for the curricula to be separate across the nations is language: there needs to be opportunities for pupils to learn English, Welsh, Irish or Gaelic as their first or second language, and to be instructed in other subjects through those languages. It is important to remember that each country has a separate national language and identity as well as being part of the United Kingdom.

Changes within the National Curriculum are often met with negativity because, as discussed in Chapter 3, they are imposed upon schools. Whilst they will have an almost instant impact upon school policy, they may not have an immediate effect on classroom practice. As a TA, you can use your experience and individual knowledge of pupils alongside teachers' expertise to drive and shape changes occurring in the classroom and use curriculum change to improve access and achievement for all.

HLTA Standards 17, 18, 19, 20 & 22

SUPPORTING THE CURRICULUM: LITERACY AND READING

If you are a TA working in the Primary classroom, you are highly likely to be involved in aspects of the delivery of Literacy. Even if you work in a Secondary setting and are not directly involved in English lessons, you will still be involved in helping children to access text through reading, interpretation of meaning and writing.

Reading in Primary schools is now taught through shared, guided and independent reading, rather than the traditional process of hearing individual children read. Listening to individuals reading, though deeply embedded in practice across schools, was seen to be an inefficient use of teachers' time (Ofsted, 1996), so a less time-consuming model of guided reading was introduced. Children are organized into smaller ability groups and are encouraged to develop skills of comprehension and problem-solving by reading aloud or silently by themselves, discussing the story and the author's meaning and by seeking guidance from the teacher when they have exhausted their own strategies. However, the original prescriptive nature of the Literacy Strategy meant that teachers were trying to achieve this in 20 minute sessions with the class only divided into two, with many schools finding this to be impractical (Ashcroft and Lee, 2000). According to Ofsted (2002a) by 2001 some schools chose to take guided reading out of the hour and teach it at another time.

A recent study of guided reading in three classrooms (Fisher, 2008), found little evidence of discussion or evaluation, suggesting that the success of guided reading is dependent on teachers' understanding of its importance and their ability to work together with the children to move it forward. Unfortunately, a study of 51 classrooms by Hurry and Parker (2007) found that most discussions were teacher-driven and that, whilst teachers modelled comprehension skills, they did not enable pupils to generate their own questions.

Whilst it is important to have some teacher-led time, children need to learn to interpret text, to find meaning, and should be encouraged to do this independently and with their peers. The techniques used in guided reading could also be applied across other subjects, Key Stages and text types.

 Activity

These are examples of guided reading in a Primary Literacy lesson and in a Secondary Science lesson:

Example 1

The TA selects a fiction book which meets the class's lesson objectives for that week. She makes sure she is familiar with the story, characters and the development of the plot.

At the beginning of the lesson, the TA introduces the book and the group are invited to discuss what they think the book is about based on the choice of cover, the title and any descriptions on the book. The children are encouraged to make predictions of what might happen during the story.

The children then read the book in silence up to a suitable point where there is a change in the story; an ideal place to ask the question 'what might happen next'. The TA asks the children to discuss the possible scenarios amongst themselves, with little or no direction of the discussion by the TA.

The children are asked to read forward into the book to find out what happened and if their ideas were correct – the TA sets this as a challenge with prizes for the first children to find out and the children who were correct.

Example 2

A class of Year 7 pupils are divided into groups of six or seven in Science.

One group is given a non-fiction book about the planets in our Solar System, whilst the rest of the class are working on other tasks as part of a carousel of activities. This group is asked to read independently about a particular planet, then to discuss the information as a group in order to devise questions that a tourist to that planet might ask before visiting.

This is part of a larger project culminating in a display about Environment, Earth and the Universe.

Consider how you might use guided reading techniques with an individual or group of pupils you work with.

How could you encourage them to use their own skills of problem-solving before seeking help?

How could you help them develop skills of comprehension?

HLTA Standards 18, 21, 29 & 30

As a TA, you might also be involved in specific interventions designed to give support to children with difficulties in literacy. In September 2008, Every Child a Reader was launched nationally, following a three-year pilot where inner-city teachers were given training in Reading Recovery to give intensive support to those children with greatest need in terms of being able to meet age related expectations in reading. Reading Recovery is an early intervention strategy based on the work of Marie Clay (for further information see www.readingrecovery.ac.nz) comprising daily half-hour sessions involving reading, letter recognition and writing. Reading Recovery is usually delivered by teachers, with these teachers also supporting the delivery of literacy interventions such as Early literacy Support (ELS) or Wave 3 by TAs for children whose difficulties are not as great (DCSF, 2008b). Burroughs-Lange and Douëtil (2007 p. 31), in the Institute of Education's report following a two-year study of 500 pupils involved in the pilot, concluded that 'children who received Reading Recovery made 20 months' gain during the year and were comfortably within average levels for their age'.

HLTA Standards 17, 18, 19, 29 & 30

SUPPORTING THE CURRICULUM: CREATIVITY

The word 'creativity' is used in education circles all the time, but what do we actually mean? A report for the DFCS (then DfEE, 1999) by the National Advisory Committee for Creative and Cultural Education (NACCCE) was commissioned to make recommendations about the creative and cultural development of children, to analyse (then) current practice and to suggest future changes. In addition to changes to the National Curriculum (addressed in 2000), the report made recommendations to schools, which included the need for schools to promote the creative development of pupils, to make provision for creativity in both the formal and informal curriculum, to improve teachers' expertise in this area and to give a greater emphasis to formative assessment to improve the quality of teaching and learning (NACCCE, 1999). They defined creativity as 'imaginative activity fashioned so as to produce outcomes that are both original and of value' and discussed the propositions that creativity can be taught and that it can be achieved by everyone. Whilst it recognizes the importance of creativity in arts-based subject and that there is a case for specialized work and specialist support in some areas, creativity also spans all areas of the curriculum and it is this wider ethos that schools should seek to embrace.

Following this report, in 2002 the DfES funded the Creative Partnerships project, 'designed to develop the skills of young people across England, raising their aspirations and achievements, and opening up more opportunities for their futures' (Arts Council England, 2008). A teaching and learning initiative across over 30 areas in England, the project continues to be funded into 2009 and beyond, following a successful programme of collaboration, research and development between specialists, schools and young people.

In 2003 the QCA conducted a three-year project, Creativity: Find it! Promote it!, investigating how teachers can implement creativity in the classroom across Key Stages 1–3. They discovered that 'promoting pupils' creativity can improve pupils' self-esteem, motivation and achievement; develop skills for adult life and develop the talent of the individual'. The QCA materials feature within a key strand of Creativity explicitly discussed within Excellence and Enjoyment – A Strategy for Primary Schools (DfES, 2003), part of the recently revised Primary Strategy.

In the 10 years or so since the original NACCCE report, the government has placed creativity at the heart of the Primary and Early Years curriculum; with Creative Development being one of the six areas of learning in the Early Years Foundation Stage (EYFS) framework (see DCSF, 2008a). In Secondary settings, formative assessment, an important tool for the development of creativity, is recognized as being a key factor in successful and dynamic teaching and learning (discussed later in this chapter).

These documents state the need for pupil creativity to be developed, thus creative approaches to teaching and learning must be needed; can one exist without the other? In order to harness creativity in our pupils, we must first recognize what creativity is and be able to teach the finer points of creativity to these pupils, ourselves demonstrating a creative approach. This, perhaps, leads to a definition of creative learning, discussed by the National College of School Leadership:

> Creative learning is much more than an allocation of more time for humanities and the arts. At the heart of these successful schools lies a culture of creativity that can best be described by a combination of relationships, organisation, teaching and learning. (NCSL, 2003: 3)

Spendlove and Wyse (2005: 8) linked the notion of creative learning to a creative act, exploring a definition as 'creative learning is learning which leads to new or original thinking which is accepted by appropriate observers as being of value'. Craft *et al.* (2006) give emphasis to the development of new knowledge giving rise to tangible outcomes, whilst Spendlove and Wyse (2007 p. 26) place an emphasis on thought based on 'the belief that all creative learning requires a distinct process of thought'. Wherever the emphasis is placed, creative learning as a whole is both explicit and implicit within frameworks for teaching and learning in schools.

What are the implications for you as a TA? Creativity is more than just the arts; it is concerned with how we approach teaching and how we encourage children to approach learning. Think about the work you do with pupils: how could you improve your practice in order to encourage creativity in those pupils? In a Research Associate report published by the NCSL, Burgess (2007) identified six key messages for those wishing to embrace creativity, one of which was *child-centredness*. He concluded that each of his research schools had 'celebrated the centrality of the child in encouraging teachers to develop each child's confidence, self-discipline and understanding of their learning and make learning vivid, real and meaningful with many first-hand experiences' (Burgess, 2007: 19).

HLTA
Standard
7

 Activity

Consider a lesson that you support pupils in regularly and where you feel you know the subject well.
How could you develop pupils' creativity in this lesson?

Here are some ideas:

- Encourage the children to make up their own questions.
- Ask them to think of as many ways as possible to reach an answer.
- You could start off a story and then take turns with the pupil(s) to decide what happens next.

SUPPORTING THE CURRICULUM: FORMATIVE ASSESSMENT

Often, the word 'assessment' conjures up images of examination halls and rows of frightened looking teenagers. Whilst some methods of assessment involve exams, this is not all there is to it. There are essentially two modes of assessment: summative and formative. Summative assessment is the end of topic, term, year or course examinations or tests, whilst formative assessment is continuous assessment throughout the period of study. Summative assessment is sometimes criticized as only providing a snapshot of pupils' ability in an area, whereas it should have an important function for setting goals and understanding where a pupil needs to improve. In essence, summative assessments need to be used *formatively*; they need to inform the next stage of learning.

Black and William (1998) studied the results of nine years of international research into assessment in schools and identified five key factors for improving learning through assessment:

1. Providing effective feedback to pupils.
2. Actively involving pupils in their own learning.
3. Adjusting teaching to take account of the results of assessment.
4. Recognizing the profound influence assessment has on the motivation and self-esteem of pupils, both of which are crucial to learning.
5. Considering the need for pupils to be able to assess themselves and to understand how to improve.

In order for pupils to progress, they need to understand where they are at in terms of their own learning, where they need to go and how they can get there. Teaching needs to be flexible and appropriate; teachers and TAs need to be reflective and adaptable. Clear communication between teachers, TAs and pupils will ensure that assessments are interpreted correctly and are more likely to lead to successful outcomes.

 Activity

What formative assessment methods have you used or seen employed in the classroom?

HLTA Standards 22, 23, 24 & 25

You will probably have suggested methods such as questions and answers, discussion, marking, praise and feedback; however, often these are heavily teacher-led. It is important to consider strategies where children are in control of their own learning and assessing their own work, for example via self or peer-assessment techniques. We will discuss the effective use of questioning later in the chapter.

Assessment for Learning, or AfL, is a government-driven initiative embedded in the Primary and Secondary National Strategies, giving 10 principles of using assessment effectively in the classroom (Assessment Reform Group, 2002). They focus mainly on formative assessment and its use in ensuring pupils understand where they are at and where thay are going. One of the principles states: 'assessment for learning should recognise the full range of achievements of all learners'. As a TA, for some pupils you are going to be the person that notices all of their achievements, no matter how small. This is an integral part of AfL, as without recognition and praise, there is little to motivate learners.

 Activity

The following two examples show self and peer assessment activities in the classroom.

Example 1

In a mixed ability Primary classroom, some pupils are afraid to put their hands up to answer questions for fear of getting the answer wrong. Whilst the teacher works on strategies to resolve this, they need a technique which can be implemented straightaway to be able to assess individual pupils' understanding in lessons. The teacher employs a 'traffic lights' system: each pupil is issued with a red card, a yellow card and a green card.

It is explained to the whole class that these are to be used to indicate levels of understanding: if a child feels confident they place a green card on their desk, if they understand some but not all parts the card is yellow, and if they are struggling they use the red card. The teacher also plans opportunities for children to hold up cards during some plenary sessions.

One child commented, 'I like the red cards as I don't like putting my hand up even if I'm stuck'.

Example 2

In a high ability Year 9 English lesson, the pupils are working in groups to prepare a debate on a subject of their own choice. Each group is divided into two to form the 'for' and the 'against' cases.

Before the planning begins, the teacher gathers the class together to discuss what a good debate is and what features each argument needs. The pupils then decide on the most important features and set these as criteria for assessment.

In a later lesson, each team presents their debate to the rest of the class. The groups not debating then use the criteria decided by the whole class to assess the debating group's work and to give them feedback. Each group is assessed in this way.

Suggest ways in which you could incorporate self or peer assessment methods into your work with pupils, perhaps in a specific subject area.

This could also apply outside of National Curriculum subjects, perhaps to help pupils recognize strengths or weaknesses elsewhere.

> HLTA
> Standard
> 24

Personalized learning, tailoring the learning experience to meet the needs of all pupils as individuals, is an intrinsic part of the principles of AfL and has direct links with Every Child Matters; when we consider that in order for every child to achieve each of the five ECM outcomes then their curriculum must be flexible and individualized. Under ECM, schools have increasing responsibility to get this right, hence there is a drive for personalized learning which goes beyond differentiation and beyond individual school subjects.

> HLTA
> Standard
> 9

Smith (2007) identified five key areas for successful personalised learning:

- Assessment that gives a broad picture of whole-school and whole-subject issues as well as data on individual progress that can be used to develop sharper personal targets.
- Teaching and learning that raises standards for everyone.
- A curriculum that gives every child their full entitlement as well as wider choices through the enriching activities of an extended school day.
- Organizing the school so that all children's needs are catered for, including those whose needs are complex and difficult to meet.
- Choices and opportunities both inside and beyond the classroom that will creatively support a diverse range of needs.

These principles rely upon a whole-school drive for the same goal, involving all staff including you, the TA. Sebba *et al.* (2007) recognized that schools use reorganization and effective deployment of support staff, including TAs and Learning Mentors, as a response to personalized learning, to provide flexible support for specific groups of pupils. There may already be many strategies in place in your school which, when joined together, allow pupils to have a flexible curriculum. However, this involves good communication, collaborative working in its truest sense and early recognition and intervention with those pupils with the greatest needs or those who are likely to be 'missed'. Personalized learning should enable pupils to meet their individual potential while also catering for their interests and aptitudes (Hopkins, 2006).

HLTA
Standards
6 & 9

 Activity

Reflect upon your role; in which area(s) of your role are you facilitating personalized learning for identified pupils?

Can you identify any areas for improvement with regards to providing personalized learning for all pupils?

Which areas are school wide and which are things you could improve as part of your own role?

SUPPORTING THE CURRICULUM: QUESTIONING

As we discussed earlier, good teachers and TAs are able to inspire and motivate pupils. How do they do this? One way is to prompt pupils, but also to empower them and enable them to ask and answer their own questions, both as a method of formative assessment, discussed earlier, and as a method to raise self esteem.

There are many ways to use questions: teacher questions, pupil questions, dealing with misconceptions, encouraging participation without fear of 'getting it wrong', as well as developing higher order skills such as analysis and evaluation. As a TA, you will come across pupils who are reluctant to ask or answer questions, who need to be encouraged to try and to see the benefit that this can have.

HLTA
Standards
14, 17,
18, 19,
24 & 29

Activity

Consider a subject area you are regularly involved in:

- How often do you ask pupils questions?
- How often do you encourage pupils to ask their own questions, perhaps in order to answer a bigger question?
- How could you create opportunities to develop these skills further, both for the pupils and for yourself?

In 1956, Benjamin Bloom, an American psychologist, proposed that there are a number of intellectual levels necessary for learning. These levels ascend in a hierarchy and can be linked to the development of cognitive skills through questioning:

Knowledge → Comprehension → Application → Analysis → Synthesis → Evaluation

For example, the most basic level is Knowledge, the simple recalling of previously learned facts. These questions are often referred to as low-level questions and often only have one 'right' answer. Examples would be questions that start with *how many* or *name*.

Comprehension questions are frequently asked in classrooms and might start with the words *why or how*. Questions of Application ask the pupil to use previous knowledge to find the answer, for example, 'if you repeated … what would you change?'

Analysis, Synthesis and Evaluation are higher-order skills and will have several possible answers. These are perhaps the more difficult questions to use in the classroom, as they will probably require some planning to make sure each level of question is considered. For example, questions of Analysis ask the pupil to look at the information and seek out patterns, using words like *compare* or *contrast*. Synthesis questions move the pupil on further by asking them to consider the next step, using words such as *plan*, *design* or *rearrange*. The final level in Bloom's taxonomy is Evaluation, asking pupils to think about what they have done, what they might change, to assess the effectiveness of something or to justify choices. Other words to use here might be *judge, recommend* or *debate*. Chapter 9 also explores Blooms Taxonomy, but in the context of understanding how learning occurs and at what depth.

It is not simply the case that higher-order skills are developed as a child gets older; all children should be encouraged to ask and answer questions of each type at each Key Stage.

 Activity

Look up Bloom's Taxonomy.
  Using these ideas, plan the questions you might ask in your subject area. Also, consider how you can help the pupils you work with to devise their own questions at each level of Bloom's Taxonomy.

HLTA Standards 14, 17, 18, 24 & 29

For questioning to be successful in the classroom, there needs to be a climate of support and safety. For example, having a range of methods for pupils to indicate when they wish to ask or answer a question, rather than only hands up, will help them to understand that they need to take turns and to listen without being scared to stand out. Also, praise must be used regularly but in a meaningful way; children will recognize when they are being patronized or being praised falsely.

THE ROLE OF THE TA IN THE CURRICULUM

Having read this chapter, you will be aware that your role in the curriculum is more than just concerned with any direct teaching or preparation of materials. You are integral to both the overt and the hidden curriculum, giving children cues about expectations, behaviour and relationships and helping them to a positive attitude to learning. You will be involved in helping pupils to set and achieve their own goals and successes, from using subtle methods of assessment and praise, such as positive body language and phrases like 'well done', to asking higher order questions enabling pupils to assess and evaluate their own performance. When reflecting upon your role and the work that you do with children, it is important to remember that the curriculum is more that what is explicitly planned or stated (Ross, 2000) and that it involves all of the learning experiences the pupil encounters throughout the day.

HLTA
Standards
1, 2, 7,
22 & 23

 Reflective questions

- What would you consider your specific role to be within supporting the curriculum?
- Can you give examples of the hidden curriculum within your classroom?
- Where are, or could, pupils be given opportunities to identify the stage they are at and set targets for future work?

Further Reading

Drury, R. (2007) *Young Billingual Learners at Home and School – Researching Multilingual Voices.* Stoke-on-Trent: Trentham Books.

Hastings, S. (2003) 'Questioning', *The Times Educational Supplement*, 4 July, available online at http://www.tes.co.uk.

Hayes, D. (ed.) (2007) *Joyful Teaching and Learning in the Primary School.* Exeter: Learning Matters.

Le Métais, J., Andrews, R., Johnson, R. and Spielhofer, T. (2001) *School Curriculum Differences across the UK*, available online at http://www.leeds.ac.uk/educol/documents/00003560.htm

Learning and Teaching Scotland (2008) *5–14 Curriculum*, available online at http://www.ltscotland.org.uk/5to14/index.asp

Northern Ireland Curriculum (2008), available online at http://www.nicurriculum.org.uk/

Ofsted (2003) *The National Literacy and Numeracy Strategies and the Primary Curriculum.* London: Ofsted.

Rose, J. (2006) *Independent Review of the Teaching of Early Reading*, available online at http://www.standards.dfes.gov.uk/rosereview

Welsh Assembly Government Department for Education, Lifelong Learning and Skills (2008) *School Curriculum*, available online at http://old.accac.org.uk/index_eng.php

References

Arts Council England (2008) Creative Partnerships, available online at http://www.creative-partnerships.com/aboutcp/

Ashcroft, K. and Lee, J. (eds) (2000) *Improving Teaching and Learning in the Core Curriculum.* London: Falmer Press.

Assessment Reform Group (2002) *Assessment for Learning: 10 Principles,* available online at http://www.qca.org.uk

Black, P. and William, D. (1998) *Inside the Black Box: Raising Standards through Classroom Assessment.* London: King's College.

Bloom, B.S. (1956) *Taxonomy of Educational Objectives, the Classification of Educational Goals – Handbook I: Cognitive Domain.* New York: McKay.

Burgess, T. (2007) *Lifting the Lid on the Creative Curriculum,* available online at http://www.ncsl.org.uk/media-762-d9-lifting-the-lid-on-the-creative-curriculum.pdf

Burroughs-Lange, S. and Douëtil, J. (2007) 'Literacy Progress of Young Children from Poor Urban Settings: A Reading Recovery Comparison Study, *Literacy Teaching and Learning* 12(1):19–46.

Craft, A., Burnard, P., Grainger, T. and Chapell, K. (2006) *Progression in Creative Learning: Final report,* available online at http://www.creative-partnerships.com/content/researchAndEvaluation Projects/139847/?version=1

DCSF (2008a) *Early Years Foundation Stage Framework,* available online at http://www.standards.dfes.gov.uk/primaryframework/foundation/

DCSF (2008b) *Every Child a Reader Toolkit.* London: DCSF.

DfEE (1999) *National Numeracy Strategy Framework for Teaching.* London: DfEE.

DfES (2003) *Excellence and Enjoyment – A Strategy for Primary Schools.* Nottingham: DfES.

Fisher, A. (2008) 'Teaching Comprehension and Critical Literacy: Investigating Guided Reading in Three Primary Classrooms', *Literacy* 42(1): 19.

Hopkins, D. (2006) *Every School a Great School: Meeting the Challenge of Large Scale, Long Term Educational Reform,* available online at http://www.ssat-inet.net/pdf/DH_1chap.pdf

Hurry, J. and Parker, M. (2007) 'Teachers' Use of Questioning and Modelling Comprehension Skills in Primary Classrooms', Educational Review 59(3): 229–314.

Kerr, J.F. (ed.) (1968) *Changing the Curriculam.* London: University of London Press.

NACCCE (1999) *All Our Futures: Creativity, Culture and Education.* London: DFEE.

NCSL (2003) *Primary Curriculam and Creativity: NCSL Leading Edge Seminar 2003,* available online at http://www.ncsl.org.uk/media-F7B-99-randd-primary-creativity-03.pdf

Newby, M. (2005) 'A Curriculum for 2020', *Journal of Education for Teaching* 31(4): 297–300.

Ofsted (1996) *The Teaching of Reading in 45 Inner London Primary Schools.* London: HMSO.

Ofsted (2002a) *The National Literacy Strategy: The First Four Years 1998–2002.* London: Ofsted.

Ofsted (2002b) *The National Numeracy Strategy: The First Three Years 1999–2002.* London: Ofsted.

QCA (2003) *Creativity, Find It! Promote It!* available online at http://curriculum.qca.org.uk

QCA (2005) *Why Should the Curriculum Change?*, available online at http://www.qca.org.uk/qca_6085. aspx

QCA (2008) *National Curriculum,* available online at http://curriculum.qca.org.uk

Ross, A. (2000) *Curriculum: Construction and Critique.* London: Falmer Press.

Sebba, J., Brown, N., Steward, S., Galton, M. and James, M. (2007) *An Investigation of Personalised Learning Approaches Used by Schools.* Nottingham: DfES.

Skelton, A. (1997) 'Studying Hidden Curricula: Developing a Perspective in the Light of Postmodern Insights', *Curriculum Studies* 5: 177–93.

Skilbeck, M. (1984) *School-based Curriculum Development*. London: Harper and Row.

Smith, R. (2007) *What's New about Personalised Learning?*, available online at http://www.teaching expertise.com/articles/whats-new-about-personalised-learning-2232

Spendlove, D. and Wyse, D. (2005) 'Definitions and Barriers: Teachers' Perceptions of Creative Learning', presented at *International Symposium Documenting Creative Learning: What, How and Why?* University of Cambridge, April 2005.

Spendlove, D. and Wyse, D. (2007) 'Creative Learning: Definitions and Barriers' in A. Craft., T. Cremin and P. Burnard (2007) *Creative Learning 3–11 and How We Document It: What, How & Why?* Stoke-on-Trent: Trentham Books.

Stenhouse (1975) *An Introduction to Curriculum Research and Development*. London: Heinemann.

Walker, D.F. (2003) 'Curriculum Work', in N. Silverman and L. Hawver (eds) *Fundamentals of Curriculum: Passion and Professionalism*. New Jersey: Lawrence Erlbaum Associates.

Wyse, D., McCreery, E. and Torrance, H. (2008) *The Primary Review Research Survey 3/2: The Trajectory and Impact of National Reform: Curriculum and Assessment in English Primary Schools*, available online at http://www.primaryreview.org.uk

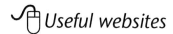 Useful websites

National Strategies
http://nationalstrategies.standards.dcsf.gov.uk

Personalised Learning
http://www.standards.dfes.gov.uk/personalisedlearning/

APPENDIX 1
PHOTOCOPIABLE ACTIVITES

LEADERSHIP TRAIT CHECKLIST

(see Activity, Chapter 2, p. 29)

Use the following checklist to identify skills you possess that could be shared:		
	True	False
I am highly organized.		
I can play a musical instrument/sing.		
I feel confident about using computers.		
I have a flair for art and display.		
I enjoy planning events such as concerts and information evenings.		
I am an effective listener.		
I have a lot of experience of working, with children with learning difficulties.		
Parents/carers often come to me for support or guidance.		
I get a lot of pleasure from books and reading.		
I feel confident in front of large groups.		
I know some strategies for dealing with unacceptable behaviour.		
I am patient.		
I prefer to be outdoors.		
I am fit and take part in sporting activities regularly.		

PRIORITIZATION GRID

(see Activity, Chapter 2, p. 33)

High Importance

Low Urgency   High Urgency

Low Importance

Make a list of the things you need to do. Give each task a number, then place each number inside a square. Those that appear in the top right hand square are of the highest priority.

ACTION PLANNING TEMPLATE

(see Activity, Chapter 2, p. 33)
Project Leader .... **School and role** .... **Date** ....

Area for Implementation	Main steps	Timescale/Personnel	Resource	Monitoring and Evaluation

SWOT ANALYSIS GRID

(see Activity, Chapter 3, p. 50)

Strengths	Weaknesses
Opportunities	**Threats**

COLLABORATIVE TEAMWORK ACTIVITY: ACTIVE SYSTEMS OF INFORMATION

(see Activity, Chapter 4, p. 56)

Use the categories listed in the first activity column, as a guide for considering what active systems of information you, as a TA or HLTA, need to be effective in your role.

Identify what systems already exist for providing you with information and consider ways to further develop active information sources in your work setting.

Teaching colleagues could also do this exercise and information could then be pooled and discussed.

This activity will help you to evaluate what information you need to carry out your role effectively and could also give senior managers and teachers the opportunity to evaluate the usefulness of current information systems.

INFORMATION REQUIRED	SYSTEMS THAT ALREADY EXIST	WAYS TO FURTHER DEVELOP ACTIVE INFORMATION SOURCES
Whole-school information		
Classroom information		
Key Stage information		
Department information		
Individual pupil information		
Other information		

COLLABORATIVE TEAMWORK ACTIVITY: TEAMWORK PROCESSES

(see Activity, Chapter 4, p. 59)

With a teaching colleague, discuss how the processes of teamwork are used in your classroom or departmental context.

Firstly consider examples of where your partnership has involved:

- liaison

- cooperation

- coordination

- collaboration

Secondly, identify any difficulties that have arisen in developing, maintaining or extending collaboration in your classroom or department and consider how these difficulties might be overcome in the future?

Difficulties experienced in developing, maintaining or extending collaborative practice.	Suggestions for overcoming these barriers collaborative practice.

COLLABORATIVE TEAMWORK ACTIVITY: ON THE SPOT DIFFERENTIATION

(see Activity, Chapter 4, p. 61)

Make a list of the 'on the spot strategies' which you use, for enabling pupils to be successful with their school activities.

Discuss and compare your ideas with the strategies used by other TAs and teachers in your school.

Consider the general examples of strategies that both TAs and teachers might use to promote learning and add your own examples to the grid below.

Create a bank of strategies which you and other colleagues could find useful when working with different pupils.

'On the spot' strategy	General example	Own example
Simplify the language used to describe a task or activity.	'Where the worksheet says ... we are going to find out ...'	
Explain words that a pupil is finding hard to understand.	Encourage older pupils to seek meaning using a dictionary.	
Focus a pupil onto one or two aspects of a worksheet or task, so that the amount of work is not overwhelming.	'You are going to work on ... ' or put post-it paper over the questions to be done so the child pulls them off and attends to those identified.	
Highlight key instructions or questions.	Use a highlighter pen to identify key words, instructions or questions.	

Use drawing or tracing to establish successful engagement in an activity.	If a pupil is good at drawing or tracing encourage the pupil to illustrate the answer first then write once some successful engagement in the work has been established.	
Help a pupil to organize his/her thinking prior to recording the information.	Using a set of symbols/pictures/or key words to encourage a pupil to sequence or order his/her thoughts before recording, or use mind maps.	
Using concrete materials to illustrate a task or concept.	Use 3D materials rather than 2D.	
Use a pupil's own interest area to illustrate a concept.	If child likes soccer explain a concept in terms of a football team, etc.	
Give a pupil some choice and ownership over the way he/she approaches their work.	'We could do this worksheet this way ... or this way ... what do you think would be best?'	
Use a recorder to establish spoken ideas or a computer to record the information.	Record suggested answers on a recorder and transcribe answers by writing or word processing.	
Other strategies used in your work context.	Use the internet to research a subject. Use software relevant to the topic.	

COLLABORATIVE TEAMWORK ACTIVITY: PERFORMING AS A TEAM

(see Activity, Chapter 4, p. 67)

Use this activity in either or both of the ways suggested below.

(a) (i)   Use this chart to reflect together as a team and consider where Tuckman's developmental stages have occurred or are occurring in the team you currently work within.

   (ii)   If our goal as a team is 'performing' then what can a team do to move more quickly to this stage?

OR

(b) (i)   Use this activity to consider the pupil groupings you work with and identify the relationship process you are going through with this small group.

   (ii)   What could you do to further the development of a 'performing' group?

Tuckman Stage	Observations which indicate this stage	Strategy for supporting progression to the next stage
Forming		
Storming		
Norming		
Performing		
Mourning		

RANK ORDER SHEET

(see Activity, Chapter 7, p. 108)

Statements	Code	Rank order
1. Pupils' inner emotions must always be considered legitimate and valid by a TA.	T	
2. TAs need to realize that, as well as the effect on pupils they have, pupils are also greatly influenced by their own families, the neighbourhoods where they live, their peers and television.	S	
3. No matter how limited the pupils' opportunities may be, TAs should give pupils responsibility to make choices and decisions.	C	
4. If pupils think that a classroom rule is unjust and should be changed but the TA disagrees, both the pupils and the TA should jointly decide on a replacement rule.	C	
5. If a pupil interrupts the lesson by talking to a neighbour, the TA should tell that pupil involved how upset they feel and discuss with them how they would feel if they were being interrupted.	T	
6. A good TA may discuss several alternative disciplinary actions when a pupil breaks a school rule.	C	
7. TAs should announce the class/group rules and inform pupils how the rules will be fairly enforced.	S	
8. TAs should nurture the pupil's creativity and self-expression as much as possible.	T	
9. TAs should be firm but fair in taking disciplinary actions with a pupil who violates a school rule.	S	

BARRIERS TO LEARNING

(See Activity, Chapter 8, p. 124)

Access to the curriculum	Access to the building, classroom, equipment
Level of work	Steps, ramps, lift, etc.
Suitability of task, e.g. age appropriate, layout/size/clarity of text	Suitability and user-friendliness of equipment
Teaching and learning methods used	
Attitudes	**Awareness**
Staff	Staff
Pupils	Pupils
Parents/carers	Parents/carers

BARRIERS TO LEARNING: EXAMPLE

(See Activity, Chapter 8, p. 124)
Example for Asha, Y7 girl

Access to the curriculum	Access to the building, classroom, equipment
Level of work	Steps, ramps, lift, etc.
Asha is working at a level well above average for her age. She is given extension work in Maths, Technology and ICT, but not in other subjects	N/A
Suitability of task, e.g. age appropriate, layout/size/clarity of text	
Often Asha is given work from an older age group, which is not always relevant to her interests and needs.	Suitability and user-friendliness of equipment
Teaching and learning methods used Asha is often left to her own devices, using worksheets. She becomes bored easily and is often off task.	N/A
Attitudes	**Awareness**
Staff	**Staff**
Some staff view Asha as being disruptive, she is often given detentions for poor behaviour	Not all staff aware of her ability/not planning with this in mind
Pupils	**Pupils**
	N/A
Parents/carers	**Parents/carers**
	Asha's parents are aware of her abilities and of her behaviour issues

CREATING A PERSONAL FRAMEWORK OF LEARNING AND TEACHING

(See Chapter 9, p. 156)

I believe that ...	Agree	Disagree	Comments
Most pupils come to school with some reluctance.			
Most learners can succeed with good teaching.			
My teaching is always rewarding and interesting for all pupils.			
Learners can be divided into two groups: those who 'want to get on' and those who 'want to get away with as little as possible'.			
All pupils can be motivated by effective teaching.			
Every learner works best with plenty of individually-given praise and positive reinforcement.			
Learners are reluctant to learn unless firmly directed.			
Most pupils like an orderly, well-managed work environment.			
More able pupils are difficult to manage.			
It is only natural for pupils to want to do as little as possible.			
Behaviour always has a reason.			
'What's in it for me?' is a reasonable question for learners to pose.			

(Continued)

I believe that ...	Agree	Disagree	Comments
On the whole, if learners fail to learn it is the fault of the teacher, the school, the curriculum, or poor resourcing.			
Over time, most learners maximize their potential.			
What learners want and what teachers want are different, therefore they will never see eye to eye about work rate and quality.			
Most pupils don't like their work to be appraised.			
Work of a low standard should be stongly criticized.			
Teachers should be prepared to put their foot down if necessary, even at the risk of unpopularity.			
If a pupil who doesn't listen the first time gets additional help, it encourages inattention amongst others.			
Staff should go out of their way to behave positively towards pupils who they know do not like work.			
The subject I support and teach demands 'natural flair': either you have it, or you haven't.			
Pupils should be threatened with punishment if they do not work.			
Learners nearly always accept constructive criticism, as they realize that it helps them improve.			
Pupils welcome work if they are given a chance to succeed.			

This form can be photocopied. © *A Toolkit for the Effective Teaching* Assistant 2009. Questionnaire adapted from McGregor (1982).

THE IMPACT OF ICT

(See Activity, Chapter 10, p. 160)

Consider how the evolving use of ICT has impacted, firstly on your school, secondly, on your pupils, and thirdly, on your own role as a TA. Discuss this also with your ICT coordinator and other colleagues.		
Impact on the school	**Impact on pupils**	**Impact on my role**

THE POSITIVE AND NEGATIVE FACTORS WHICH CAN INFLUENCE MY USE OF ICT

(See Activity, Chapter 10, p. 172)

Identify and reflect upon those factors which can affect the way we perceive the use of ICT. What are the specific skills I need to develop, and how do to turn the negative factors into positive ones?	
Positive factors	**What specific skills do I need to develop in these areas?**
Will make my work with pupils more interesting for pupils.	
Will make my lessons more diverse.	
Will enable me to help differentiate my lessons.	
Will help me to be more creative in my work.	
Will make lessons more fun.	
Will give me more confidence in my work.	
Will improve my presentation materials for lessons.	
Will help me with my administrative tasks.	
Will enhance my career prospects.	
Negative factors	**What can I do about these, and who can help me?**
Makes preparation for lessons more difficult.	
Impairs pupils' learning.	
A lack of confidence in the use of ICT.	
Takes up too much time.	
Is counter-productive due to insufficient technical resources	

Source: adapted from Cox *et al.*, 2000; John and Wheeler, 2008.

APPENDIX 2
HLTA STANDARDS

PROFESSIONAL ATTRIBUTES

Those awarded HLTA status must demonstrate, through their practice, that they:

(1) have high expectations of children and young people with a commitment to helping them fulfil their potential

(2) establish fair, respectful, trusting, supportive and constructive relationships with children and young people

(3) demonstrate the positive values, attitudes and behaviour they expect from children and young people

(4) communicate effectively and sensitively with children, young people, colleagues, parents and carers

(5) recognize and respect the contribution that parents and carers can make to the development and well being of children and young people

(6) demonstrate a commitment to collaborative and cooperative working with colleagues

(7) improve their own knowledge and practice including responding to advice and feedback.

PROFESSIONAL KNOWLEDGE AND UNDERSTANDING

Those awarded HLTA status must demonstrate, through their practice, that they:

(8) understand the key factors that affect children and young people's learning and progress

(9) know how to contribute to effective personalized provision by taking practical account of diversity

(10) have sufficient understanding of their area(s) of expertise to support the development, learning and progress of children and young people

(11) have achieved a nationally recognized qualification at level 2 or above in English/literacy and Mathematics/numeracy

(12) know how to use ICT to support their professional activities

(13) know how statutory and non-statutory frameworks for the school curriculum relate to the age and ability ranges of the learners they support

(14) understand the objectives, content and intended outcomes for the learning activities in which they are involved

(15) know how to support learners in accessing the curriculum in accordance with the special educational needs (SEN) code of practice and disabilities legislation

(16) know how other frameworks, that support the development and well being of children and young people, impact upon their practice.

PROFESSIONAL SKILLS

Teaching and learning activities must take place under the direction of a teacher and in accordance with arrangements made by the headteacher of the school.

PLANNING AND EXPECTATIONS

Those awarded HLTA status must demonstrate, through their practice, that they:

(17) use their area(s) of expertise to contribute to the planning and preparation of learning activities

(18) use their area(s) of expertise to plan their role in learning activities

(19) devise clearly structured activities that interest and motivate learners and advance their learning

(20) plan how they will support the inclusion of the children and young people in the learning activities

(21) contribute to the selection and preparation of resources suitable for children and young people's interests and abilities.

MONITORING AND ASSESSMENT

Those awarded HLTA status must demonstrate, through their practice, that they:

(22) monitor learners' responses to activities and modify the approach accordingly

(23) monitor learners' progress in order to provide focused support and feedback

(24) support the evaluation of learners' progress using a range of assessment techniques

(25) contribute to maintaining and analyzing records of learners' progress.

TEACHING AND LEARNING ACTIVITIES

Those awarded HLTA status must demonstrate, through their practice, that they:

(26) use effective strategies to promote positive behaviour

(27) recognize and respond appropriately to situations that challenge equality of opportunity

(28) use their ICT skills to advance learning

(29) advance learning when working with individuals

(30) advance learning when working with small groups

(31) advance learning when working with whole classes without the presence of the assigned teacher

(32) organize and manage learning activities in ways which keep learners safe

(33) direct the work, where relevant, of other adults in supporting learning.

GLOSSARY

Additional needs – describes needs of all children and young people at risk of poor Every Child Matters outcomes who require extra support from education, health or social services.

Audit – a systematic and objective overview and review process to compare actual policy and practice against recommended established procedures.

Common Assessment Framework – a holistic assessment tool used by the Children's Workforce to assess the additional needs of children and young people at the first sign of difficulties who are achieving poorly on the Every Child Matters outcomes.

Department for Children, Schools and Families (DCSF) – the English government department responsible for policy affecting children and young people, as part of the Government's aim to deliver educational excellence. Three new departments were set up to replace the Department for Education and Skills (DfES) and the Department of Trade and Industry (DTI).

Distributed leadership – the distribution and delegation of aspects of leadership across different staff at all levels, in order to divide tasks and responsibilities up more equitably.

Downloading: – transferring files or data from one computer to another, usually using an internet connection. To download means to receive; to upload means to transmit. Note: downloading files from the internet is a controversial activity. It is very easy to find and download illegal and copyright-infringing files through the internet.

Early Years – refers to children aged 0–7 and their provision in settings such as nurseries and children's centres.

Early Years Professional Status (EYPS) – a graduate professional status for lead practitioners in Early Years settings, equivalent to QTS.

Education Improvement Partnership – involves a group of educational settings collaborating together to address the improvement of common issues such as behaviour, 14–19 provision, childcare and extended school provision.

Evaluation – the process of critically examining and judging effectiveness, strengths, weaknesses and how well activities, interventions and initiatives are progressing.

Extended schools – offer a range of core universal services and out of hours learning activities from 8am to 6pm to respond to the needs of children, young people and their families.

Federation – a group of two or more educational settings, usually schools, which have a formal agreement to work together to improve and raise standards.

Foundation Stage – a distinct phase of education for children aged 3–5, which provides a framework and curriculum for children's learning and development in nursery and reception classes.

Handheld devices – a computer that can conveniently be stored in a pocket (of sufficient size) and used while you're holding it. Today's handheld computers, which are also called personal digital assistants (PDAs), can be divided into those that accept handwriting as input and those with small keyboards. Increasingly, mobile phone technology is taking on the role of the PDA.

Intelligent accountability – an educational setting's own view of how well it serves its children and young people and its priorities for improvement.

Interactive Whiteboard (IWB) – a touch-sensitive projection screen that allows you to control a computer directly, by touching the board rather than using a keyboard or mouse, although these can still be used. They require a computer, a projector and the whiteboard itself. You can use your finger or an electronic 'pen' to activate elements on whatever you have projected on the IWB (e.g. internet pages, files, software) and transmit to the computer.

Key Worker – a practitioner from education, health or social care services who provides a lead support and advocacy role for children and young people with more complex additional needs.

Lead Professional – a practitioner from health, social care or education services, who acts as a gatekeeper for information sharing, and coordinates and monitors provision and outcomes for children and young people who have been identified through the common assessment framework process as experiencing difficulties.

Makaton® – a unique language programme offering a structured, multi-modal (signing and symbols) approach for the teaching of communication, language and literacy skills. Devised for children and adults with a variety of communication and learning disabilities, Makaton is used extensively throughout the UK and has been adapted for use in over 40 other countries. Makaton symbols have become an integral component of key literacy software designed for use with those who have severe learning disabilities.

Monitoring – the process of checking progress against set targets in relation to an aspect such as Every Child Matters.

National Service Framework – a set of quality standards for health, social care and some education services aimed at improving the life chances and health of children and young people.

Networking – a collaborative process between staff from education, health and social care services that promotes the sharing of best practice, expertise and resources to support change and innovation.

New Relationship with Schools – the relationship between self evaluation and school improvement.

Outcomes – identifiable impact of interventions and services on children and young people.

Personalization – is where children, young people and their families, as responsible service users, are active participants in the shaping, development and delivery of personalized services.

Personalized learning – entails enabling children and young people to achieve their personal best through working in a way that suits them. It embraces every aspect which includes teaching and learning strategies, ICT, curriculum choice, organization and timetabling, assessment arrangements and relationships with the local community.

Planning, Preparation and Assessment (PPA) – time set aside for the planning and preparation of classes in schools and time for assessment of pupils. As part of the workforce agreement, teaching staff are guaranteed time away from the classroom to do this work and HLTAs are often responsible for covering this class time.

Podcasting – allows you to download audio files via the internet onto your computer and mobile music player. These files can include music, interviews, discussions and news reports (and may be a mixture of all).

Pupil Referral Unit – any centre maintained by an English local authority that provides alternative suitable and appropriate education for children and young people who are not able to attend a mainstream or special school.

Quality Assurance – a form of audit and a systematic examination of quality linked to accountability that ensures a service is of the quality needed and expected by service users.

Safeguarding – describes the process of identifying children and young people who have suffered or who are likely to suffer significant harm, and the subsequent action taken to keep them safe.

School Improvement Partner – provides professional challenge and support to leaders in schools and PRU's, to help them to evaluate their performance, identify priorities for improvement and plan for effective change.

Self evaluation – a developmental in-depth reflective collaborative process at the heart of school improvement, focused on the quality of children and young people's learning, achievement, personal development and well being.

Self review – a comprehensive overview of selected areas or aspects in an educational setting.

Specialist services – these include services for child protection, adoption and fostering, residential and respite provision, and mental health. These services target children and young people with acute or high levels of need who are at risk of achieving poor Every Child Matters outcomes.

Tablet PC – notebook or slate-shaped mobile computer, equipped with a touch screen or graphics tablet/screen hybrid technology which allows the user to operate the computer with a stylus or digital pen, or a fingertip, instead of a keyboard or mouse.

Targeted services – provide support for children and young people with additional and complex needs who are less likely to achieve optimal outcomes.

Transfer – refers to the movement of children and young people from one educational setting or school to another, as in moving from Year 6 in the primary school to Year 7 in the secondary school.

Transition – refers to the move from one year to another within a school or educational setting.

Universal services (or mainstream services) – routinely available to children, young people and their families in and around educational settings.

Vulnerable children/young people – refers to those at risk of social exclusion, who are disadvantaged and whose life chances are at risk. It includes those in public care, children with learning difficulties and disabilities, travellers, asylum seekers, excluded pupils, truants, young offenders, young family carers, and children experiencing family stress or affected by domestic violence.

Web-based text-processor – a text-processing package which is hosted on an internet server, and allows users to upload from and save to your desktop and edit anytime. Being web-based, it can be accessed from anywhere with internet access, and users can allow others to share and change documents in real time from anywhere. Google provides a free version, known as Google Docs.

Web 2.0 – this is a term describing the current trend in the use of world-wide web technology and web design that aims to enhance creativity, information sharing, and, most notably, collaboration among users. This technology is the driving force behind the development of interactive social networking sites such as Facebook, MySpace and YouTube.

Wraparound services – provision 'wrapped around' the normal school day which is available through schools, children's centres, nurseries, registered child minders and approved child carers.

INDEX

Added to a page number 'f' denotes a figure and 't' denotes a table